Rotgut Rustlers

Whiskey, Women, and Wild Times in the West

Edited by Erin Turner

TWODOT

Guilford, Connecticut
Helena, Montana
An imprint of the Globe Pequot Press

A · TWODOT® · BOOK

Text contributed by Charles L. Convis, Elizabeth Gibson, T. D. Griffith, Sean McLachlan, Barbara Marriott, Jan Murphy, Robert Barr Smith, Randy Stapilus, R. Michael Wilson, and Jim Yuskavitch

Text design by Sheryl P. Kober

Library of Congress Cataloging-in-Publication Data is available on file.

ISBN 978-0-7627-5536-3

Printed in the United States of America

10 9 8 7 6 5 4 3 2 1

Contents

INTRODUCTION

America has had criminals as long as there have been laws to be broken. Bank and stagecoach robbers, cattle rustlers, smugglers, counterfeiters, gamblers, racketeers, bootleggers, crooked politicians have an iconic place in the history of the United States, particularly on the American frontier. Perhaps it was the size and freedom the vast open space of the West provided for wrong-doers to hide out and potentially escape that pushed them to commit their crimes. They could practically disappear into thin air because the country is so large and because communication was once so slow. But, as these stories will reveal, most of the bad guys and gals were served justice and either spent time in prison, were murdered by other criminals, or hung for their crimes. In the end their lives ended badly, but fortunately, the stories of their varied lives and terrible crimes live on in the history of the United States.

THE DEAUTREMONT BROTHERS

Oregon's Last Train Robbery

When Southern Pacific Railroad Train Number 13 came to a slow stop a little before 1:00 p.m. on October 11, 1923, in Tunnel 13 on the summit of Siskiyou Pass in southern Oregon, the eighty-plus passengers aboard must have thought it odd. They only had a few minutes to sit in the darkness and wonder what was going on before a huge explosion rocked the front of the train, breaking out windows on the passenger cars and sending a bright flash of light and thick, billowing smoke through the tunnel.

Conductor J. O. Marrett, assuming a boiler explosion, tried to calm and comfort the panicked passengers as best he could, then stepped out of the car into the black, smoky darkness of the tunnel and began to carefully make his way to the front of the train. It would be some minutes before he realized what the forward crew members already knew—that a brutal and vicious robbery was in progress.

Chugging south to San Francisco, Train Number 13 had originated out of Portland, Oregon, and was carrying, in addition to paying passengers, twenty deadheading railroad employees and was pulling four baggage cars.

Tunnel 13 was located just south of Ashland in the Siskiyou Mountains, a remote and wild place in those days. The steep, winding grade through the mountains to the tunnel required additional "helper" engines to get trains to the summit. Just before reaching the tunnel, the trains stopped at Siskiyou Station, where the helper engines were unhooked. Then, because the ride down the other side of Siskiyou Pass was also steep and a train could gain 4 or 5 miles per hour extra speed before reaching the tunnel, company policy required its engineers to conduct a brake test, slowing down the train before reaching the east end of Tunnel 13 on its way down the mountain. It was all a routine, except for today.

On this day, three brothers—nineteen-year-old Hugh DeAutremont and the twenty-three-year-old twins, Roy and Ray DeAutremont—were waiting for the train to reach the tunnel. They were out to make a big, one-time heist that would set them up for a life of leisure, forever free from financial worries. Rumor had it that Train Number 13, called the Gold Special because in past years it transported gold between Portland and San Francisco, was carrying $40,000 in cash on this run.

Now, hidden in the brush along the tracks, Hugh and Roy, armed with Colt .45 automatic pistols, waited at the east end of the tunnel where the train would enter, while Ray, clutching a 12-gauge automatic shotgun, positioned himself at the west entrance.

Their plan was simple. The train, having conducted its brake test before entering the 3,100-foot-long tunnel, would be traveling slowly enough for Hugh and Roy to hop aboard. They would then make their way to the engine car cab and order the engineer to stop the train with the engine outside the exit end of the tunnel and the rest of the train inside. Ray, waiting with his shotgun at the tunnel exit, added extra firepower if needed. They would then blow open the mail car door with dynamite, uncouple the rest of the train, and order the engineer to pull the mail car out of the tunnel, where they would take its valuable cargo and then disappear into the rugged mountains as rich men.

An hour earlier they had run wires from a detonator hidden in the woods to the tracks and stashed a suitcase filled with dynamite in the bushes so that everything would be ready to go. The brothers had stolen the explosives and accessories, ironically, from a Southern Pacific Railroad Company work site. Everything was in place, and now all they needed to do was wait for the train to arrive. They had planned it out so well that nothing could possibly go wrong.

The DeAutremonts were not an atypical family for that time period in American history. Ray and Roy were born on March 31, 1900, in Iowa, and Hugh in Arkansas in 1904. They were the middle children in a family of five brothers. Their father, Paul, was of French extraction and their mother, Belle, German. They were Catholics and regular churchgoers.

A barber by trade, the father also tried his hand at farming and ranching and owned a general store for a while. In addition to Arkansas and Iowa, the family also lived for a time in Colorado and New Mexico. Eventually Paul and Belle divorced, and he moved to Eugene, Oregon, to work as a barber.

Following in their father's footsteps, Roy and Ray moved to Oklahoma to attend barber school, but Ray did not care for the profession. One day he jumped a train and rode the rails to Portland, arriving in 1918.

While Roy remained in Oklahoma and opened his own barbershop, Ray became involved in the labor movement, specifically with the Industrial Workers of the World party. In November 1919 he was arrested, which was not an uncommon practice for harassing labor activists, and sentenced to one year in a Washington State reformatory on charges of "criminal syndicalism."

Roy came to Oregon when he heard about his brother's arrest, and upon Ray's release, the two lived together in a Salem apartment, scraping by on what work they could find. Some scholars of the DeAutremont case believe that this was a radicalizing period for the two brothers, with Ray's anger and bitterness over his arrest eventually affecting Roy as well.

Ray took off for Spokane, Washington, in 1921 to find work and then went to Chicago where he hoped to join up with "gangsters." Failing to make a connection, he returned to Oregon by the end of the year and hooked up once again with Roy.

The twins, who were always close, began talking about pulling off some major heist that would permanently solve all their financial problems—an idea that first occurred to Ray when he was serving his reformatory sentence from 1919 to 1920. In 1922 the two even went so far as to plan several bank and general store robberies in Oregon and Washington, casing the locations but backing out at the last minute.

Over the next year the brothers spent time with family in Oregon, attended church, and worked at a number of jobs. Then Ray hopped a train during the winter of 1922–1923 and went to visit his younger brother Hugh, who was attending high school in New Mexico, where his mother Belle remained after her divorce. It was here that he pitched to Hugh the idea of helping him and Roy with a holdup, suggesting that the younger brother come up to Oregon after he graduated.

When Hugh graduated in June 1923, he headed up to Oregon to join Ray and Roy, and they began discussing a plan to rob a Southern Pacific Railroad mail car. Their date with destiny was drawing closer.

The brothers began exploring the Southern Pacific Railroad's route from Portland to northern California, looking for a promising ambush location. But the three just weren't finding a place they liked until Ray remembered Tunnel 13 and the Siskiyou Summit, over which he had traveled on his way to visit Hugh in New Mexico. Their spot was chosen, and they began to plan the details for a late October robbery of the Gold Special.

They went to Portland in early September 1923 and bought a used Nash car, which they drove to their father's house in Eugene, taking the opportunity while passing through Oregon City to steal the explosives, detonator, and wire they would use in the robbery.

They visited with their father for a few days, then loaded the Nash with camping gear and other provisions and departed on September 18, telling him they were going hunting in Washington's Puget Sound area. Then they turned south down the Pacific Highway to the Siskiyou Mountains.

Just a little below the summit of Siskiyou Pass, they pulled off the road and concealed the car. Here they camped for about a week, and then moved to another site not far away to spend a few days practicing setting up the explosives and getting familiar with handling their weapons. They did a good deal of target shooting. They also burned their tent and other belongings that might be used to identify them if discovered by the authorities before relocating to a small cabin they found on nearby Mount Crest.

They stayed here for the better part of a week, making their preparations for the robbery, for which they had set a date of October 11.

Next, they sent Hugh to get the car with orders to drive it back to their father's house in Eugene, store it there, and then hop a train for a lift back to the Siskiyou Summit. Because of the very limited road system in the area, attempting a getaway by car would almost certainly result in capture by the authorities. The plan, instead, was for Roy and Hugh to hide in the mountains once the robbery was successfully completed. Ray would make his way back to Eugene, pick up the car, then come and retrieve his brothers and the loot. At that point they would be free to make their escape.

But things went wrong. On the way down the mountain on September 26, Hugh crashed the Nash into a cow that was loitering in the road, crunching in the touring car's front end. He made it into Ashland, where he got it repaired, but had to spend a couple of days in town while the work was being done. He finally pulled into Eugene on September 29, leaving the car at his father's house and hopping a train to Ashland. While hanging around the Southern Pacific Railroad yard waiting for a train to come by so he could hitch a ride to the Siskiyou Summit, Hugh was questioned by suspicious security guards. Although they let him go, the episode unnerved him. Instead of waiting for a train and risk getting caught, he hiked up to the Mount Crest cabin from Ashland, reuniting with Ray and Roy on October 9.

The appointed day finally arrived. At noon the brothers set out from the cabin on foot for Tunnel 13. In addition to their weapons, they carried with them the detonating machine wrapped in a pair of blue overalls, three backpacks to carry away the loot, three pads that had been soaked with creosote, which they would strap to their feet to confuse bloodhounds, a one-pound can of pepper for the same purpose, flashlights, and a suitcase containing sticks of dynamite.

Upon reaching the tunnel, they attached the wires from the detonator and hid the suitcase by the tracks. Hugh and Roy made their way to the east tunnel entrance. Roy hefted his shotgun, sat down at the west entrance, lit a cigarette, and waited.

But now the waiting was over. The brothers could hear the train approach, slowing down enough during its brake test to allow a person to leap aboard as it passed by. Just before the train entered the tunnel, Hugh and Roy emerged from the brush and swung themselves onto the engine car.

Hugh stole up on engineer Sidney L. Bates and fireman Marvin L. Seng. With pistol drawn, Hugh ordered that the train be stopped with the engine outside the west end of the tunnel and the remaining cars inside. Roy watched from the back of the engine car by the oil tank.

As the engine emerged from the tunnel and the train came to a halt, Ray suddenly appeared, brandishing his shotgun. Mail clerk Elvyn E. Dougherty opened the door of the mail car to see what was going on. When he poked his head out, Ray fired his shotgun, but missed. Dougherty quickly slid the car door shut and locked it. Hugh Haffney, in the baggage car, was also peering out his car door. Seeing what was happening, he, too, slid his car door closed and locked it.

The DeAutremont brothers had everything under control and everyone where they wanted them. All that was needed now was to blow the door off the mail car, grab the $40,000, and make clean their escape. The high life was in their grasp.

Ray and Roy went up to the engine cab where Hugh was covering the engineer and fireman. They ordered both trainmen to get down off the cab and marched them out of the tunnel to the front of the train where they would be protected from any debris thrown by the explosion they were about to set off.

They placed the suitcase of dynamite by the mail car door, attached the wires, and ran for cover as Roy rammed down the detonator plunger.

But the robbers had no experience using explosives and used far more dynamite than the job required. Instead of just blowing off the door, the explosion tore apart poor U.S. Postal Service mail clerk Elvyn E. Dougherty and virtually demolished the mail car. Baggage man Haffney, in the next car over, was knocked unconscious by the blast.

Immediately after the explosion, while conductor J. O. Marrett was still attending to the passengers, brakeman Charles Orin "Coyle" Johnson jumped from one of the rear cars onto the tracks and made his way through the dark, smoky tunnel to see what had happened, holding a red lantern to light his way. Rail accidents including derailings and boiler explosions were not unheard of—between 1890 and 1905 there were as many as 7,000 such incidents in the United States. That is probably what Johnson was expecting to find. Instead, he ran into Roy DeAutremont.

The brothers now had a dilemma on their hands. The plan called for uncoupling the mail car from the rest of the train so that the engine could pull it out into daylight. At that point the trio could search it until they found the $40,000 they sought. But the explosion filled the tunnel with smoke and flames, making it difficult to see and breathe. They brought fireman Seng back to uncouple the car, but he was overcome by the fumes and had to retreat. Now there was a problem. Then the brakeman blundered into Roy's clutches.

Roy told him that that it was a robbery and demanded that Johnson help uncouple the mail car. The brakeman explained that once the uncoupling lever was raised, the engine had to be moved forward to separate the cars. So Roy sent Johnson forward to tell engineer Bates, who was being covered by Hugh and Ray, to pull the engine and mail car out of the tunnel. But when the brakeman suddenly appeared out of the smoky tunnel, red light in hand, Ray and Hugh panicked and opened up on him with both pistol and shotgun. Johnson fell to the ground, dying. One of the two DeAutremonts, it's not known which, shot Johnson one more time to finish him off.

Now Hugh brought engineer Bates back into his cab and ordered him to pull forward. Unfortunately for the brothers, the mail car had been so badly damaged by the explosion that, even after several tries, it wouldn't budge.

Stunned at how badly things were going, the brothers examined the smoldering carcass of the mail car, strewn with the body parts of the mail clerk, and considered their options. The mail car was so hot and smoky that, in their estimation, by the time it was safe to go inside to loot, the law would probably have arrived on the scene. It looked like it was time to cut their losses.

Roy and Ray held a brief consultation on what they should do. They decided to kill the engineer and the fireman and run for it. Roy shot the fireman two times with his Colt .45. Ray climbed up into the cab of the engine where Hugh was still guarding the engineer and yelled to Hugh, "Bump him off and let's clear out of here."

Hugh shot Bates in the head with his handgun. Then the three brothers ran off into the forest, leaving behind four dead men and the empty backpacks they had brought to fill with stolen cash.

By now conductor Marrett had made his way to the mail car accompanied by a medical student passenger, twenty-three-year-old Lawrence E. C. Joers, who had offered to help with anyone who might have been injured in the explosion. Finding their way to the front of the train through the dense smoke, they discovered the engineer, brakeman, and fireman lying on the ground. Still thinking they were only injured from an accidental explosion, the medical student began to give the engineer artificial respiration. But as he applied pressure to the chest, blood spurted out, revealing gunshot wounds. Now it dawned on them that there had been a robbery and multiple murders. Joers soon found the detonating wires along the track. Marrett ran for an emergency telephone located outside the tunnel and called for help.

Before long, another train steamed up the grade carrying a doctor and law enforcement officers, who collected evidence. Within hours search parties were combing the area, but no sign of the would-be robbers could be found. Southern Pacific Railroad immediately offered a reward of $2,500 for their capture.

In the wake of the bungled robbery attempt, the three DeAutremont brothers hightailed it to a cache where they had stored some supplies for their escape. They holed up there for nearly two weeks. After what seemed like an adequate period of lying low, Ray borrowed Roy's handgun (Ray had lost his during the robbery) and jumped a train to Medford, intending to continue on to Eugene to retrieve the Nash.

But as Ray walked through town, much to his horror, he spotted a newspaper with pictures of himself and Roy under the caption, *Have you seen the DeAutremont brothers?* There was a $14,400 reward being offered for them dead or alive. That was enough for Ray, who returned to the hideout to tell Roy and Hugh that the law had identified them as the killers.

Now it was time to run and run hard. The three made their way through the mountains toward the coast. By early November they were on the Klamath River in California, where Ray decided to strike out on his own while Hugh and Roy continued moving south to Grenada, California. Here, Roy took a job on a farm, and Hugh kept moving.

Unbeknownst to the three brothers, a massive manhunt that included searches on foot, with bloodhounds, and by airplane had been launched. Wanted posters were also being distributed worldwide. Nevertheless, it would be three and a half years before the Tunnel 13 killers would be brought to justice.

The robbery had been such a disaster—the murder of four men and a price on their heads without a penny to show for it. What other mistakes had they made that enabled their names to be connected to the crime so quickly?

The investigating officers found a wealth of evidence at the crime scene and at the cabin on Mount Crest. But two pieces of evidence gave them most of what they wanted. For one thing, the serial number of the handgun that had been dropped at the crime scene identified its purchaser as Ray DeAutremont. But the best evidence came in the form of the coveralls that the brothers had used to wrap up the detonator. Authorities bundled it up and sent it to Professor Edward Heinrich of the University of California at Berkeley. He conducted a series of forensic tests on the garment, but his best results came when he simply looked into one of the pencil pockets and found a wadded up piece of paper. He unfolded it carefully. It was a U.S. Postal Service registered mail receipt for a letter sent by Roy DeAutremont to his older brother, Verne, who was living in New Mexico.

From those two pieces of evidence, investigators were quickly able to figure out the robbery plot. Hugh was eventually linked as well through handwriting analysis of the aliases he had used at hotels and from the purchases he had made of equipment used in the robbery attempt.

On November 23, 1923, six indictments were issued against the brothers—four counts of murder and one count each for attempted burglary and larceny. More than two million wanted posters were printed and distributed worldwide. The three-year manhunt would cost $500,000.

While on the lam, Ray ended up in Detroit. He was eventually able to contact Roy in California, who joined him there in 1924. They worked their way south, intending to eventually escape the country. Instead they ended up in Ohio, where Ray got married and had a baby girl. In early 1927 Roy and Ray went to Steubenville, Ohio, to look for work as coal miners. But the law was closing in. Ray saw a wanted poster of the three of them, with Hugh's picture marked "captured."

After Roy and Hugh had split up in California, Hugh traveled through the Southwest for a while and then journeyed to Chicago. There he joined the U.S. Army in April 1924 under the name James C. Price. He was assigned to duty in the Philippines.

But the Philippines were not far enough away for Hugh to hide. Before too long the authorities' massive wanted-poster distribution campaign was finally going to pay off. In late 1926 Price's sergeant, Thomas Reynolds, was in San Francisco and saw one of those posters. He immediately recognized Private Price as Hugh DeAutremont. Reynolds took a stroll over to the Southern Pacific Railroad office and told his story.

There had been many false leads and disappointments over the years in the manhunt for the DeAutremonts, but the agents thought this might, finally, be the real thing. They sent one of their men to Manila in February 1927 to check the story out.

By mid-March the agent was back in San Francisco with Hugh DeAutremont in custody. By the end of the month, Hugh was transferred to the custody of Ralph Jennings, sheriff of Jackson County, Oregon, where the crime had taken place.

Three months later an agent from the U.S. Department of Justice arrested Ray at his house in Steubenville. Later that day, local police officers nabbed Roy as he was leaving work at a mill.

The two brothers had been fingered by a former coworker who had recognized their pictures from a wanted poster. It was over.

On June 27, 1927, the three brothers were delivered to the Oregon State Penitentiary in Salem to begin serving life sentences. While serving his time, Hugh founded a prison magazine called *Shadows*. Roy worked as a barber, and Ray learned several languages at the prison school and became a modestly talented painter.

Hugh was paroled in early 1958 and moved to San Francisco to work as a printer. Less than three months later, he was diagnosed with stomach cancer and died on March 30, 1959. Roy was diagnosed with schizophrenia, transferred to the Oregon State Hospital, and given a lobotomy. He was eventually paroled and died in 1983 in a nursing home in Salem. Ray was paroled in 1961 and worked part-time as a janitor at the University of Oregon. He died in 1984.

It was years after their robbery attempt that the DeAutremont brothers learned that Train No. 13 carried only its usual cargo of mail on that October day. There was no $40,000 aboard. It was also Oregon's last train robbery.

The three brothers are buried next to their mother at Salem's Belcrest Memorial Cemetery. All three of their names are on a single headstone inscribed side by side, just as they were on those wanted posters so many years ago.

Vincent Silva

The Man Who Fooled a Town

On October 23, 1892, the residents of Las Vegas, New Mexico, woke up to a picture-perfect winter scene. The previous night's storm had covered the streets and walkways in brilliant white. Shop fronts gleamed with a just-scrubbed look from the night's fierce wind. Windowsills laden with snow glittered and gleamed.

The brilliant sun reflecting off the icy streets caused early risers to view the main street through squinted eyes. Then eyes fell on the town bridge. There, gently swaying back and forth in the slight breeze, was Patricio Maes, hanging from the metal girder on the bridge. His clothes, stiff from cold and ice, fit him like boards; his cocked head faced heavenward, as if he were viewing the sky; his sightless eyes saw nothing.

The night before, a bitter wind had swept along the streets of Las Vegas, bringing with it a cold that settled into the marrow of a man's bones. This weather had driven an unusually large crowd to seek comfort in Silva's Imperial Saloon. The conversations thundered off the walls. Red-bearded Vincent Silva, looking dapper and handsome as usual, oiled his way around his customers, stopping here and there to have a quiet word with someone.

Meanwhile, the wind quieted and snow began falling. The white flakes piled up quickly and covered the dusty roads of Las Vegas. As midnight approached, Valdez, the bartender, shouted out that he was feeling sick and was closing the bar. Complaints and surprised looks were exchanged among the men. Silva's never closed; it was a twenty-four-hour-a-day operation. Reluctantly the men left the saloon, faced with the choice of going home or freezing outside in the cold.

When the bar emptied, Silva locked the door and started for home. However, a short time later, shadowy figures began making their way through the snow to the saloon's side door. Vincent Silva had called an emergency meeting of his secret outlaw band, the White Caps. Silva, a respected and wealthy citizen of Las Vegas, was not all he appeared to be. Silva's handsome looks, powerful bearing, and red hair made him a charismatic man. Most of the townspeople held him in high regard as a successful businessman and the owner of the Imperial Saloon, a large affair with a bar, billiards, and a dance hall.

Silva came to Las Vegas with his wife, Telesfora, in 1875 and started his business. Four years later the Atchison, Topeka, and Santa Fe Railway arrived, making his saloon even more successful.

Wealth and success were new to Silva. He was born of poor parents in the countryside of Bernallilo County, New Mexico. He married Telesfora Sandoval, a plain-looking village girl who presented a remarkable contrast to his handsomeness.

Before moving to Las Vegas, Silva and Telesfora lived in the mining town of San Pedro. Silva operated a grocery store, and his wife took care of the candy counter. An avid hunter, Silva spent his weekends looking for game. His familiarity with the countryside served him well in later years.

In Las Vegas people admired Silva as a family man. He was the doting father of an adopted daughter. Eight years earlier, someone had abandoned the newborn Emma in a Las Vegas stable. Unable to bear children, Telesfora begged her husband to adopt the baby. It was not long before both parents were completely enamored with the child. As further evidence of his family responsibilities, Silva had welcomed Telesflora's younger brother, Gabriel, into his household and employed him as a bartender in his saloon.

Silva was more than a family man, however. He had another side—a dark, evil side that only his outlaw band knew. Greed had slowly turned the simple man into a crime lord. While he smiled and sympathized with the citizens of Las Vegas, his men were rustling cattle, robbing, and murdering innocent people.

Vincent had built an organization with some of the cruelest, most immoral men in the West; men with no conscience and no compassion. Some of his gang members bore very descriptive names. They called Martin Gonzoles y Blea "the Moor" because of his dark complexion; Manuel Gonzales y Baca, "Toothless"; Antonio Jose Valdez, "the Ape"; and Ricardo Romero, "Pugnose." Antonio Jose Valdez also earned the name "Pussyfoot" for the way he walked.

Not all of the outlaws were tagged by their physical appearance. Guadalupe Catallero, "the Owl," was Silva's spy and personal aide. Five feet tall and weighing about one hundred and ten pounds with crossed eyes, the Owl had the appearance of a helpless and harmless man.

The Owl looked so inconsequential, people often ignored him. He would sit on his haunches on the side of the street or by a storefront in apparent slumber. However, he was wide awake; he would listen, take everything in, and then report his findings to Silva.

Also in the gang were three men of extreme importance to Vincent: Julian Trujillo, Jose Chavez y Chavez, and Eugenio Alarid. These three were members of the Las Vegas police force. They had worked over the years to see to it that Vincent Silva was not accused or even suspected of crimes.

Vincent Silva was an uneducated man; he could barely read or write, but his cunning, ambition, and ruthlessness made him the leader of this group: His men followed him without question.

To keep his façade of respectability in the community, Vincent had to keep his unlawful acts away from public scrutiny. He bought a ranch, Monte Largo, in an inaccessible section of the San Pedro mining district. Monte Largo was a place of deep gorges and scissor peaks, an ideal hiding place for his rustled cattle and horses.

It was to Monte Largo that Refugio Esquivel, a local rancher, traced his stolen horses. There he found his brand altered into Silva's brand. After rescuing his stock, Refugio stormed into Silva's saloon and accused him of cattle rustling.

Silva feigned innocence. There was no proof, so who would believe Refugio? However, the humiliation of a public accusation in his own saloon shook Silva's confidence. For years missing cattle and unsolved murders had plagued Las Vegas, but no one had ever suspected the respectable Vincent Silva. Someone must have talked. Silva believed that there was an informer in the White Caps, and he thought he knew who it was.

Silva acted the part of a fair man, and the fair thing to do was to have the alleged traitor put on trial and judged by his peers. And so it was on that snowy night in October that the band of thieves gathered on the second floor of the Imperial Saloon for a clandestine meeting.

Just days before, Patricio Maes, a Silva gang member, had placed a notice announcing his resignation from the Partido del Pueblo Unido political party. He stated that he was now a member of the Republican party.

The Herrera brothers, who wanted a party that represented the people, originally started the Partido del Pueblo Unido. These men rode around the countryside punishing those they believed had stolen or illegally obtained land from the poorer peasants. While they threatened people and destroyed barns and crops, they never physically attacked anyone. The party was nicknamed the White Caps after the headgear they wore on raids. When Pablo Herrera was murdered, the party was leaderless and disbanded. Vincent Silva secretly re-formed the party into a gang of thieves, murderers, and cattle rustlers. He kept the White Caps name for his gang. They were also called the Forty Thieves, a name that accurately described the membership.

Silva took the published announcement of Maes's resignation personally. To him it was not a resignation from a political party but a display of disloyalty and untrustworthiness. He also believed that Maes was the leak.

Silva set up court to try Maes on the charge of being a White Cap traitor. He appointed himself attorney general and fellow outlaw Polanco the defending lawyer. Toothless, also called the Dull One, was the judge.

Both sides presented their arguments. The gang members voted on a verdict, but "Judge" Toothless felt the verdict was unfair and refused to announce it. In an angry tirade directed at Toothless because of his refusal, Manuel Gonzolez y Baca hurled insults at the men, reminding them of the importance of capital punishment. The discussion heated up as men chose sides and began to make their points physically. It was apparent to Silva that each member of his band had his own opinion about the accused and was not willing to listen to other arguments nor blindly follow Silva on this matter.

Silva stopped the trial, ordered three gallons of whiskey, and after the refreshing break, called for another vote. The vote was unanimous—death to the traitor. Patricio Maes fell to his knees pleading for mercy, proclaiming his innocence, and begging for forgiveness for any transgressions. But the liquor had done its job, and the gang members were now in agreement with Silva and unmoved by Maes's pleading.

A noose dropped over Maes's head, and the gang led their victim through the deserted, stormy streets to the iron bridge spanning the Gallinas River. When they reached the bridge, the assassins allowed Maes to say his prayers. When he finished, one end of the rope was tied to a girder. Then Silva and a gang member picked up Maes and threw him over the bridge. Unfortunately, the rope knot was not tight, and it slipped, causing Maes to fall, smashing against the ice of the frozen river.

Two men climbed down to the ice, threw the loose end up, and the men on the bridge hauled Maes's body up. They tightly secured the rope end to the metal bridge girder and let him hang. Then, in ones and twos, the gang members drifted off, leaving Maes to his death dance in the howling wind. The next morning a large crowd gathered around the bridge to view the swinging corpse.

The *Las Vegas Optic* reported the hanging with a small notice: "Patricio Maes was taken by a mob early Saturday morning and hanged from the Gallinas River bridge at Las Vegas." That seemed to be the end of the matter.

Meanwhile, Captain Esquivel, the father of Refugio, was quietly investigating the rustling of his family's horses. Captain Esquivel had enough evidence to prove the illegal activities of the White Caps. Unfortunately, it was all circumstantial. Even so, he was able to get a grand jury indictment against Silva. On November 7, 1892, Vincent Silva's trial began. At the trial Silva's alibi could not be broken. The charges were dropped, and Silva was freed.

After that Silva became a very cautious man. He did not fear the local police but the Sociedad de Muta Protection, a vigilante group. Taking several gang members with him, Silva went into hiding in a cave near the village of Coyote (now called Rainsville). From this hideout, a mere twelve miles from Las Vegas, Silva and his band continued their criminal activities.

A deserted Telesfora was forced to find a way to support herself and Emma, by now a student at the Las Vegas Academy. She opened a lunch counter in town and fearing for the safety of her brother, Gabriel, insisted that he give up his work at the saloon, which continued operating under the management of a gang member. Although he was no longer managing the saloon, Silva did not stay completely away from the town. He made clandestine night forays into West Las Vegas to visit his mistress, Flora de la Pena.

Silva knew his safety depended on stealth and secrecy, and he worried about the two people closest to him. His young brother-in-law, Gabriel Sandoval, knew too much about Silva's illegal activities. His other worry was for the safety of Telesfora and his child.

Telesfora was the opposite of Silva in many ways. Her short, dark, and fat appearance made a sharp contrast to his large frame and redheaded good looks. Despite her unattractiveness she was well respected in the community and known as a kind and compassionate woman. Her demeanor was quiet; Silva's was one of boldness and bravado. She was blindly dedicated to Silva and very much in love with him; he openly kept a mistress. What the two had in common was their love for their daughter, Emma. Now Silva was to use that love to protect himself.

On January 23, Guadalupe Catallero pulled up to the Las Vegas Academy in a horse-drawn carriage. He told Emma he was taking her home for lunch. Instead, he drove her to Silva, who took her to Taos and enrolled her in a local school.

When Telesfora found her daughter missing, she was frantic, consumed with worry and fear for her beloved child. By kidnapping Emma, Silva hoped to silence both his brother-in-law and his wife. He planned on using Telesfora and her brother's love for Emma and their fear for her well-being to force them into cooperating with him. But Silva soon worried that even this measure was not enough. Enlisting the help of his three police officers, Jose Chavez y Chavez, Julian Trujillo, and Eugenio Alarid, he planned a murder.

The three policemen met with Gabriel Sandoval. Convincing him that he was aiding in the rescue of Emma, they led him to an abandoned mill in West Las Vegas. There Silva jumped out of the darkness and stabbed Sandoval, his own brother-in-law, to death, while the three police officers held his arms. The policemen, with the help of the Owl, carried the body to the back of Silva's saloon, where they stripped it and threw it in the privy pit.

Silva had plans to leave for Mexico with his mistress, but he needed more money. Silva and five of his gang members broke into the William Frank mercantile store in Las Vegas and helped themselves. They also stole the safe. The *Las Vegas Optic* described it as "the most audacious act in many years."

The thieves dumped the broken safe by the road about a mile from the store, setting fire to the accounts, books, and papers. They took the cash, amounting to twenty-five dollars. The merchandise, which was worth more than five hundred dollars, was never recovered.

On May 19, 1893, a notice of a reward for the capture of the outlaws appeared in the *Las Vegas Optic*. On the list was Vincent Silva, wanted for stealing. Also on the list were rewards for the capture of the robbers of the William Frank Store and the murderers of Jacob Stutzman and

Abran Abulafie, all by persons unknown. What the authorities did not know at the time was that all of these crimes were perpetrated by Silva and his band of forty thieves.

On the day that this notice appeared, events took a horrific turn in Vincent Silva's life. Needing more money for his flight with his mistress, Silva sent his wife a message. The message told Telesfora that he, her brother, and Emma were all well and that she was to pack her things and join them.

That evening, Silva's man Genovevo Avila picked Telesfora up and headed toward Silva's ranch. Along the way, Vincent joined them. When they reached the ranch, Silva dragged his wife into the small house and demanded money. She handed him all she had—two hundred dollars. Not satisfied, Silva demanded her jewelry. When she protested, he pulled out his knife and killed her. He dragged her body to a deep arroyo at the southern end of the village and flung her to the bottom.

Furious, Silva jumped on the bank until it collapsed and covered her body. After he'd killed his wife, his mood drastically changed. Pleased with himself, he opened up his stuffed money belt, and gave each of his five gang members ten dollars.

The men were in a state of shock over the killing of Telesfora. But shock turned to anger when Silva handed out the meager sum of ten dollars each from his bulging money belt.

As the men headed for the village, Antonio Jose Valdez walked up to Silva, put a .45 to his head, and shot him. They dragged his body back to the bank of the arroyo, tossed it over, kicked sand down to cover it, and went their separate ways after dividing up the money and jewels.

The fact that Vincent Silva, Telesfora Silva, and Gabriel Sandoval were all now dead did not slow down the activities of the White Caps. Over the next few years, innocent men were murdered, and cattle continued to disappear. Finally, William T. Thornton, the governor of New Mexico, offered pardons to anyone who came forward with information on the crimes.

It was not until April 10, 1894, that Manuel Gonzales y Baca told the district attorney about the crimes of Vincent Silva and the White Caps. Among the many crimes he reported were the hanging of Patricio Maes and the murder of Gabriel Sandoval. He said nothing of the murder of Telesfora and Vincent Silva.

When the news of Vincent's heinous crimes became public, the townsfolk were appalled. A man they had respected, trusted, and admired had betrayed them. An intense hunt for Silva turned up nothing. Vincent Silva and his wife seemed to have disappeared without a trace.

Vincent's mistress, Flor de la Pena, took Emma into her home and raised her along with her son, Hilario, who may have been Silva's child.

Eventually, the Silva gang began to fall apart. Several gang members had been captured and hanged. Dishonest policemen Julian Trujillo and Eugenio Alarid had earned life sentences in prison. Jose Chavez y Chavez escaped and went into hiding. And Vincent Silva was still "missing."

A year later, Guadalupe Caballero, the Owl, solved the mystery of Vincent and Telesfora Silva's whereabouts and explained to the authorities how they had been killed. On March 17, 1895, Antonio Jose Valdez led the officials to their graves in the arroyo. The March 18 edition of the *Las Vegas Optic* reported the events:

> *Some excitement was caused here yesterday by the bringing in of the bodies of Vincent Silva and his wife. Silva was the leader of the gang of cutthroats who made so much trouble in this county two years ago. He has been badly wanted by the officers since the gang was broken up, and there were rumors that he had been killed and also that he was in Arizona or Colorado. Yesterday Hon. Manuel Baca and a party went out about 12 miles north of here on information obtained from some of the former gang, and found the bodies of both Silva and wife buried near each other. It is understood that Silva was murdered to obtain money supposed to be in his possession and his wife was killed to keep her from informing on the murderers.*

Finally, after two years of searching, the authorities found Vincent Silva, a man who led two lives. It was a shock to the town to discover that the man they respected as a successful businessman, loving husband, and devoted father was a killer, thief, adulterer, and kidnapper. With his cleverness and wit, Silva had managed to fool a town for more than twenty years.

The Two Faces of Ned Christie

Hero or Villain?

Deputy U.S. Marshal Dan Maples, a well-respected lawman, was in Indian Territory searching for outlaws. He and his small posse—which included his young son Sam—camped close to the Big Spring, a plentiful source of water. Maples and a posse man went into town for supplies and, on the way back, walked into an ambush. It happened as they were crossing Spring Branch Creek, using a log that served as a bridge.

Jefferson, in the lead, saw somebody's shiny revolver in a thicket ahead. The holder of the revolver fired twice, and Maples went down. He managed to pull his revolver and fire four times into the thicket, but the attacker vanished. Officers investigating the murder scene soon found a black coat with a bullet hole in it, what was left of a whiskey bottle in the pocket.

Maples died the next day, and at least one local citizen's life would never be the same. Ned Christie's existence in Oklahoma was about to become news.

Over the years a great deal of chatter has abounded over Ned Christie as a career outlaw, and most tales paint him as a wanton killer. Consider this passage from the WPA Writer's Project back in 1938:

> *Eleven murders were credited to Christie. Among his victims were two officers, an Indian woman, and a half-breed boy. He was born a killer, cold blooded, ruthless; no one knew when or where he would strike next . . . [A]long the isolated paths to the lonely cabins of settlers he stalked relentless in his maniacal hatred.*

Christie was a Cherokee, described as a tall, lean, good-looking man who wore his hair long in the old tribal fashion. He came of a well-known, respected family, for he was one of the sons of Watt Christie, an expert blacksmith who came west sometime in the 1830s to settle in the Goingsnake District of the Cherokee Nation.

Watt was also an active, successful farmer aside from his smithing trade. He had several wives, then a common and legal practice. Watt's extended family eventually produced eleven children, seven boys and four girls . . . or maybe it was twenty-one, depending on which account you read.

Ned was deeply bitter over the encroachment of white immigrants into the Cherokee Nation, the advance of the railroads, the planned allotment of parcels of land to individual Cherokees, and increasing agitation for statehood for the entire territory. He certainly opposed all of these things as a violation of Cherokee sovereignty, and he did not mince words about his position.

Thus far he had been a peaceful man, save for a charge of killing a young Cherokee, of which he was acquitted. But because of the events on the dark night near Big Spring, he was now suspected of the murder of Deputy U.S. Marshal Maples, a well-known veteran federal officer.

Maples and his posse were camped close to Tahlequah, the Cherokee capital. Whatever Maples's mission, it appeared to be fairly routine, at least as routine as any job the marshals had to do. The territory was dangerous country, where any lawman was at risk. In the end more than sixty deputy marshals would die in the line of duty in this wild area, described by a newspaper of the time as the "rendezvous of the vile and wicked from everywhere."

At the time of the murder, Christie was in Tahlequah. As a tribal legislator he had come to attend a special meeting of the Cherokee Council. The Cherokee National Female Seminary had burned down, and that tragedy had deprived the Nation of both a handsome building and the venue for the free education of young Cherokee women. The council met in emergency session to decide what action to take to replace their school.

The marshals arrested one John Parris, who lived in a disreputable part of Tahlequah called Dog Town and had spent some time on the wrong side of the law. Parris has been variously described as a drinking companion or an accomplice of Christie in the Maples murder. After his arrest the hunt for Ned Christie began.

Christie and Parris were probably together on the evening of the shooting and ended up in Dog Town. That evening, according to one account, Parris and Christie left a friend's house very drunk. That was not long before Marshal Maples was murdered nearby.

In the most reliable version of what happened that night, Parris and Christie met three other Indian men. One of the three was the egregiously bad Bub Trainor, and one of the others had seen the inside of a federal prison at least twice.

A story later surfaced that another man had watched in the darkness as Bub Trainor had stolen Christie's coat as he had slept, then worn it to cut down the marshal. That same tale asserts that the dying Maples's return fire tore through Christie's coat and knocked the neck from a whiskey bottle in the pocket. Christie had bought a bottle of moonshine from Nancy Shell, who ran a Tahlequah bootleg joint, and the bottle in his coat was still plugged with a piece of Nancy's apron, torn off as a makeshift stopper. That bit of glass and strip of apron were damning evidence against Christie.

Christie woke next day to find himself one of the suspects in the killing of Maples. Also on the short list of murderers were Parris, Parris's brother, and two other Cherokee men. All of them had been spotted near the creek at about the time of the murder. Nancy Shell identified the scrap of cloth that plugged the broken bottle's neck. She also admitted that she had sold the bottle to Christie and Parris.

Christie might have come in and surrendered to stand trial in Fort Smith, but he chose to stay away from the fort. According to one tale he wanted to turn himself in, but others convinced him that he should run. In another story Christie sent a messenger to Fort Smith, asking district judge Isaac Parker to set bail, something Parker could hardly do for a man accused of the ambush murder of a federal officer.

In September 1889 veteran Deputy Marshal Heck Thomas led a serious attempt to arrest Christie. He took a posse of four men, including Deputy Marshal L. P. Isbel out of Vinita. The lawmen managed to avoid Christie's watchers, moving in slowly at night, until Christie's house was surrounded. Then Christie's dogs started barking, and the fight was on.

Christie fired from a loft window while his wife and son reloaded his rifle and pistols and handed them up to him. In an effort to break the stalemate, the posse set fire to Christie's gun shop near the house. But as Isbel leaned out from behind a tree, Christie drilled him through the right shoulder. The marshal went down, badly hurt, and Thomas hurried to help Isbel, fixing a temporary dressing around the wound.

As the flames from Christie's shop spread through the brush around the house, Christie's wife ran from the house, followed by his son, then

Christie himself. Thomas fired on the fleeing figures through the smoke, putting a bullet through the younger Christie's lung. Christie himself took a round from Thomas's rifle. It smashed into his temple, tore out his right eye, and ripped loose much of the structure of the nasal bones. Christie kept going, however, and vanished into the woods. Thomas and two of his posse briefly looked for their quarry, but Isbel was badly wounded, and Thomas's most pressing task was getting him back to medical help at Fort Smith.

Christie, Christie's son, and Isbel would all recover from their wounds. Isbel's arm was paralyzed, however, and he bid good-bye to the marshal service. Christie was terribly disfigured, no longer the handsome man he had been. From that day forward, deeply bitter, he spoke no word of English but conversed entirely in Cherokee.

Christie's kin and his friends improved his fortifications while he recovered from his terrible wound. The new lair was not far from his old home but this time was built within a rock formation on a hill that afforded good views in every direction. The rock formed a thick wall that no bullet could possible pierce.

Christie was undisturbed for a while, for it was obvious that only a very strong posse had any chance to root him out. Some people thought it would take U.S. troops. And in the interim Christie rebuilt his home on a new site, strategically close to a spring. The new place would be called Ned's Fort. The walls were two parallel lines of logs, the space between the logs filled with sand. The walls inside were lined with oak, giving even more protection against rifle bullets. Upstairs there were no windows, only firing ports for defense.

Christie finished his new place in 1891, and a little while later the law tried again. This time the leader was an experienced deputy marshal named Dave Rusk. Rusk was a one-time Confederate officer and a crack shot. He had been a lawman for more than fifteen years when he set off to besiege Christie.

He chose a posse composed mostly of Cherokees who were not well disposed toward Christie, but his first try at Ned's Fort ended in fiasco with four of his Indian posse men wounded. For the moment he retired, but Rusk was tough and persistent. He would come again.

Rusk was back on the hunt in October of 1892. This time he led five other deputy marshals, but again the mission ended in failure. Rusk called to Christie to give up, which may have been a mistake. For

Christie answered the challenge to surrender with a gobbling sound one writer called the "Cherokee death cry" and gunfire, and two deputy marshals went down, badly wounded.

Now several women and children ran out of Ned's Fort, and they told the lawmen that not only was Christie inside the fortress, but also three other Cherokee men. Rusk looked about for a better solution than going head-on against this bulletproof house. He found his answer in a rickety wagon, which the lawmen soon filled with brush and logwood. They set fire to it and then rolled it flaming into the side of the fort, hoping to burn Christie out. Trouble was, the battered wagon disintegrated on contact with the log wall, and the fire went out before it could do major damage.

Their next weapon was several sticks of dynamite lashed together. The fuse was lit and one of the posse threw the package against the side of Christie's lair. As the dynamite struck the wall, however, the fuse fell loose, and so that attempt fizzled out. Now the deputies sent a messenger into Tahlequah with instructions to wire headquarters at Fort Smith for more help. The rest of the lawmen returned to their futile siege of the log building. In the end they ran out of ammunition and had to retreat.

Another expedition against Ned's Fort was led by Paden Tolbert, a tough, experienced deputy marshal. Tolbert talked the matter over with U.S. Marshal Jacob Yoes and Judge Parker and quietly recruited four more men, plus a fifth man to cook for the group. Even their initial meeting was held in the dead of night. Nobody was going to take a chance that some early warning might reach Christie.

Next day the group took the train to Fort Smith, where they met John Tolbert, Paden's brother, and five more men. The group then met up with three more posse members, including Sam Maples, young son of the dead deputy marshal. One version of the fight that followed has Christie besieged by no fewer than twenty-seven men.

And the posse acquired an unusual piece of crime-fighting equipment. It was a small cannon, about four feet long, with forty rounds to go with it.

Other lawmen joined the posse before it moved west across the Arkansas, including Heck Bruner, one of the best of the deputy marshals, and the experienced Bill Smith, who was part Cherokee. The posse now numbered about twenty-five men, and Cherokee sheriff Ben Knight—no partisan of Christie—agreed to guide them into the heart of Christie's lair.

Logically, Christie should have known this small army was coming. The lawmen could not move rapidly, and there could be no hiding so many armed men and a mule-drawn wagon loaded with a cannon and heaps of supplies from the vigilant eyes in Christie country.

The trip in was uneventful, however, and shortly after nightfall the party reached a spot behind a ridge not far from their target. Dinner was tinned sardines and crackers, for the lawmen did not build a fire. In spite of the size of their force, they still had some hope that their approach had gone undetected.

At about four o'clock the next morning, the lawmen moved to their positions. Tolbert, Rusk, and two others moved the wagon to the point they had selected to get the cannon into position. With the little gun ready to fire across a creek in front of Ned's Fort, the law was ready.

At about daybreak a man carrying a water bucket emerged from the cabin and headed toward the spring. Tolbert shouted to the figure to surrender, but the man dropped the bucket and dove back inside the house.

Tolbert shouted again. He is said to have told Christie that they were prepared to stay this time until Christie was taken, and that he had no means of escape. Nothing happened. Then Tolbert shouted to Christie to send out any women and children who were inside the cabin. In response, three Cherokee women and a child emerged from the cabin door. Cherokee lawman Knight asked one of them who was inside helping Christie, but the women would not speak.

Now Tolbert tried again, yelling to the cabin that the posse would not leave until Christie was captured or dead. The answer was gunfire. The battle continued as the morning wore away, and gradually a group of onlookers began to form. Among them was Christie's father, Watt. Ben Knight went to Watt and asked him to help persuade his son to surrender. The father refused.

The lawmen turned to the little cannon, loaded it with black powder and something called a "bullet-wedge" projectile, and opened fire. But the heavy log walls held up through thirty-seven rounds, dented and splintered but still intact. With only three rounds left, Tolbert tried doubling the powder charge, but all that accomplished was splitting the barrel of the cannon. Night was falling by now, and Tolbert began to send his men back to camp in pairs for something to eat.

He began to explore other ways to get into the fort. His eye lit on the rear axle of the wagon that had disintegrated during the earlier siege. It was still intact. He sent men to Christie's own sawmill then, and they brought back heavy boards and used them to build a rolling barricade atop the axle, a sort of mobile shield to cover an approach to Christie's fort. The thing would be guided by the tongue of the destroyed wagon, used as a sort of lever to push the structure near the building.

The plan was for Charlie Copeland, an officer, to carry an explosive charge, six sticks of dynamite, advancing behind the shield as three more officers pushed it toward the cabin, with the remaining officers providing covering fire. When they got near enough, Copeland would dash to the cabin wall and place his charge of dynamite against it.

And so, about midnight, four officers rolled the oak shield close to the logs of the cabin wall. As planned, Copeland placed the dynamite, lit the fuse, and sprinted back to the protection of the shield. They pulled the shield back a safe distance as the fuse smoked and sputtered.

A colossal blast caved in the wall of the fort and knocked over a stove inside. Now fire followed the explosion, and by dawn great gusts of flame were shooting up from the structure, garish against the coming light. Gunfire from the fort had died away. All the posse had to do now was wait.

With one side of his fortress blown out and flames enveloping the cabin, Christie had no options left. Out of the fire and smoke, he ran suddenly, a pistol in each hand, gobbling his war cry and firing on the marshals hidden behind trees and logs and rocks. He must have known that he was running to his death, charging straight ahead into those flaming rifles. And, in fact, he overran lawman Wess Bowman, who was lying on the ground. Bowman simply rolled over and shot Christie in the back of the head as he ran by.

The rest of the posse closed in then, holding their fire, but young Sam Maples ran up and emptied two revolvers into what remained of Christie. The marshal's son had waited a long time to avenge his father.

An enterprising photographer emerged from the crowd of spectators and took everybody's picture. The lawmen hauled Christie's body into town and thence to Fayetteville, where everybody, the living and the dead, was loaded on the Fort Smith train. At various points Christie was propped up to take the usual photographs. In one of them somebody laid a Winchester across his folded arms. The posse also had their pictures taken again, and there was general rejoicing at the fall of a man most white people thought was Lucifer incarnate.

Not so among the Cherokee Nation. Many people, especially fellow Keetoowahs, saw the fallen man as a hero who had resisted the encroachment of the white man's law. He was admired for his courage as well. Watt Christie claimed his son's body and returned it to a family burying ground near Rabbit Trap.

So passed Ned Christie, both vilified and canonized by reams of prose of greater or lesser accuracy. His story was powerful fodder for any number of writers, some of whom were not above making up a "fact" or two to embellish their tale. Other more reliable authors simply uncritically accepted the original story that Christie cold-bloodedly shot down Marshal Maples from ambush.

The notion that Christie had in fact murdered Maples was badly shaken when, in 1922, an elderly blacksmith came forward to insist that Christie was innocent. He had seen Christie lying on the ground drunk, he said, and watched Bub Trainor pull Christie's coat from him. The blacksmith, one Dick Humphrey, somehow suspected dirty work and hid to watch what happened next. And he saw Trainor talk to Parris, then check his own revolvers, and head toward the log bridge across the little creek.

Why didn't Humphrey come forward? Because Trainor had a great many friends among the outlaw fraternity, he said, and even after Trainor was shot down a few years later, Humphrey was still afraid to speak. Only as an old man did he decide to tell his tale to a newspaper in Tulsa. Christie was, probably, innocent and became a hunted man only because of the lies Parris told the lawmen to save his own skin, plus the damning evidence of the coat with its hole and the whiskey bottle's broken neck.

And so ended the saga of Ned Christie, hero or villain, wrongfully accused victim or callous murderer. Leaving aside the myths and legends, one thing is certain: Christie was a very tough cookie indeed, an exceptionally brave fighting man, a dead shot, and a man of conviction.

Henry Starr

More Banks Than Any Other Man in America

Ex-marshal Floyd Wilson was riding with a fellow detective, hot on the trail of a budding outlaw know as Henry Starr. Unfortunately, the second detective had fallen some distance behind Wilson when the lawman rode up on his quarry. Alone and unsure of just how dangerous this new outlaw might be, the lawman pulled his Winchester out of the saddle scabbard and shouted to Starr, "Hold up! I have a warrant for you!"

Starr dismounted and drew his own rifle, yelling to Wilson that he should be the one to hold up, and both men opened fire at a range of only about thirty yards. Wilson probably fired first, although that shot may have been simply a warning. In his usual whiny manner, Starr later asserted that he had "pleaded with him not to make me kill him, but he opened fire, the first ball breaking my saddle and two others passing close by."

In fact the officer's rifle jammed after that single round, and Starr shot him down. Wilson pulled his pistol as he lay on the ground, but Starr shot him again, and then once more, and finally drove a third round point-blank into Wilson's chest. The last round pierced Wilson's heart. Starr turned away from the fallen officer, whose clothing still smoldered from the muzzle blast from Starr's rifle, swung up on Wilson's horse, and rode away. Starr's outlaw career was off with a bang.

Starr was related by marriage to Belle Starr, the Bandit Queen, much celebrated in print and celluloid. Though Belle was one of the West's most enduring legends, she was no queen, and she was also one of history's all-time overrated criminals. But Henry himself was the real thing, all wool and a yard wide; the papers called him the Bearcat, but his real name truly was Henry Starr.

Through the years Starr gained a reputation as the country's greatest bank robber. When he started taking other people's money, the outlaw's favorite means of escape was the horse; by the time he finished his crooked career, he and the rest of America's robbers were carrying off their loot in automobiles.

Henry Starr was part Cherokee, born in Fort Gibson, Indian Territory, in December 1873. His father was George Starr, called "Hop," son of notorious old Tom Starr and brother to Sam Starr, the husband of the celebrated Belle. His mother, Mary Scott, was a much-respected lady. Starr got what he described as a sixth-grade education, then entered the hard adult world of work and choices.

Henry did some plowing and cow punching for a while, then graduated to stealing horses. He apparently considered himself something of a free spirit, born of the Cherokee lands, not a man ever to be constrained by mere laws. As he himself told a Kansas newspaper:

> *It was God overhead and nothing around. The world, our world, was ours and none to dispute . . . We had been taught that it was ours, to have and to hold so long as grass grew and water ran, ours to hunt on, ours in which to follow in the footsteps of our fathers, to do with as we wished.*

Although he fancied himself an unfettered soul, or maybe because he did, Starr was given to blaming other people for his own shortcomings. And he blamed quite a lot of them: his stepfather, his boss, a lying witness, peace officers he said were venal and crooked, even what he called the bloody and corrupt federal court at Fort Smith.

He said, for example, that as a youngster, on his way to the site appointed for tribal payments, somebody he didn't know asked him to carry a valise to the place. Later, again according to him, deputy U.S. marshals stopped him and found whiskey in the bag. He was, he said, badly mistreated by the lawmen, feeling the "murder-breeding leg-irons and chains." "Let any young man of ambition," he declaimed, "be shackled to a worthless perjurer and be carried 200 miles away from home, all the time being pointed out as a horse thief, to face a charge for which there is no iota of evidence . . . and what respect would he have for a law with such representatives?"

All of these people and entities, Starr believed, drove him to a life of crime. Starr's self-justification predictably excused his passage down the paths of unrighteousness, straight to a long career stealing other people's money, beginning in the summer of 1892, when he started out robbing a country store with a couple of second-rate hoodlums for backup.

He also stuck up the railway station at little Nowata, in company with career thugs Ed Newcomb and Jesse Jackson. As so often happened with Starr's confederates, however, the law quickly caught up: Newcomb served a long prison sentence, and Jackson killed himself in jail. Starr got away.

With practice Starr got pretty good at larceny, and he raised his sights. In December of that year, he visited Coffeyville, Kansas, where he bought wire cutters and gun holsters in preparation for greater things. Starr apparently saw nothing wrong in jumping bail after one of his early crimes, leaving people who believed in him holding the bag, nor did his conscience seem to bother him when he hid out at the home of a friend and then stole the friend's money, about $300, a substantial nest egg.

Floyd Wilson was probably the only man Starr ever killed, but that was hardly due to Starr's peaceable nature. The outlaw surely did a lot of pistol waving in his robbing days, and a good deal of indiscriminate shooting as well. Fortunately for the general public, he never hit anybody else, unless he did some quiet murdering that is not recorded.

Despite the outright murder of Wilson, Starr the outlaw started off slowly. Much of his early robbing was bush league, holdups of country stores, stealing from store tills and individual citizens indiscriminately. For instance, he and one Milo Creekmore stuck up a little country store in Lenapah, looking for a stockman's $700 that was supposed to be held there. They followed that with another store robbery in which they robbed the clerk of some $500, magnanimously giving back to the fellow $10 of the $500 so that he might have something with which to do business.

Starr and his growing gang certainly were not getting rich. They were, however, beginning to build a reputation. Late in March 1893, Starr and outlaw Frank Cheney struck the Caney Valley National Bank in Caney, Kansas, riding off with about $2,000. According to Starr he and Cheney had already "sacked the town of Choteau, just to keep in form, without any trouble at all." And then, on May 2, Starr and his embryo gang—six men in addition to Starr—stuck up a Katy train at Pryor Creek in Indian Territory, making off with some $5,000 in jewelry and money.

The gang members seem to have considered themselves professional criminals rather than warriors for the working day and lived high on the hog. They expended at least one hundred rounds of ammunition per day in practice, Starr boasted, and ate "every delicacy to be obtained."

In June of 1893 Starr followed up his success on the Katy with an ambitious attempt to rob a bank in Bentonville, Arkansas, but Starr was cautious at the start of this one. He had the gang's rifles brought into town in a hired buggy to escape attention. But once the robbery began, the citizenry of Bentonville quickly learned that their bank was being robbed. These stout people reached for their weapons, and Starr ran for his life amidst a torrent of gunfire. One of his men, Link Cumplin, was badly shot up, although he managed to stay on his horse and clear the town. Like other Starr accomplices Cumplin would finish the year dead from his wounds. One townsman took a round in the groin and another was wounded in the chin, but the gang was in full retreat with a posse hot on their heels.

The gang would never ride together again. One, a morose man inevitably called "Happy Jack," was shot down two months later; a second was killed by lawmen in 1895. And in 1894 Cheney also ate his last meal, which was an officer's bullet to the head.

As for Starr, he evaded the posse but was arrested not long afterward in Colorado Springs. After an ill-conceived jailbreak attempt, he faced a multitude of charges at Fort Smith. He was convicted of several robberies, and to add insult to injury, the People's Bank of Bentonville sued Starr for $11,000 looted from the bank. Starr denied the claim, even though he was carrying much of the money when he was arrested.

But the big charge, the deadly one, was the murder of Wilson. That trial, too, ended in conviction, and Starr faced Judge Isaac Parker for sentencing. Judge Parker was famous for his stern lectures to condemned criminals, hanging sentences, and dwelling at length not only on the vileness of their earthly crimes but also on the imminent and daily danger posed to their immortal souls. The judge gave Starr a twenty-minute speech on morality and salvation and sentenced him to die.

That should have been the end of Henry Starr, but it wasn't. The United States Supreme Court reversed the conviction, and the matter was remanded and set for a second trial. Meanwhile, Starr remained in the Fort Smith jail with as choice a collection of murderers and other worthless scum as any lockup has ever held.

Crawford Goldsby, the bloody-handed felon better known as Cherokee Bill, smuggled in a pistol. Nobody could get at Cherokee Bill, however, and he seemed to have plenty of ammunition. The standoff might have continued indefinitely, except for Henry Starr. Starr boldly walked into the cell where Cherokee Bill had taken refuge and talked him out of his weapon.

On retrial Starr was again convicted of the Wilson murder and again sentenced to death. And again the Supreme Court reversed. Judge Parker left the bench not long afterward and was replaced by Judge John Rogers. Judge Rogers entertained a plea of manslaughter, and Starr went off for a stiff prison term of thirteen years and eight months. Starr could behave well when he wanted to, and after his mother appeared before the Cherokee Council, that body appealed to President Theodore Roosevelt for clemency. In 1901, impressed with the story of Starr's cool intervention with Cherokee Bill, the president telegraphed Starr: "[W] ill you be good if I set you free?" Starr said he would, and so, by the beginning of 1903, Henry Starr was a free man.

Starr settled in Tulsa and married a schoolteacher, Miss Ollie Griffin. Starr was not without worries, however, for the Arkansas authorities had still not forgotten Bentonville; Starr was safe, for the time being, for Oklahoma authorities refused to extradite him, relying on an attorney general's opinion that such an action would be unlawful as it affected a member of the Civilized Tribes. So Starr remained free and, for a time, apparently stayed away from the outlaw trail.

Eventually the lure of the bank heist and easy money were too much for Starr. With Kid Wilson, an old criminal associate now on parole from New York, he struck a country bank in Tyro, Kansas. Things got so hot as a result that Starr and Wilson fled all the way to Colorado, where they robbed a tiny bank in Amity. Moving on to Arizona, Starr settled there under an alias. Traced by a letter he sent to Oklahoma, he was arrested in Arizona and returned to Colorado, where an unsympathetic court gave him seven to twenty-five years in the Cañon City penitentiary. In the fall of 1913, after his usual good behavior, Starr was paroled, on the one condition being that he not leave the state of Colorado.

And for a while he didn't. He opened a small restaurant, but that venture did not prosper, and in due course Starr abandoned the eatery and left Colorado, taking with him the comely wife of a local merchant. There followed a long string of robberies in Oklahoma, none of them big paydays. Rewards were posted—"dead or alive" this time—but Starr was hard to find, even though he was living in Tulsa. He even had the audacity to write the governor of Oklahoma, denying he had anything to do with any robberies, a profoundly unconvincing tactic reminiscent of Jesse James.

But Starr's luck was about to run out. For in March of 1915 he decided to replenish his funds by raiding the bank in Stroud, a prosperous town about dead center in Oklahoma. He rode into town on horseback with six hoodlums to help him, a force that should have sufficed to cow the citizens of peaceful Stroud. And this gang should have been enough to accomplish the bank robber's ideal, the dream for which the Dalton Gang had gotten itself destroyed in Coffeyville twenty-three years before. They were going to rob two banks at once.

On March 27, 1915, at about 9:00 a.m., Starr and his crew rode into Stroud and set to work. At first the robbery went according to plan. Starr divided his force into two parties of three men, and they entered simultaneously the First National and the Stroud State Bank. Starr led the column that would raid the State Bank, brandishing a short rifle he had stuffed down his pants leg. As his partners covered two bankmen and a customer with pistols, Starr got $1,600 in loose cash, and then he demanded that bookkeeper J. B. Charles open the safe or Starr would kill him.

"You'll have to kill me, then," said Charles coolly, "because I don't know the combination." Starr then threatened bank vice president Sam Patrick, who just as coolly told the outlaw leader that the safe had already been opened for the day's operating cash but was then reclosed and its time lock reset for the next day. Frustrated, Starr snatched Patrick's diamond stickpin and herded him, Charles, and a customer out into the street.

Over in the First National, Starr's companions found the safe open and swept up more than $4,000. When Starr joined them, they collected four bank employees and five customers to use as human shields. Herding these nine men in front of them, along with the hostages from the State Bank, the whole bandit gang walked deliberately toward their horses. But word of the holdup had spread through the town, and armed citizens were beginning to collect.

Their first shots were ineffective, and Starr's gang blazed away up and down the street to keep the townsmen at bay. Starr, hiding behind bankman Patrick, snapped a shot at one Charley Guild, a shot that drove the shotgun-toting horse buyer quickly to cover behind a building.

More of Stroud's angry citizens were opening up on the outlaws. One in particular proved to be an especially deadly marksman. Seventeen-year-old Paul Curry had seen the robbery unfold from the yard of his parents' home nearby. Curry now ran into a butcher shop and came out with a sawed-off Winchester rifle. Taking cover behind some barrels in front of his father's grocery store, young Curry smashed Starr's leg with a round that tore into the outlaw's left thigh. When the bandit raised his weapon to return the fire, Curry yelled, "Throw away that gun or I'll kill you!" Convinced that this cool, tough youngster meant what he said, Starr dropped his weapon and fell back on the ground.

By this time the rest of the gang, abandoning their leader, had run to the stockyards, where they had tethered their all-important horses. They mounted up in haste and began to ride hard for safety, but bandit Lewis Estes was having trouble controlling his horse. Young Curry fired once more, and the bullet smashed into Estes's shoulder, breaking it and tearing into a lung. Waving a pistol, the outlaw forced two of the hostages to help him climb into the saddle, and all five bandits rode clear of the town.

Estes managed to stay on his horse for about a mile and half until he fainted from loss of blood and was pitched out of the saddle. His companions, as compassionate for him as they had been for Starr, took his horse and left him on the ground. Recovered by a posse, he was returned to town and taken to the office of Dr. John Evans, where Starr already lay. The bandit leader readily admitted to his identity and encouraged the close-mouthed Estes to do the same.

As the doctor dug the rifle bullet out of Starr's leg, Starr asked, "What did the kid shoot me with?" A hog rifle, somebody said, and Starr reacted with embarrassment. "I'll be damned. I don't mind getting shot, knew it had to happen sooner or later. But a kid with a hog gun—that hurts my pride."

Starr did have the good grace to congratulate Curry on his courageous stand. The young man told Starr he would use the reward money, $1,000, to get an education, and Starr is reported to have said, "You're all right, boy."

Meanwhile, a posse pursued the fleeing bandits, and the telephone—that new and handy crime-fighting tool—sent lawmen, volunteers, and even state militia chasing after the remains of the gang from all directions. Much of the pursuit was by automobile, and the pursuers came very close. But in the end they were foiled by the cross-country mobility of the mounted bandits and their own inability to quickly hire or borrow horses for the pursuit.

At his trial Starr entered a plea of guilty, to everybody's surprise, and then went off to prison in McAlester with a twenty-five-year sentence. Estes got five years. While in prison Starr went into his good behavior mode, and he was back on the street again in less than four years. His chief aid and support in this quick return to liberty was one Kate Barnard, who was Oklahoma's first commissioner of "Charities and Corrections."

To her credit Kate was a holy terror to slothful or uncaring officials and did much good in improving conditions in state hospitals. She also cordially detested the penal system, which she considered medieval, and thought herself a perceptive judge of the character of those confined there. "I have studied men," she said, "until I know from the shape of their hands and head, the gait of their walk, and the contour of their faces, much of their mode of life and the character of their thoughts."

She was convinced that Starr would now walk the paths of virtue and thought he had made "one of the sincerest efforts at reformation of all the 20,000 convicts I have known." Maybe this redoubtable lady did have some powerful insight into the souls of felons, but in Starr's case she—and others, including the prison chaplain—had been thoroughly bamboozled.

Starr now settled in Tulsa and became involved in the burgeoning film industry. He bought an interest in a firm called the Pan-American Motion Picture Company, and with it produced a silent movie, *Debtor to the Law.* This film, an account of the Stroud debacle, used many of that town's citizens as actors, including young Curry, playing himself. *Debtor to the Law* was very successful, and other films followed.

At that point in his life, after serving prison sentences in Colorado and Oklahoma, Starr had every chance to change his outlaw lifestyle. And for a while it seemed that he would do so. However, not even the bonds of matrimony—he was married twice—could wean Starr off the excitement of being a professional criminal.

In spite of the fact that he had not had much luck robbing banks in Arkansas, Starr decided to hit yet another Arkansas town. This time he tried the People's National Bank in the little town of Harrison, not far from Bentonville.

On February 18, 1921, Starr and three other men drove into Harrison in a Nash automobile and entered the bank. None of them wore a mask, although Starr seems to have worn a pair of cheap glasses, perhaps as a rudimentary disguise. The outlaws had every expectation of a successful haul, for there was some $30,000 in the bank.

At first the holdup went just as planned. The robbers pushed up to the cashier's windows and covered bank president Marvin Wagley and cashier Cleve Coffman, pushing out of the way Ruth Wilson, a bookkeeper for a grocery firm who was in the midst of making a deposit for her boss.

"Hands up!" yelled the bandits. They repeatedly warned Coffman to "keep quiet; don't move." One of them then went inside the working area of the bank while a second man began to herd everybody else toward the vault. Starr had thoughtfully brought along a pillow case, which he now opened. At gunpoint, he told Coffman to do what he was told. "You work with me and I'll work with you." By now the robbers had to watch not only Coffman, Wagley, and Ruth Wilson, but two other female employees and three more customers. Starr and his men also leveled their weapons at sixty-eight-year-old William J. Myers, who was a director and onetime president of the bank.

Myers had just entered his office at the rear of the bank, walking right into the middle of the robbery in progress. Having no other option, he dutifully raised his hands and followed one robber's orders by walking into the bank vault. But Myers apparently believed in prior planning, for he had long since arranged for a back door to the vault—what he called his "bandit trap"—specifically for just such an occasion. He had also secreted a loaded 1873 Winchester at the rear of the vault.

Starr finished sweeping the depositors' money into a sack, and he now ordered Coffman to open the safe. Coffman began to turn the dial, with the outlaw leader looking over his shoulder. When the door swung open Starr started to reach inside. At that moment Myers opened fire from inside the vault and Starr went down. "Don't shoot!" he is supposed to have yelled. "Don't shoot, don't shoot anybody. I am the one that is shot; don't shoot a man who is down."

Myers advanced out of the vault, his weapon trained on Starr. Oddly enough, the outlaw asked Myers to remove the cheap glasses he was wearing. Myers did so, then pressed on after Starr's companions, who had not stayed to fight or save their leader. They ran for it, in fact, tearing out of town in their automobile and leaving their boss behind. Myers ran outside and blazed away at the Nash as it raced off down the street, hitting one tire and blowing out the windshield.

Hastily organized citizens' posses pursued, but all they found was the Nash, abandoned and set on fire. In the days to come, authorities would arrest three other men for complicity in the crime, but for now all eyes were on the desperately wounded Henry Starr. At first, Starr would not reveal who his cohorts were, and simply asked to see George Crump, once a U.S. Marshal. Crump was not in town, but his son was, and the younger man positively identified Starr.

So once again the celebrated king of the bank robbers was down and hurt and back in the hands of the law. Once more he had been shot down by an ordinary citizen who objected to Starr's larcenous ways, and this time the hurt would be permanent.

As he lay on a cot in a jail cell, Starr was visited by Coffman, the bank cashier, and on another occasion by an official of a bank in Seligman, Missouri, who identified Starr as one of the men who had robbed his bank the previous year, just before Christmas. Lawmen spent some time with him too, and at last Starr began to give them some information. He also told one physician, Dr. T. P. Fowler, that "I was in debt $20,000 and had to have money, so I turned bank robber again. I am sorry, but the deed is done."

Myers's bullet had lodged in the outlaw's spine, from which it was carefully removed by Dr. J. J. Johnson. Starr survived the operation, but the doctor opined that Starr's life was now chiefly in danger from blood poisoning. He also ran the risk of fatal uremic poisoning, the doctor said, because the slug had torn through one kidney on its way to the backbone.

The doctors did all they could for Henry Starr, but it soon became obvious to them, and to Starr, that he was finished. His present and ex-wife were both contacted, along with his mother and son. Staring death in the face, Starr now began to lose some of his outlaw cockiness. "I am going to die," he said, "and I am anxious to make my peace with God." He also said he would give some useful information to the sheriff, which he did.

This time there would be no encore for Starr. He lasted four days, slipped into a coma, and died.

Few honest depositors and bank employees would shed a single tear. They would not miss in the slightest a boastful professional criminal who lived off the sweat of other people. No amount of weeping and learned lamentation about society's evils would change the fact that Henry Starr was a career thug, a thug by choice, a thug who found it easier to steal what other people earned than work for himself.

Henry Starr was blessed by nature with considerable intelligence and an iron constitution, both of which he chose to squander in robbing other people, running from the law, and wasting his years sitting in prison. Boastful and arrogant, it is the real measure of the man that on the day before his death, sliding toward oblivion, he still bragged to his doctors that he had "robbed more banks than any man in America."

Where he was going, that dubious record would do him precious little good.

When George Birdwell Robbed the Wrong Bank

The Usual Hazards of Daylight Banditry

The gang drove into Boley, Oklahoma, and turned up Main Street, and Pete Glass stopped the Buick, pointing north, just south of the bank. Glass waited in the car while George Birdwell and Champ Patterson got out, Birdwell carrying a 1911 Colt .45 semiautomatic pistol, Patterson with a sawed-off shotgun beneath his overcoat. As they entered the bank, treasurer Wesley Riley looked up from his conversation with Horace Aldridge, suspecting nothing. D. J. Turner, the president, got up from his desk and moved up behind the bars on the teller's window to serve Birdwell. He found himself looking into the bad end of the Colt pistol.

"We're robbing this bank," Birdwell said. "Hand over the dough! Don't pull no alarm!"

Turner said nothing but began to pull bills out of the cash drawer, sliding them under the bars to the bandit. Meanwhile, bookkeeper Herb McCormick saw what was going on, slid softly to the floor, and crawled back toward the vault, hoping to get to the rifle he kept there. And then, as Turner pulled out the last bills in the drawer, the alarm fired with a deafening din, both inside the bank and outside, and in the four other stores wired into the system. "You pulled that alarm," yelled Birdwell. "I'll kill you for that!"

And the doughty Turner looked the bandit right in the eye: "You bet I pulled it!"

Riley, standing helplessly in front of Patterson's shotgun, saw what was coming. "Don't hurt nobody, please!" he pleaded, but his only answer was obscenities. Infuriated by Turner's defiance, Birdwell's mercurial temper exploded, and he drove four .45 slugs into Turner at point-blank range. Turner staggered back and went down, clutching at the desk for support as he fell.

McCormick reached the vault and his rifle, and, as the bank president fell, the bookkeeper put a bullet into Birdwell's neck. Blood spurting from the wound, the outlaw dropped his pistol and the sack full of about $700 in loot. "I'm shot," he cried, no longer bold and arrogant. "Hold me! I'm . . . " And down he went.

Patterson ordered Riley and customer Horace Aldridge to pull what was left of Birdwell to the bank door and get him outside. Under the malignant stare of the shotgun, they did. Glass, hearing the firing, now came running into the bank, pistol in hand. He fired random shots toward the back of the bank as he and Patterson fell back toward the door, still trying to scoop up bills scattered across the counter and floor and stuff them into their pockets.

Outside, the outlaws saw citizens headed their way, running toward the bank carrying rifles and shotguns. The hostages took advantage of their captors' confusion to drop what was left of Birdwell on the sidewalk and run for it, disappearing down a side street. Riley's coat was ripped by a bullet or buckshot aimed at Patterson, but both he and Aldridge escaped without being hurt.

His forced labor and human shields suddenly gone, Patterson bent over to pick up Birdwell. Hazel, who owned the town's big department store, had told the sheriff that he and his shotgun were ready for a bank robbery, that he might "git me a pretty boy for breakfast." Now he took a shot at Patterson.

Glass crawled toward Birdwell, as Patterson saw shopkeeper Hazel on his store's veranda and fired at him. Glass realized that Birdwell was quite dead and saw the giant form of Sheriff McCormick heading for him, followed by more citizens who had armed themselves at the Masonic Temple. Glass, seeing that the fat was in the fire, abandoned Birdwell's corpse and ran to the Buick. Patterson, stubborn or stupid or both, was still tugging at Birdwell's corpse when a citizen named Zeigler shot him again.

Miraculously untouched by the hailstorm of lead, Glass slammed the Buick into reverse and began to turn around and make tracks for the highway. At that point, retired sheriff John Owens, kneeling in the center of Main Street some fifty yards from the Buick, coolly put a bullet into Glass. Roaring backward, the car crashed into a parking lot wall and stopped. Everybody within range poured bullets into it until the car was junk and Glass was a corpse. Birdwell and his boys had taken on the wrong town.

In 1932 Boley's five-block Main Street boasted forty stores, including Hazel's two-story department store and the Farmers' and Merchants'

Bank. Boley was a successful all-black community, one of about two dozen such towns in Oklahoma in those days. Across the street from the bank stood the Masonic Temple, an impressive three-story structure. The bank, whose president, Turner, had also served as mayor for ten years, was the town's centerpiece. He had been worried about bank robbery, with good reason.

In the first three months of 1932, bandits stuck up Oklahoma banks for some $62,000, a lot of money to small depositors. In Boley a hoodlum named Charles Arthur Floyd began to create a reputation for himself. He was called "Choc" by his friends, but the rest of the reading public called him "Pretty Boy."

Then and later, people who should have known better called Floyd a latter-day Robin Hood. They gave no thought to the little people whose savings were wiped out by his raids. There was no friendly FDIC to protect depositors if a bank was driven to bankruptcy by robbers. Unless the bank had insurance, the depositors were out of luck.

Floyd and his gang had already struck the banks at Paden and Prague, not far away from Boley, robbing both in the same day. And just the January before, a gang had robbed the bank in the little town of Castle, just six miles down the road from Boley.

Turner said flatly that he would defend the town's savings at all costs and when Turner said something, he meant it. His bank had installed a brand-new electric alarm system. It triggered automatically when the last bills were removed from a teller's drawer, whether the bills were snatched by a robber or removed under duress by a bank employee.

The alarm made a noise like the last trumpet and was tied into four businesses in downtown Boley: Hazel's department store, Shorty Bragg's barbershop, Aldridge's pool hall, and John Owens's meat market.

Butcher John Owens was a formidable man indeed, a retired peace officer who always wore a black Stetson with a bullet hole in the crown, a memento from a gunfight. He and other citizens of Boley kept their shotguns and rifles close at hand, and more weapons were stashed in the Masonic Temple.

Anybody who tried to hold up the bank would also have to come through Sheriff Lankston McCormick, all six feet seven of him, very tough and very capable. Anyone who wanted the hard-earned money of Boley's people would have to buck most of the rest of Boley's determined citizenry as well. But George Birdwell didn't have the sense to stay away.

Companion and sometime accomplice to Pretty Boy Floyd, Birdwell was later described by a lawman as "the man who planned these activities and handled the machine gun in their raids." Birdwell had been a cowboy and an oil field roustabout. At least one story goes that at one time he was even a church deacon. Whatever Birdwell's history, he had turned robber, presumably because there was more money in the larceny business. Birdwell was a veteran criminal and well known for his volatile temper. He nevertheless had the reputation of being a devoted father who not only took care of his wife and his own four children but also looked after his two nephews.

Nobody knows for sure how many banks Birdwell and Pretty Boy Floyd stuck up together. They robbed the bank of little Morris a couple of times, and banks in Shamrock, Konawa, Maud, Earlsboro, and Tahlequah, in addition to the banks in Paden and Castle. They held up the American State Bank in Henryetta, Oklahoma, early in November 1932 and got more than $11,000, a notable haul for those impoverished days.

Of Birdwell's helpers at Boley, Champ Patterson was an experienced outlaw, and Birdwell's brand-new bank robber was a black gambler from Boley called Pete Glass. It may have been Glass who suggested the Boley raid to Birdwell, for the cocky Glass boasted that he was going to "show the gang how to rob a colored bank."

Pretty Boy Floyd refused to join in the Boley venture. This disappointed Birdwell, but it certainly didn't stop him. He decided to take on the Farmers' and Merchants' Bank by himself with only the two men he had.

Two days before Thanksgiving, Birdwell and his cohorts drove their big black Buick down to Boley to reconnoiter the town and its bank. They hung out at Horace Aldridge's pool hall, shooting a few games and watching the bank across the street. Neither Birdwell nor the rest of the bandits aroused suspicion until they left town. They made the mistake of saying something ungentlemanly to Bennie Dolphin, a pretty secretary who worked for Dr. W. A. Paxton, whose office was across the street from the bank.

After breakfast the next day, allowing time for the Boley bank to open, the three climbed in their Buick. Patterson, who usually drove the getaway car, took the wheel, but somewhere near Boley, he moved over so that Glass could drive. The outlaws' plan—insofar as they had any plan at all—was to drive up Main Street and stop just short of the bank. They would park on the wrong side of the street, pointed north, the direction away from the highway.

Once Patterson and Birdwell had the cash and returned to the Buick, Glass was to back up a short distance, making a U-turn as he did so, and then drive hard to the south, to the highway and safety. It would have made more sense to park facing south to begin with and save a few precious seconds when they ran. The right side of the car would face the bank, giving the men two doors to jump into instead of just one.

It was the day before Thanksgiving, and many farmers were in town to buy supplies. Some bought shotgun ammunition because quail season opened the following day. Also in the bank was Herb McCormick, the brother of Sheriff Lank McCormick, and the bank's treasurer, Wesley W. Riley, who was talking to Horace Aldridge, a customer. Out on the street, Sheriff McCormick was making his rounds, dressed in high boots with his trousers stuffed into them, a plaid shirt under a sheepskin coat, and a cowboy hat.

Now the robbery had been averted in blood, and the sheriff shouted for a cease-fire. Dr. Paxton ran across Main Street toward the bank, his shotgun in one hand and his medical bag in the other. Turner was semiconscious on the floor, soaked in blood. Herb McCormick knelt beside him, unable to help.

Turner, still clinging to life, was loaded into Dr. Paxton's car for the trip to the hospital at Okemah. Turner's wife drove up and jumped into Paxton's vehicle, but neither her love nor the doctor's ministrations could save the gallant bank president. He died on the road.

Patterson survived his multiple wounds to reach Okemah.

The next day, according to the *Daily Oklahoman*, Champ Patterson, unable to talk because of his neck wound, confirmed by nodding his head that the dead bandit was the infamous George Birdwell.

A crowd of over five thousand people turned out for Turner's funeral on November 28. Boley was jammed with mourners, only about a quarter of whom could crowd inside the church for the funeral services. Among those making eulogies was a man representing the Oklahoma Bankers Association. Scattered through the crowd were more than fifty peace officers in plain clothes, alert to the possibility that Floyd might "come to claim revenge," as one paper put it.

Pretty Boy Floyd didn't show up. He left the state before the year was out, never to return except to get himself buried at the biggest funeral ever seen in Oklahoma. Within two years he would be cut down by lawmen in the dirt of an Ohio cornfield.

In addition to laudatory letters, McCormick also received a $500 reward from the Oklahoma Bankers Association for killing Birdwell, and Boley's "vigilance committee" got another $500 for exterminating Glass. Governor "Alfalfa Bill" Murray invited McCormick to Oklahoma City, where the governor conferred on him the honorary rank of "Major."

And so he was known for the rest of his life.

John Richard "Rattlesnake Dick" Darling

The Perils of Rattlesnake Dick

John Richard Darling took the name Rattlesnake Dick, apparently after the more famous outlaw of the same name in California. He started out with petty crimes and drunkenness but was twice sentenced to prison. He could hold his own in the epic of Nevada outlawry, but his life was more tragic than violent.

One morning in late summer 1863, Dick woke up and discovered that he had enlisted in Company D of the First Battalion, Nevada Territorial Volunteers, Captain Baldwin commanding. With the regular soldiers transferred east for the Civil War, volunteer units had difficulty maintaining strength for protection against Indians. Company D did most of its recruiting in Virginia City, Gold Hill, and Dayton saloons.

Surprisingly, when Dick got over his hangover, he felt pride in being a soldier. He ran to tell the joyous news to the woman who claimed to be his wife. She thought him an idiot and refused to live at Fort Churchill, his new duty post. For this ingratitude, Dick beat her up, and she decided to stay at a ranch 3 miles from the fort.

Before long, Dick began thinking seriously about his marital rights. On Saturday, September 12, 1863, he rode out to his beloved's new home, anxious to reestablish a more intimate relationship. But Monday's *Virginia Evening Bulletin* reported: "A gentlemen just in from the fort informs us that on Saturday the notorious Rattlesnake Dick was shot by his wife, the ball passing through his body and falling to the ground."

The next day's newspaper had more—and more accurate—details. When Dick arrived for his visit, his wife had met him with a double-barreled shotgun and "both barrels took effect in his left chest, seriously if not mortally wounding him."

But Dick survived his wifely welcome. He walked out to the road in front of the ranch, where Captain Baldwin picked him up and returned him to the fort. His nameless wife, now disillusioned with matrimony, disappeared from history. When Dick's enlistment ended in spring 1866, he turned to crime for a living, beginning with the nonviolent variety.

We don't know why Dick was over at Austin, but on the stage back to his Virginia City home, he met a young lady from Austin whose husband had sent her on a vacation to the States. Dick stole her watch and money, and when he reached Virginia City, his spending spree included many of the Comstock saloons. Pawning the watch financed his drinking as well as the purchase of companionship from one Bertha, whom he met in a saloon.

But when they reached Bertha's upstairs room, Dick passed out just outside her door. She had the bartender call the police, who arrested Dick, perhaps for obstructing traffic. Released the next morning, Dick returned to the saloon with a hangover and a club. He sneaked up behind the bartender, knocked him senseless, and then rushed upstairs to even his score with Bertha.

Bertha wasn't home, so Dick sat down to wait. He whiled the time away by sampling her stock of refreshments, and Bertha returned to find him passed out again. Dick was arrested and taken back to jail, but the bartender had to admit that he hadn't seen who hit him, so Dick was released on bail.

Rattlesnake Dick charged back to Bertha's place, but she convinced him that they had no future. She, too, disappeared from history.

The proceeds of Dick's petty theft lasted only ten days. Then, it would appear that he turned to violent crime. The Virginia City newspaper for the last few days in May reported that Dick and a companion named M.M. Woods had broken into a locked saloon on Virginia City's main street and nearly beaten a customer, Patrick McCauley, to death. Jessie Case, the young woman who kept the saloon, had had to run an errand, so she had locked up, telling McCauley, the only customer, that she'd be back shortly.

Jessie returned to find the back door broken open, blood all over the floor, and McCauley unconscious and beaten so badly, he was hardly recognizable. Blood covered his face, and broken glass littered the floor. When he recovered enough to talk, McCauley said that he worked on a ranch on the Carson River, about 25 miles away, and that he had been robbed of $300. He had no idea how his assailant or assailants got in and attacked him. The May 26 *Territorial Enterprise* "earnestly hoped that the police could obtain some kind of clue leading to the arrest and conviction of the scoundrels concerned in this high-handed piece of villainy."

Police Captain George Downey learned that Dick had been living across the street at the Occidental Hotel for four or five days and had suddenly disappeared. Before the disappearance he had been hanging out at the saloon in question. The police found McCauley's wallet in Dick's room, and the hotel proprietor said Dick had told her that he was going to nearby Washoe Valley to visit his father. Downey tracked his man to Ophir in Washoe Valley, where he was hiding out in an old house, and there made the arrest on the day following the crime.

The newspaper reported that McCauley eventually identified Dick as one of the two men he saw in the bar, although he did not know which one had struck him from behind. The police never found Woods. Dick claimed that Woods told him that he had won $100 from McCauley and that McCauley had pulled a knife on him. Then, Woods said that he hit McCauley with a bottle and left the saloon, telling Dick that he was leaving the state. Dick even claimed that he was not in the saloon when Woods did the crime. The judge turned a deaf ear to those statements.

So did the jury. After its guilty verdict, Judge Richard Rising sentenced Dick to fourteen years in prison at hard labor. But the transcript of the testimony before the magistrate, upon which Dick was held in custody until he went to trial, throws grave doubt on the trial jury's quick verdict, the judge's heavy sentence, and the newspaper's presentation of the facts.

Victim McCauley testified before the magistrate that he entered the saloon on Friday, May 25, between nine and ten o'clock. He saw two men there. One asked him to play cards, and McCauley said he did not have time. When he turned around to leave, he was struck on the back of the head. He had about $160 in gold and silver, and when he came to, he only had $28 in loose coins.

McCauley identified Dick as one of the men in the saloon but could not say which of the two hit him as his back was turned. He was sure that Dick was not the one who asked him to play cards. McCauley was out in the street when he regained consciousness. He said that he had entered the saloon to light his pipe, and he was there only two or three minutes.

On cross-examination, McCauley said that there was no one behind the bar when he entered. He had seen Dick in the saloon before and had bought him a drink. At that time, Dick was with the same man that he saw there when he was attacked.

Jessie Case testified that she saw McCauley in her saloon between ten and eleven o'clock. She served him a drink, and he drank with Dick, a frequent customer, and another man whom she did not know. After five or ten minutes, the three men left and she closed and locked the saloon, putting the front door key in her pocket and the rear door key in her money drawer. She returned in about an hour and the front door was still locked, but the back door was ajar. She saw blood in the back room.

Constable Augustus Ash testified that he saw McCauley between ten and eleven o'clock washing himself behind Ash's office. Then Ash went to Jessie's saloon, where he found the front door unlocked and a broken bottle and blood in the back room. He and Police Chief Downey went to Ophir and arrested Dick, who was lying on a bed with his boots on.

Dick's lawyer did not let him testify. Five years would pass before his version reached the authorities. The action taken then suggests that Dick may have been innocent of this crime and railroaded into prison.

Dick's prison term began June 30, 1866. Five years later, Richard Rising, the trial judge, wrote Nevada Lieutenant Governor Frank Denver, saying that he thought five years was a sufficient sentence, and he would concur in Rattlesnake Dick's application for a pardon. He said his very stiff sentence reflected the community's feeling at the time about violent crime.

"I would say that at the time of his sentence, many outrages and crimes had been and were constantly being committed in this city, and to endeavor to create a terror upon evildoers," Rising wrote. "I imposed upon those convicted very severe punishments."

Dick's fourteen years was the longest sentence Judge Rising had ever given for robbery and assault. Two months later the governor responded with a pardon for Dick.

But we have more than the trial judge's letter of regret. Dick's statement of facts surrounding the conviction, filed in his application for pardon, states that on Friday, May 25, 1866, he had been in Jessie Case's saloon with McCauley and Woods. Woods had brought him a note from a sick woman in Ophir saying she wanted to see him. He left immediately, and McCauley and Woods started playing cards. He reached Ophir about three o'clock in the afternoon and stayed all night with a man named Kelley who kept a saloon there.

While Dick was there, Woods arrived, saying that he'd had trouble with McCauley about the card game. Woods said that McCauley threw a knife at him, and then he struck McCauley on the head with a bottle and left the saloon.

"It's too hot for me here," Woods had said, and he left town.

The next morning Constable Ash and Police Chief Downey arrested Dick. Downey told him that if he could find Woods, he would not want Dick. But Downey "was determined if he could not find Woods to convict me of the charge," Dick said in a statement.

Dick's statement also charged McCauley with later robbing another man and with betraying his own brother into the California State Prison. He said another of McCauley's brothers was hanged.

Finally, Dick denied having anything to do with the robbery of McCauley. He also mentioned that he had once been a soldier.

Dick's petition for a pardon had drawn the written support of the committing magistrate, the district attorney, the constable and the police chief who arrested him, the U.S. Marshal, and two of the trial jurors.

Rattlesnake Dick got his pardon in 1871, but his perils continued.

Just over a year later, in November 1872, Dick was back in prison for robbing Colonel M.N. Stone on the highway below Silver City, a few miles from Virginia City. Colonel Stone was a lawyer, and in late October he was making frequent political speeches for his party. On the evening of October 24, while traveling in a buggy after making a speech, he was held up by two masked men wearing linen dusters.

The taller of the two men resembled Rattlesnake Dick. Apparently the shorter man did all the talking. The shorter man removed Stone's purse and watch from his pocket. The purse contained $55. Then he told Stone to get back in the buggy and "drive like hell," which Stone did.

The next morning Stone and Deputy Sheriff B.P. Lackey went to the holdup scene. They followed the boot tracks of the robbers to a fresh buggy track out in the sagebrush. The buggy had come from the direction of Carson City and returned in that direction.

"Probably rented there," Lackey said. "The town's full with the horse races going on."

The next day, Lackey and Stone learned that Rattlesnake Dick and one Edwin Booth had rented a buggy in Carson City the afternoon of the robbery, returning it the next day. They had also borrowed a couple of linen dusters to wear. The deputy and Stone went out to the races and saw Dick there. Later that afternoon, Stone and Dick had a conversation.

"How much would you pay if I found your watch for you?" Dick asked.

"A hundred dollars. How soon can you get it?"

"I'll meet you in an hour at Frisbie's Saloon. Bring the money."

But when Stone told Lackey and Sheriff Swift of this conversation, they insisted on arresting Dick immediately. Stone wanted to wait until Dick appeared with the watch, but Swift made the arrest anyway.

Stone went to the station after Dick was brought in, without the watch. Dick reminded him that he was to pay $100 for the watch.

"I meant I'd pay it if the watch was found with the men who robbed me," Stone said.

"If they'll release me, I'll find the robbers and the watch."

The sheriff left with Dick, and they returned in twenty minutes. This time Dick had the watch. Again Dick asked to be released, offering to find the robbers. The sheriff refused to release Dick and returned in about fifteen minutes with a William Chamberlin in custody. Apparently, Dick had given Sheriff Swift Chamberlin's name.

When Stone saw Chamberlin in the sheriff's office, he accused him of being one of the robbers. After initial denials, Chamberlin admitted leaving Carson City with Dick in a rented buggy.

All three suspects were charged with the robbery, and Will Campbell appeared as attorney to represent Booth. Before the trial began, the district attorney dismissed the charges against Booth, probably on condition that he testify against the other two. Trial Judge Seawall then appointed Campbell to represent Dick and Chamberlin. Campbell protested the violation of ethical rules, pointing out that he could not represent men who had a conflict of interest with each other and with his former client. Furthermore, he argued, he could not be expected to cross-examine Booth about matters told him by Booth in confidence. Judge Seawall insisted that he defend Dick and Chamberlin.

A witness testified at the trial that he had seen three men in a buggy going toward Carson City from Silver City on the night of the 24th. It stopped in front of a saloon, and two men went inside while a third stayed in the buggy. He also testified that Dick had admitted to him that he was one of the two men who went in for drinks and brought out a drink for the man in the buggy. In the preliminary examination before trial, Chamberlin had admitted that he, Dick, and Booth were the three men in the buggy at that time.

Dick testified in his own defense. He said Chamberlin had robbed Stone and that he knew where the victim's watch was because he had seen the chain protruding from under the pillow where it was hidden. He did not know who put it there. He denied doing it himself.

After two days of testimony, the jury found both Dick and Chamberlin guilty. The judge sentenced each to ten years in prison. Considering himself a silent observer of Chamberlin's robbery, Dick probably shook his head in confusion. Perhaps he looked at Campbell, shaking his head at the impossible situation his attorney had been forced into.

Dick served eight years of the sentence without difficulty, although he once served a month in the dungeon for possession of a large knife. But in July 1880 he killed Chamberlin by striking him over the head with a pick. Dick, a trusty at the time, was working alone with Chamberlin in the prison quarry. Dick claimed that Chamberlin attacked him with a pick handle, and he acted in self-defense. The prison authorities must have believed Dick because he was not prosecuted for the killing or even disciplined for it.

Dick was released in 1881, at the conclusion of his ten-year sentence. He appeared briefly in Virginia City and then disappeared.

In addition to seeking a new environment away from old acquaintances and suspicious police, Dick tried honest employment. He got hired as a brakeman on the Carson and Colorado Railroad. This narrow gauge line connected with the Virginia and Truckee at Mound House to run southerly through Lyon and Esmeralda Counties, terminating in Inyo County, California, after a distance of 293 miles.

Dick made his new home in Hawthorne, Nevada, at about the midpoint of his employer's line. But unfortunately his new job had not changed enough of Dick's customary behavior. In August 1883 Dick got into a saloon argument with James Warren, an ex-convict better known as Jimmy Fresh. Each accused the other of stealing money from a prostitute.

While on his way to work the next morning, Dick met Warren on the street. Warren drew his pistol, saying, "You'll not threaten my life again," and shot Dick in the face. He pumped two more bullets into Dick's dead body after it fell.

The newspaper account of Dick's final affray said he was forty-three and a native of Kentucky. After service in the War against Mexico [impossible unless he was a seven-year-old drummer boy], he had moved to Salt Lake City and lived with the Mormons. He married but deserted his wife to come to the Comstock after the silver discovery of 1859.

"He had been in numerous deadly affrays," the newspaper reported, "and was regarded as a desperate character. Darling's life was an eventful one, and if written up would furnish material for a first-class dime novel."

BEN KUHL

A Nevada Tragedy

Besides providing the West's first train robbery, Nevada gave us the West's last holdup of a horse-drawn stage. And the resulting murder trial became a legal landmark in the development of admissible criminal evidence.

Jarbidge hardly seemed part of Nevada. The stage road came southwest from Rogerson, Idaho, through increasingly rough country, crossing the state line 8 miles north of town. Snowdrifts up to 30 feet deep made Jarbidge the most isolated mining camp in Nevada. Jarbidge's name came from an Indian word for devil. Yet it had become the state's leading producer of gold in the years leading up to the First World War.

The December 5, 1916, evening stage from Rogerson, due in Jarbidge between 5:00 and 6:30, was late, to no one's surprise. Snow had been falling heavily since midafternoon, and with the plunging temperature, the freezing wind, and the precarious descent into the narrow Jarbidge River canyon, no one expected driver Fred Searcey to be on time. But at 9 p.m., Postmaster Scott Fleming, anxious about his mail, started asking questions. He learned from Rose Dexter, who lived at the north end of town a half mile from the post office, that she had heard a loud crack, "like a high-powered gun" at about 6:30 that evening. Shortly after, the stage passed with two men sitting on the seat. One of the men seemed slumped over, and the other had his overcoat collar turned up around his ears. Knowing Searcey well, Rose hollered, "Halloo," but did not get an answer. The stage disappeared in the darkness, and she thought no more about it.

"I thought it might be someone shooting a mad coyote," Rose said about the noise she had heard.

A hastily summoned search party carrying kerosene lanterns found the stage in a dense willow thicket, its horses tied to a tree. The stage was just 200 yards off the road and a quarter mile from the business part of the town. Fred Searcey lay dead on the seat, a bullet wound behind his left ear and a gaping exit wound in his mouth and right cheek. Frozen blood had caked on the seat and floor, and the horses shivered from the cold. The second-class mail sack had been ripped open and its contents strewn about. The first-class sack, in which cash was sometimes sent, was missing. The storm raged too much to continue the search, but guards were posted on all trails to make sure no one left, and the citizens waited until daylight.

The next morning, fairly certain that the killer was still among the 1,500 residents of the town, Constable I. C. Hill and Justice of the Peace J.A. Yewell organized a new search party. It included J.B. McCormick, an experienced hunter. McCormick saw dog tracks near the stage and examined them carefully. He blew out the new snow and got a good print in the old snow underneath.

"I believe these tracks were made by one of them old tramp dogs that don't really belong to nobody," he said. "Let's keep our eyes open and see what we can see. Maybe the dog will come back."

"Well, he's a big one," another said. "Could be that big yeller one that hangs around that rounder name of Ben Kuhl."

"That one on a peace bond for jumping a claim?" someone asked.

"Yep. He's a tough one, I hear."

"They say he's served time in California," another said.

"Hell, he's also done state prison time in Oregon."

Sure enough, at about ten o'clock, one of the camp's dogs came by as though following a trail. McCormick and the others watched and followed as the dog went directly to a place in the brush, about 20 feet off the trail, where the fresh-fallen snow still covered the missing first-class mail sack. They dug it up. By then, they knew that it had contained $2,800 in cash being mailed to the Success Bar and Cafe to cash checks. The cash was gone, but a bloody palm print had been left behind on a torn letter.

"Anybody recognize the dog?" someone asked.

"Seen him around with that Kuhl."

"Let's tell the sheriff."

The search party also found where the killer had waited for the stage, evidently jumping on it as it went past. Footprints and the dog tracks led through the trees and across a bridge. There they found a blood-soaked overcoat, a sack of coins, another sack of registered mail, and a shirt and bandana weighted down with stones in the stream. The shirt resembled those usually worn by Kuhl, and it had the letter "K" marked in ink immediately below the collar. It appeared to have been washed to get rid of blood.

When Justice of the Peace Yewell confronted Kuhl with the overcoat, Kuhl said, "I never owned an overcoat in my life. I wear a mackinaw." But the coat belonged to a friend of his and would have been available for him to wear. In fact some citizens said they had seen Kuhl wearing it.

Kuhl was not popular. He had been a cook at the OK Mine for about a month but was fired when he tried to jump another man's claim. Now he did odd jobs in the camp while waiting for his trespassing trial. He lived in a floored tent with some other drifters. Already known as a troublemaker for the claim-jumping incident, he had previously served a year in the Oregon State Prison for animal larceny and four months in the Yuba County, California, jail for petty theft.

"I hear he needed money," someone said.

"Yeah, to hire a lawyer and to pay a fine for the claim jumping if he gets off that easy."

"He's got more to worry about now."

A search of the tent Kuhl shared with Ed Beck and Billy McGraw produced a .44 caliber revolver, the hammer resting on the one spent cartridge. The gun, found under Kuhl's bed, belonged to Beck, who said he had loaned it to McGraw. The night of the killing, Beck had asked McGraw for the gun, saying Kuhl wanted it for hunting. McGraw delivered the gun to Beck. Kuhl and Beck were seen in the Success Bar and Cafe at about eight o'clock, shortly before Searcey's body was found. They had bought a round of drinks and seemed to be drawing attention to their presence in the bar and to the time.

It took two days for Elko County Sheriff Joe Harris and District Attorney Edward P. Carville to come from the county seat. They had to ride trains east to Ogden, Utah, north to Pocatello, Idaho, and west to Twin Falls, where they changed to the stage. A few men provided Kuhl with an alibi, but he, Beck, and McGraw were arrested and charged with murder.

Kuhl, a slender man standing nearly six feet tall with light blue eyes, was thirty-three. A native of Indiana, he had a wife and an infant son in Salt Lake City and had been in Jarbidge about four months.

Beck, also thirty-three, was a native of Finland and had been in town only a week. Although he had been in the United States for fifteen years, he could barely speak English. He was a heavy drinker.

The trial was originally set for April 16, 1917, but Jarbidge continued to suffer through one of the worst winters in its history. On April 3, Carville and Harris again made the long trip to collect evidence and check on witnesses. They returned to Elko and asked the court to postpone the trial to September. Edwin E. Caine had been appointed by the court to defend Kuhl. Judge Erroll Taber agreed that the defendants could be tried separately, and he set Kuhl's trial for September 18, with Beck's to follow. He asked the press to not report Kuhl's trial, as it might prejudice the jurors selected for Beck's case.

District Attorney Carville prosecuted the cases. C.H. Stone, supervisor of the Federal Bureau of Investigation in Bakersfield, California, was the most important of his forty-six witnesses. Stone, a fingerprint expert, identified the palm print found on the envelope as that of Kuhl. Many people testified that they had seen Kuhl wearing the overcoat that had been found near the river.

The jury found Kuhl guilty on October 7, 1917, after eighteen days of trial and two hours of deliberations.

Beck's trial began on October 8. He testified in his own defense. He said that Kuhl had told him that he and Searcey had arranged a frame-up in which it would appear that Kuhl was holding up the stage. He needed a gun to carry out his part. Kuhl and Searcey were to divide the proceeds of the false holdup between them. Beck said that he got the gun from McGraw and gave it to Kuhl. After the crime Kuhl had told Beck that Searcey would not go through with the deal and he, Kuhl, had "bumped him off." Kuhl also told Beck that he had taken about $2,000 and would split it with Beck if Beck kept quiet about what Kuhl had told him.

McGraw also testified in Beck's trial that he gave the gun to Beck on his original understanding that Beck and Kuhl wanted the revolver to go deer hunting. Later he learned about the simulated holdup.

Beck was also found guilty. McGraw's trial was scheduled to be the last. After he testified against Kuhl and Beck, his charges were dropped.

Beck was sentenced to life imprisonment; Kuhl, to death. The convicted man had a right to choose between hanging and shooting, and Kuhl chose to be shot. The court set his execution date for January 18, 1918. That date was changed from time to time as Kuhl appealed his conviction.

The Nevada Supreme Court decided Kuhl's appeal on September 5, 1918. Kuhl's lawyer pointed out that no court in any English-speaking country of the world had ever allowed palm prints into evidence. The court affirmed the conviction, and the new execution date was December 20, 1918.

One week before the execution date, Kuhl persuaded the State Board of Pardons to look into his claim that he had acted in self-defense. He told the board that the robbery was a frame-up between him and Searcey. He said that sometime before the crime, he had told Searcey that he needed money to develop some mining claims. Searcey then told him that he had previously arranged a false holdup in Idaho and had gotten away with it. They agreed to wait until money was being sent to a Jarbidge bar to cash checks and then work the false holdup. They agreed that Searcey would delay the arrival of the stage to give Kuhl enough time to stash the plunder and get to the post office before the stage arrived so that he would have an alibi.

Kuhl said they rehearsed the holdup once at the selected point, about a mile and one half from Jarbidge. On the night of the crime, he met the stage at the agreed point. He and Searcey sat on the box and discussed the "job" as they moved toward the town.

Kuhl said that Searcey told him that a sack in the stage boot held \$300 and there was \$2,800 in greenbacks in the first-class mail sack. Searcey was willing to give up the \$300, but he refused to cut the mail sack open and give up the greenbacks.

An argument followed, and Kuhl claimed that Searcey went for his gun. Believing that he had been double-crossed and that his own life was in danger, Kuhl then shot Searcey, grabbing his body to keep it from falling off the stage. That, he claimed, is how his clothing became bloody.

Kuhl held Searcey's body up as the stage passed Mrs. Dexter's house, where she called out to them. After he tied the horses in the willow thicket, Kuhl took the first-class mail sack into the brush, where he removed the \$2,800. Then he washed up, made his way back to his tent, and joined the search party looking for the missing stage. In fact he helped take Searcey down from the box and was not sure until then that he had actually killed the man.

On December 13, by a vote of three to two, the board of pardons commuted Kuhl's sentence from execution to life imprisonment. The acting governor, the attorney general, and Chief Justice Patrick McCarran of the state supreme court voted to commute. The two associate justices of the supreme court opposed.

The *Reno Gazette*, claiming "inside facts," reported that the first vote was to not commute, the chief justice siding with his two associates. Then he changed his mind. The *Gazette* also claimed that the evidence produced at the trial supported Kuhl's story before the board of pardons.

Beck was paroled in 1923 after serving six years of his life sentence.

Kuhl came up regularly for parole during the 1920s and 1930s and was regularly turned down. For twelve years he was in charge of the prison bake shop, during which time he took a master baker's course by mail from the Chicago School of Technology. He also studied music and directed the prison orchestra for three years.

In an April 21, 1936, letter to the governor, Kuhl's expression is an impressive witness to the change in his life since he had so brutally murdered Fred Searcey almost twenty years before. He wrote:

> *For the last eight years my duties have been with the prison library. Our present collection of literature comprises some of the most cherished gems of ancient lore. I worked unceasingly for years before my labors were rewarded. Now we have a total of five thousand volumes, obtained through popular subscription from the many good people of our state, and we are indeed proud and sincerely grateful to every one who has contributed to this most worthy cause. Our greatest achievement has been the inauguration of our Prison School, and we trust that this program may be adequately supported by our Legislature and made a permanent policy of the institution.*

Over seventy citizens of the Carson City area signed a petition at this time asking that Kuhl be granted parole. Wardens and other prison officials added their letters in support of Kuhl's petitions. [One such warden, Carl Hocker, was later captain of the security staff at San Quentin and a friend of this writer when, as a deputy district attorney for Marin County, California, he prosecuted cases arising in that prison.] No one ever mentioned any behavioral problems. But Kuhl's prison folder contained a letter from prosecutor Carville, by then a district judge, reminding the parole board that he considered the original death sentence completely appropriate. He thought the reduction to a life sentence was all the mercy the state owed Ben Kuhl.

Kuhl's prison folder contained many letters from his wife and mother. His mother had married again and lived in Kalamazoo, Michigan. His father lived in Walla Walla, Washington. Kuhl's wife Minnie, short for Minnier, divorced him after his conviction, but her second marriage must have ended because she resumed using the Kuhl name in her letters. On November 3, 1927, she wrote the governor, enclosing a letter she had recently received from Kuhl.

This letter, dated October 8, 1927, started this way:

> *My darling Minnie: At last your long wanted letter reached me. My goodness, Pet, I just knew something was terribly wrong. You poor, dear kid, I really am sorry for you. Yes, sweetheart it seems as though all our sorrows come at once. But try to be cheerful; there will be better times surely some day. I think you have done so wonderful all these years. God bless you; I am proud of you. And my little man was sick, too. My that is tough. But glad to know he is better.*

Minnie ended her letter to the governor:

> *It is not my idea to make an extended plea for mercy, but I do so hope you may feel that justice has been served and that more good will come to three of us from his liberation than from his continued confinement.*

Mrs. Kuhl also included a letter from her son to the governor. These remarks suggest that most of the letter was written by Minnie and copied by the boy:

> *I have always loved my Papa Ben, as I remember him. He has been in the Nevada State Prison about eleven years now, and it seems that I don't know what a father's love is since he left us so many years ago.*
>
> *I know my papa wasn't a bad man or criminal. He just got in with rough associates and they influenced him to do*

> *wrong. It seems that things have just gone entirely wrong in the last few years. My mother has just been under a very serious operation, and she is in need of someone to help her out. She is worried about the home and she thinks it is liable to be taken away from us. This winter she knows will be a very hard one for us unless Papa Ben could come home to help us, and help cheer my mother because God only knows her worries, needs, and sorrows.*
>
> *I work as much as possible in the summer and after school so I can help my mother. I am trying to get an education, trying to grasp the present opportunities but unless Papa Ben comes home I'm afraid I'll have to give up.*
>
> *I know that your decision will be for the best, because only efficient and capable men are chosen to be at the head of any state's executive department. I shall certainly appreciate your kind consideration and trouble and more power to Nevada's State executive, Governor Fred B. Balzar.*

Eighteen years later, on May 7, 1945, Ben Kuhl finally got his parole. He was sixty-one, the oldest inmate in the prison and the inmate who had served the longest time. The parole certificate was signed by the attorney general, two justices of the state supreme court, and by the head of the board, Edward Carville, then the state governor. The parole contained the special condition that Kuhl leave Nevada and never return.

But Kuhl's "better times" never came. We don't know what happened. Some say Kuhl went to California, where he soon died of disease. Others say he was hitchhiking toward northeastern Nevada when he was struck and killed by an unidentified hit-and-run driver. The latter story is more likely true, as he had promised the parole board that he would remarry his wife if released. She and their son still lived in Salt Lake City.

Perhaps the boy learned that Papa Ben was an unpopular claim jumper and petty thief who brutally killed an acquaintance. But perhaps he also learned that his father improved his life through self-education and community work inside a prison until free citizens and prison officials joined in his request for parole. The district attorney who'd worked to convict Kuhl in a landmark evidential case was the same man who, as governor, paroled him.

Lawrence Kelly

Smuggler of Opium

In March 1891, Lawrence Kelly snuck onto his four-ton sloop with another illegal batch of opium. The sixty-five half-pound cans he carried would fetch a tidy profit. But only if he was careful. The law had been getting too close to him lately, so he decided to travel a more circuitous route. That day, he sailed from Victoria, British Columbia, to Olympia, Washington. From there, he walked to the train station at Tenino 20 miles away, carrying the opium in a satchel. At Tenino he boarded a northbound train.

Unfortunately for Kelly, U.S. Customs agent Charles Mulkey of Tacoma boarded the same train. While walking through the smoking car, he spotted the bag Kelly was carrying and immediately became suspicious. He walked over, seized it, and began to search it, despite protests from Kelly. Inside he found the cans of illegal opium. He placed Kelly under arrest, and when the train stopped at Castle Rock, Mulkey took Kelly and George Davis, the man sitting next to Kelly, off the train and back to Tacoma, where Kelly appeared before the U.S. Commissioner.

How did Lawrence Kelly become a smuggler of opium? His early life shows no signs of defiance; in fact, it seems just the opposite. Kelly was born about 1839 in the British Isles. When he was a young man, he joined the British Army and then later became a sailor. His British sloop docked at New Orleans just after the American Civil War broke out, so he deserted the ship and joined the Confederate Army. He served with distinction, fighting until General Lee's surrender on April 9, 1865.

Shortly after the end of the war, Kelly emigrated west, sailing around South America on the ship *Young America* and ending up in the Puget Sound area. His name first appeared in a newspaper about 1872, when he was caught smuggling Canadian silks into the United States. He was fined $500, which he easily paid, but this punishment didn't curb his smuggling. He soon had enough money to build a nice home on Guemes Island, just across Guemes Channel from Anacortes. His house was perched high on a bluff, and Kelly had an awe-inspiring view of the Guemes Channel, Bellingham Channel, and Rosario Strait.

In 1877 he married Lizzie Coutts, when he was thirty-two and she was sixteen. Shortly after their wedding, he transferred the title of his house to her name, so that if he were ever to be arrested, the house could not be seized to pay his fines. Judging by that act, it seems he never planned to make a living by legitimate means. For a time, he and Lizzie easily lived off the money he made as a smuggler.

At first Kelly used an ordinary fishing sloop to carry illegal goods from Canada to Washington State. He didn't even bother to paint over its bright red color—he could outrun the law, anyway. He knew all the coves and bays like the back of his hand, and his small boat could travel easily in shallow water through which the bigger customs boats couldn't navigate. He smeared pot black and tallow on his boat to make it glide more easily through the water. And if someone chased him and he couldn't get away, he just dumped the smuggled goods overboard so that he wouldn't be caught with them.

Smuggling was not an unheard-of crime in the United States in the nineteenth century. During the Civil War, liquor, blankets, and wool were smuggled from Canada for use by soldiers. Smuggling increased dramatically, however, when the railroads began to import large numbers of Chinese workers as laborers for canneries, hop fields, mines, and public works. Though this caused some difficulties with white workers, Chinese laborers were desirable because they worked hard, took fewer breaks, could be paid less, and did not drink.

Then the Exclusion Act of 1882 prevented Chinese laborers from entering the United States legally. Smugglers saw an opportunity in the Puget Sound area. In no time at all smugglers began to sneak Chinese workers into the country, and Kelly joined their ranks. The smugglers took the Chinese immigrants to places where a large number of Chinese were already living so that they would blend into the population. Sometimes the smugglers hid the immigrants in the smaller San Juan Islands to wait for the perfect opportunity to take them to the United States mainland. Smugglers generally received $50 per alien, so smuggling was a good moneymaking operation.

Chinese workers used large amounts of opium, and soon the illegal trade of that commodity grew, too. A refinery in Victoria cranked out as much opium as the Chinese workers could ever want. Opium could be imported legally, but it was very highly taxed, so the drug was often smuggled into the country to avoid the customs duty.

Whether his cargo was human or other, it made no difference to Kelly. He would smuggle anything. But once his activities were discovered, the law was perpetually at his heels. He was first arrested on December 21, 1882. Customs agent Thomas Caine had noticed that Kelly frequently used the Swinomish Slough, near LaConner, as one of his drop-off points. On December 21 Caine hid in the Slough and waited for Kelly to show up. For some reason Kelly was suspicious. As he approached the area where Caine was hidden, he quietly jumped into the water and swam, pushing his boat in front of him. In spite of Kelly's stealth, Caine could still see the boat when it appeared out of the early morning fog. He waited until the sloop got close, then ordered Kelly to surrender. Kelly did, without a fight. He was carrying forty cases of Chinese wine and a man from China, both illegal. Fortunately for Kelly, the Chinese man testified at Kelly's hearing that he was not a "coolie," or illegal Chinese immigrant, but actually a merchant with business in Portland. The smuggling charge was dismissed, and Kelly was fined a mere $150 for the illegal importation of Chinese wine. Kelly returned to smuggling immediately.

In July of 1883, Kelly again was caught with illegal goods and assessed a fine of $390. Four months later, on November 17, he was fined $20. And he went right back to smuggling. The fines were just penny-ante annoyances to Kelly.

In 1886 Kelly expanded his base of operations. He bought some property on Sinclair Island from Thomas P. Hogin, which he also put in his wife's name. From high on a bluff, this house had an advantageous view of the waterways. He could see the Strait of Georgia and Canada on the other side. He also could easily watch for customs ships.

Kelly and his wife had six children who attended school on Sinclair Island. Kelly even became a member of the school board. The townspeople seemed to be aware of Kelly's occupation, but they didn't harass him about it. Perhaps some even sympathized with him. By the late 1880s, he was smuggling mostly opium from Victoria. He would stash the opium on the island until weather conditions were right and a successful delivery on the mainland was likely. Then he would take the opium to Port Townsend, Seattle, or some other Washington port. He generally made $12 on each pound of the drug.

Not long after moving to Sinclair, Kelly had another serious brush with the law. Customs inspectors seized his Whitehall boat on May 16,

1886, in Tacoma. Unfortunately for Kelly, he had just loaded 567 tins of opium, equivalent to 364 pounds. Officers took him to jail, where he was held on a bail of $3,000. In the end, Kelly was fined only $100, but the seizure of his boat threatened to end his career.

Somehow Kelly's luck had not yet run out. In fact, he got right back into the business and seemed to work with impunity. Dozens of his deliveries around the Puget Sound area went undetected, even though the customs boats were getting stronger and faster and smugglers were getting caught more and more frequently. Kelly and the others devised new tricks to keep from getting arrested. Kelly would put the opium in a weighted sack, tie the sack to a rope, and tie the rope to a ring bolted into the hull of his boat. The boat dragged the opium along under water so that a casual inspection of the ship would detect nothing on deck. Sometimes Kelly tied a sack of opium to a float when customs inspectors came near, and then he would retrieve it when the inspectors were gone.

The smuggling of Chinese immigrants became more dangerous, too. To hide them, some smugglers resorted to sewing them into potato sacks, then stashing them in some small cubbyhole of the ship. Anyone who inspected the ship might conclude that the ship was transporting a cargo of vegetables. Sometimes the Chinese would be left on an uninhabited island or on barren rocks to wait for a boat to take them to the mainland. Rumors spread that smugglers would sometimes toss the illegal immigrants overboard in order to avoid arrest. Kelly always denied doing that, but he did admit that he sometimes just delivered the Chinese back to Vancouver Island and let them believe they were in the United States.

No matter how clever the smugglers were, the law was closing in. Herbert Foote Beecher, son of the famous evangelist Reverend Henry Ward Beecher, came to Washington in 1883. For two years he plied the waters between Port Townsend and the San Juans in his gospel ship *Evangel*. He had heard all kinds of stories about Kelly and other smugglers, and it wasn't long before the information he obtained led to arrests, larger fines, and confiscation of greater amounts of opium. Kelly was captured several times and paid increasingly higher fines.

Efforts like Beecher's led to Kelly's 1891 arrest by Customs agent Mulkey aboard the train. When he appeared before the U.S. Commissioner in Tacoma, Kelly denied ownership of the satchel. He said that Mulkey had planted the opium in his bag while he was in the washroom. The commissioner did not believe him and sentenced him to two years at the McNeil Island Federal Penitentiary. Amazingly, Kelly's neighbors on Sinclair Island did believe him. They tried to petition for his release, but they were unsuccessful.

Customs officers converged on Kelly's hideout at Sinclair Island. They took his ship *Alert* and sold it for $3,221.83 to pay off his fines. They couldn't prove he had participated in previous shipments of illegal opium, but they thought they could at least charge him with entering and leaving foreign ports without proper paperwork. They claimed he had been to Victoria and back several times without declaring his manifest.

While he was at McNeil Island, Kelly's fines mounted to the point where he had to sell off his island property in order to pay them. To support herself, his wife kept house for a man in Anacortes whose wife was hospitalized. After his release, Kelly went to Anacortes in a drunken rage and threatened his wife with a gun. She alerted the police, but Kelly had disappeared.

In 1896, Kelly was almost caught when he stole a box of tools from carpenter D. J. Davis of Anacortes. A man named J. H. Young became suspicious when he saw Kelly and another man sneaking toward the wharf, so Young asked Davis to check on his tools. They were missing, so Young, Davis, and J. A. Crookham formed a search party. Marshal Stevenson, J. W. Bird, H. H. Soufle, R. McCormick, and George Layton formed another.

At first neither search party could find the two men, but then Young spotted Kelly in a boat off Guemes Island. The marshal's party followed the Fidalgo Island shore and circled around Burrows Bay. Young's party sailed across the bay to Cypress Island, where they found two men and their camp but no boat or tool chest. Somehow Kelly had slipped away again. The next day the marshal went back to the island to resume the search. He found a cabin and a dog. Stevenson, Bird, and Soufle snuck up to the cabin and peered inside. There they found Kelly asleep, so they pounded on the door and demanded to be let in. Kelly opened the door, and he was immediately arrested. He resisted briefly, and when he tried to get to his rifle, Stevenson knocked him down and handcuffed him.

The posse returned to Anacortes. While their boat docked, Kelly jumped overboard and disappeared into the water. He somehow swam away, even though handcuffed. A week later a man named Ipsen spotted two men and a boat on the beach near Deception Pass. He watched them for a short time and became convinced they were smugglers, so he disguised himself as a settler and approached their camp. By the time he arrived the men were gone, but a search of their tent yielded about $5,000 worth of opium. Ipsen suspected that the stash belonged to Lawrence Kelly, but others didn't think so. They figured that Kelly knew the Puget Sound area too well to let himself be trapped on an island by a high tide.

The next day 100 feet of cable was stolen from a local sloop, five boxes of codfish were taken from Matheson's wharf, and a rowboat was stolen from W. Mathews's landing on Guemes Island. Because Kelly was known to be in debt due to his fines, he was suspected of the thefts, but no proof of his guilt ever surfaced.

About this time Kelly purchased the sloop *Katy Thomas,* built on Waldron Island in 1894 by Ashton Thomas and his brothers, Ellery and John. Ashton Thomas named the boat for his wife, Kathryn, who sewed the sails for the boat. The Thomas family used the boat in races up until 1897. The boat outlived Kelly—it was still in use some sixty years after it was built.

By the turn of the century, Kelly was slowing down, and in 1901 he was captured in Seattle. He had just arrived from Vancouver Island and had booked a room at the Granville Hotel. He left two suitcases full of opium in his room while he went out for the evening. Unfortunately he was picked up for drunkenness that night, and while he was in jail, the Seattle police received a tip from Vancouver Island police. They sent an investigator to Kelly's hotel room, where they found the opium. Amazingly, he paid only a $5 fine and the opium was not even confiscated.

The next day a Seattle policeman followed Kelly when he left for New Westminster on Vancouver Island. Kelly checked in at the Fraser House, went out for dinner and a stroll, and then returned to the hotel. Once Kelly was in the hotel, the policeman decided he could probably take a break, but that was just what Kelly was counting on. During the night he snuck out and crossed back into Washington. A few months later, as he debarked a steamer in Portland, he was arrested for possession of $800 worth of opium. He spent several months in the Multnomah County jail.

In January 1905 Kelly was spotted on a train not far from the Canadian border. Customs agent Fred F. Strickling had heard that Kelly was going to try to smuggle opium on the local train, so he boarded the train at its northernmost stop in Sumas, near the Canadian border. He figured he would have no trouble intercepting Kelly on his way north. At each train stop, he asked the conductor if anyone had boarded. Finally the conductor answered in the affirmative: A man had boarded the train at Nooksack.

Strickling strode down the aisle until he found the man the conductor had described. He approached the man and told him that he needed to look inside his valise. Kelly was defiant and refused. When Strickling insisted, Kelly shoved him out of the way and fled down the aisle. Before Strickling could react, Kelly jumped off the train. Strickling pulled the emergency cord, and the train stopped. Inside Kelly's luggage were sixty-five tins of opium. Strickling ordered the engineer to back up the train to the place where Kelly had jumped off.

Luckily for Strickling, Kelly knocked himself out when he jumped. Strickling quickly handcuffed him, confiscated his gun, and took him on the train to Deming. Kelly's face and shoulders were cut up from his rough landing in the cinders along the track, so the Deming station agent asked a local doctor to patch up the prisoner. Shortly afterward Strickling escorted Kelly to Sumas and on to Bellingham, where he was arraigned before U.S. Commissioner H. B. Williams. He was released on $1,000 in bail, and he promptly skipped town.

Kelly was captured by Fred E. King and Fred C. Dean on July 18, 1905, near Anderson Island. His boat was full of opium at the time. He received a two-year sentence at McNeil Island but was released early for good behavior. The moment he was released, a U.S. marshal hauled him straight back to jail in Seattle for the earlier offense on which he had jumped bail. In May 1909 Kelly was sent back to McNeil Island for a one-year sentence.

After his release Kelly found that going straight meant hard times. He "retired" from his life of crime in 1911, when he was about seventy years old. He contacted the Daughters of the Confederacy and was admitted to a Confederate soldiers' home in Louisiana, where he died. So ended the twenty-five-year career of one of the most notorious smugglers on the Pacific Coast.

Johnny Schnarr

An Accidental Rumrunner

Johnny Schnarr checked his supplies one last time. His boat was in tip-top shape, and the typical winter storms had not yet touched the region. A few minutes later, Schnarr and his partner, Harry, motored away from the dock at Victoria, British Columbia. Their destination was San Francisco. Their cargo was prime Canadian rum. November 8, 1920, was off to a promising start.

Schnarr set a course through the Strait of Juan de Fuca and out to the Pacific Ocean. He picked up his contraband at Pedder Bay, then headed for the open sea. The operation seemed to be going so well, he decided to risk a little catnap. He had been up for almost twenty-four hours straight and was exhausted. He left Harry at the helm.

Two hours later, Schnarr awoke from his nap. Harry was struggling with the wheel. Schnarr pushed him out of the way and attempted to gain control of the boat. Once he had her stabilized, he got his bearings. He was astounded—somehow Harry had turned the boat nearly 180 degrees! In a chastened voice, Harry admitted he really didn't know that much about sailing.

Schnarr cursed Harry and put the boat back on course. He was able to get them around Cape Flattery, the northwestern tip of Washington, but then the motor began to cough and sputter. Schnarr was able to fix the problem, but the boat was using so much gas and oil that he knew they would not have enough fuel to get all the way to San Francisco. They stopped at Astoria, on the mouth of the Columbia River, to stock up on fuel. But their bad luck continued when they left town. The tide was out, and they ran aground on a sandbar. They had to wait six hours before the tide came in to float them off the sand.

The next two days were uneventful, and they made good progress. Schnarr set the course and figured nothing else could go wrong. He decided to risk taking another nap, despite the unreliable Harry. Harry stayed true to his character. He couldn't hold the course. The boat ran aground again and the resulting crunch woke Schnarr from his sleep. The stranded boat was being pounded mercilessly by the waves. The men had no choice but to abandon ship. They struggled through the waves and collapsed on the shore. Once he was rested, Schnarr realized that some of the cargo might be saved. Between waves, Schnarr waded back to the marooned boat. He opened the hatch cover and pulled out a sack of liquor. When the next big wave receded, he made a break for the beach. He dropped the sack to the sand and rested a minute before going after another load. Eventually Schnarr and Harry were able to recover seventy of the 110 cases of liquor before the boat was completely broken up by the waves.

Schnarr's career as a rumrunner was not off to a very good start. But he had not chosen this career on purpose. It had happened by accident.

Johnny Schnarr began his life on November 16, 1894, in the small town of Chehalis, Washington. He had two older brothers, August and Gus, and a younger sister, Minnie. When he was six years old, the family moved to a twenty-six-acre plot on Coal Creek, 3 miles from Chehalis. When he was eleven, the Brown Logging Company wanted to build a railway through the county, and the Schnarr property lay right in the path the company wanted to use. In exchange for their property, the railroad built the Schnarrs a new log house in another location.

In 1910, Johnny's older brothers went to work at a logging camp on Cracroft Island, about 150 miles west of Vancouver Island, British Columbia. The next spring young Johnny joined them. After logging operations finished in the fall, the brothers looked around for trapping prospects. They camped on the east side of Vancouver Island and spent the winter there. Here Schnarr developed skills he would one day use in his future career. In addition to all he learned about trapping, he also learned a lot about sailing, weather, and the sea. He even learned to make dugout canoes from watching the Indians.

The following summer the boys got handlogging rights for an area on the Adams River. In the fall and winter they trapped on Butte Inlet. The next summer, the Schnarr brothers worked in a logging camp and again spent the winter trapping. The following spring, they tried their hand at fishing on the Klinaklini River. There, Johnny Schnarr met his future employer, Fred Kohse. Out fishing one day, the Schnarr brothers helped Kohse get his small rowboat unstuck from a gravel bar. To thank them, he gave them a ride in his sailboat, which was anchored at the mouth of the river. When they got to Victoria, Kohse offered them jobs at his boathouse. August and Johnny accepted; Gus Schnarr returned to Chehalis. While working for Kohse, Johnny learned a lot about fixing engines and navigating a boat on the ocean.

Schnarr took a five-year hiatus from fishing and logging to serve his country in World War I, but he returned to his home state after the armistice. He resumed his life as a logger near Hoquiam. While there, he received a letter from Kohse, who asked if he would be willing to run a boatload of liquor for a friend named Harry. Harry needed someone good with engines.

In Victoria, Kohse introduced Schnarr to Harry. Harry offered Schnarr $500 to drive his boat to San Francisco and back. Schnarr would be the ship's mechanic, navigator, and rumrunner. The Volstead Act of January 1920 had made it illegal to import liquor into the United States, but Johnny Schnarr took Harry up on his offer anyway. The boat turned out to be a little smaller than Schnarr would have liked, but he had already accepted the job. As it turned out, he had reason to be wary; his partner proved completely unskilled.

After Schnarr and Harry wrecked off the Oregon coast, they stashed the liquor on the beach, then walked north to what was probably the Cape Blanco lighthouse. By the time they returned for their cargo, someone had stolen all the booze. They were stuck in Oregon with no money and no way home. Finally Harry's girlfriend sent cash to pay their return fare. Harry paid Schnarr $100 despite the fact that they had not been able to deliver their cargo. Then they parted ways.

Schnarr returned to Chehalis and resumed logging for a while, but in March of 1921 he received another letter from Kohse. He wanted Schnarr to run liquor from Canada into Washington State. He would split the profit three ways among Schnarr, himself, and his partner, Billy Garraro. The boat he would use was 18 feet long and had a 1-cylinder, 5-horsepower engine. Its top speed was 5 knots. Schnarr liked the terms and accepted the offer.

His first delivery was to Anacortes, Washington, on the northern tip of Fidalgo Island. His customer was Consolidated Exporters, located about 5 miles north of downtown. The company would become one of Schnarr's top customers. The boat he used was in top shape, and he no longer had to deal with an unreliable shipmate. Schnarr's only worry was the U.S. Coast Guard cutter *Arcata*, which had a top speed of 12 knots and carried a cannon with a range of 4,000 yards. Although the *Arcata* was faster than Schnarr's boat, it generally patrolled much farther south. For a while Schnarr made his runs undisturbed.

In the first month, he made more than $1,000 in just five or six trips. He and Garraro picked up the booze in Victoria, then they sped toward their destination, taking turns steering so that they didn't get tired. When they came within a certain range of the shoreline, Schnarr would stop the boat. He then exchanged flashlight signals with his customers waiting onshore. If he received the appropriate signal in return, he would drop a skiff in the water. This small boat would be used to haul the liquor to shore. Schnarr usually stayed with the getaway boat while Garraro rowed the booze to shore and collected the money.

At first Schnarr carried about seventy-five cases of booze on each trip, but demand was great. Kohse bought a new boat big enough to haul 110 cases at a time. The boat was faster, too—too fast for the Coast Guard to catch. But just in case, Kohse and Schnarr changed their method of operation just a bit. Instead of picking up the booze directly from the supplier in Victoria, Schnarr motored out to Discovery Island, a small island in Haro Strait, and picked up his liquor there.

Conducting business this way was less obvious to the authorities. But an additional hazard developed. Some men, too lazy or too stupid to mess with the business end of rumrunning, waited until other rumrunners were already in the process of making their runs. They would steal the liquor at gunpoint and sell it to the nearest customer. Mickey, Happy, and Ted Eggers were the most notorious of these pirates.

Kohse started demanding a bigger percentage of the profits, but Schnarr thought that arrangement was unfair since he was taking all the risks. He severed his relationship with Kohse, and Billy Garraro left with him. Schnarr took a break from rumrunning to work on a boat he had designed himself. He hired a Japanese carpenter and shipbuilder to build the boat to his specifications and borrowed money to buy an engine for it. He found a powerful 6-cylinder, 80-horsepower Marmon car engine. He spent about three weeks installing it on the boat, which he called *Moonbeam*. Its top speed was 17 or 18 knots, and it was able to carry about seventy-five cases of liquor.

In the fall of 1923, the boat was ready to go. Autumn was the perfect time to get started. Schnarr generally avoided making deliveries in the summer because the nights were too short. He needed to be able to make the round trip to and from the delivery point under cover of darkness. Ready for a busy season with a new boat, he already had several customers lined up. Some of them were men he had met while working for Kohse.

The first of these were brothers-in-law Carl Melby and Pete Peterson. They supplied liquor to the greater Seattle area, using a Cadillac and a Studebaker to carry their liquor loads. The cars were specially outfitted with heavy-duty springs so that the weight they were carrying would not be noticeable.

To confuse the authorities, Schnarr used a different drop-off location every time he delivered to Melby and Peterson. He delivered liquor to ports all over Puget Sound, from Port Angeles to Anacortes. Unfortunately the lucrative relationship was threatened when Schnarr noticed that Peterson was shorting him. He threatened to end their association unless Melby handled all the money. After looking into the situation, Melby noticed that he had been shorted, too. He put an end to those shenanigans, and the liquor deliveries continued.

One time Schnarr was making a run to a small bay about a mile east of Port Angeles. By the time he arrived, a strong wind had whipped up, causing 20-foot waves. His contact, Barney Sampson, suggested that they tie up at the government wharf in Port Angeles to wait out the storm. Schnarr agreed, not wanting to test his luck twice in one night. Schnarr was astonished when the harbormaster told him that the Coast Guard cutter *Arcata* was tied up on the other side. Before the sun came up the next morning, Schnarr left the harbor before he could be caught.

Run-ins with the law weren't the only hazards of Schnarr's trade. Submerged logs and debris were frequently a problem for Schnarr and other rumrunners. Puget Sound was always full of them due to the region's logging activity and storms. More than once Schnarr's boat suffered damage from logs he couldn't see until he had run into them. Another hazard was fog, which could roll in thick and fast. Schnarr knew Puget Sound so well that he was usually able to reach his destination despite fog, but one time he sheared most of the blades off the two propellers when his boat cruised over submerged rocks. He limped back to port at about three knots with only one blade left. On another trip he almost collided with an ocean liner but managed to avoid it in the nick of time.

In 1923, a new man came to Seattle to enforce Prohibition. He was a tough ex-cattleman from Wyoming named Carl Jackson. He immediately hired more men to patrol the wharves. Schnarr had to be more careful about where he dropped off his liquor. His friends in the local police force usually tipped him off when there was going to be a raid, but he did have a close call or two. One night, just as Garraro reached the beach with his skiff full of thirty cases of booze, Prohibition agents popped out of the forest. Fortunately the raid didn't seem very organized, and Garraro, Melby, and Peterson were able to split up. They raced through the trees on foot while Schnarr watched helplessly from his position offshore in the *Moonbeam*. Fortunately, the men escaped, though Carl was shot in the sole of his foot.

Another close call came later that winter. The Shore Patrol caught Schnarr's team near Deception Pass on the north end of Whidbey Island. Just as they were about to offload their cargo into the rowboat, lights came on and the Shore Patrol started blasting away. In his haste to escape the spray of bullets, Garraro cut off the anchor rather than haul it in. Once again, the smugglers avoided detection. Or so Schnarr thought. The next day a customs inspector came around the Victoria docks and found a lead bullet lodged in the hull of the *Moonbeam* and knew what had happened. Rather than argue the case, Schnarr paid the man the $500 fee. He didn't want to be out of commission too long, or he'd be out much more than that in lost profits.

In the spring of 1924, a new threat arrived in the waters. The U.S. Customs Service launched ten new boats in the Puget Sound area. Their top speed was about 18 knots, the same speed as Schnarr's own boat. He knew he'd need a new engine. This time he bought one that he figured wouldn't have to be replaced for quite a while. With a 300-horsepower Fiat airplane engine that reached a top speed of 30 knots, he would easily outrun the Coast Guard and the Customs Service. He adapted the airplane engine for use on the boat, but he couldn't change the fact that this type of engine had no gears. That meant it had no reverse, so he would have to be sure he was pointing the boat in the right direction before starting it.

For the next two years, Schnarr had a steady job running rum into Washington. He ran booze all year except during the longest days of summer. Soon he realized that he needed a bigger boat. He could only carry seventy-five cases, and many customers wanted 100 or more at a time. He designed a new boat 48 feet long with a 9-foot beam. Luckily the new boat's construction was already in the works when some friends borrowed the old boat to make a run and lost it when the Coast Guard shot it up and then forced it into a crash landing on a beach. The friends escaped unhurt, but Schnarr's own rumrunning business was out of commission for a month while he put the finishing touches on his new boat. Schnarr took the rare opportunity for a little leisure. He spent some of his spare time at the horse races at Willow's Fairgrounds and Race Track, where he met his first wife. He married Pearl Bromely in December 1927 in Tacoma. Pearl had a daughter named Doreen by a previous marriage, and two years later the couple would have a son named Johnny. Eventually they bought a house on Vancouver Island, where they frequently treated their friends to hunting and fishing trips.

Meanwhile, Schnarr finished building his new boat, the *Miss Victoria*. This one had two 300-horsepower Fiat engines, but the design of the cabin proved difficult for loading and unloading cargo. In the fall of 1928, Schnarr built a new boat with a 400-horsepower Liberty airplane engine. Fully loaded with 125 cases, it could still go 30 knots. He called this boat *Miss Victoria II*.

He set off on a trip to deliver to Melby on Dungeness Spit near Sequim. Initially the weather was good, with only a light breeze. But when the tide started to come in, huge breakers formed in the shallows. Schnarr must not have realized the seriousness of the conditions because he proceeded with his delivery as normal. As the *Miss Victoria II* approached shore, Schnarr looked for his flashlight signal. When he saw it, he sent his assistant, a man named Griffith, to shore in a flat-bottomed skiff loaded with liquor. As Griffith approached the shore, one of those big waves caught the small boat and flipped it over, dumping Griffith and the booze. Fortunately another wave caught Griffith and deposited his unconscious body on the beach. Miraculously he was unharmed. Even more miraculous, Griffith managed to recover all the liquor. Not even one bottle was broken. After resting, Griffith rowed back out to the *Miss Victoria II*. He was swamped one more time by the waves on his way out, but this time he was ready for it. He climbed aboard the skiff again and reached the *Miss Victoria II* without further incident.

Schnarr used the *Miss Victoria II* for about two years before he needed an even bigger boat. By that time many rumrunners had been caught, but the demand for liquor was just as strong as ever. Schnarr figured he could pick up the slack and make two or three deliveries on one trip if he had a bigger boat.

The new boat was 45 feet long with a 10-foot beam and two 400-horsepower engines. Now he could carry 200 cases and still reach a speed of 30 knots. He named the new boat *Kitnayakwa* after a river in northern British Columbia. He chose the name because he figured it would be hard for witnesses to remember if he were ever spotted. On one of his first trips in that boat, the Coast Guard tried to run him down. He didn't have any rum onboard, so he could easily go 40 knots. The cutters still could go only about 17 knots and their cannon fire fell well short of the mark.

One December night Schnarr had an incident that was too close for comfort. He was on his way to make a delivery at Discovery Bay, behind the Quimper Peninsula. He didn't spot the Coast Guard cutter until it was about 100 yards away. He quickly got up speed, but the cutter started firing. He couldn't continue on his present course toward a bay or he'd be trapped, so Schnarr quickly turned the boat around 180 degrees and passed within 100 feet of the cutter. The wash from Schnarr's boat spoiled the sniper's aim just a bit. By the time the bulky cutter turned around, Schnarr was well out of range. Five more cutters were out there waiting to ambush him, but with his superior speed, Schnarr got away easily. The next day he had to repair eighteen bullet holes in the hull of his boat. He lost some of his liquor, but otherwise he was unharmed. Later, he learned that $25,000 had been offered for the capture of his boat.

One time on a stormy night delivery, the boat's engine suddenly died. As Schnarr repaired a plugged gas line, a hose came loose. Gasoline sprayed all over the work area and on Schnarr. As Schnarr struggled to complete the repair, a wrench slipped from his hand and struck an electrical contact. The force was enough to create a spark, and the spilled gas was quickly ablaze—along with Schnarr's arm. Billy Garraro quickly helped put out the fire but not before Schnarr's arm was seriously burned. The boat was not badly damaged, and the two men made their delivery as usual. Though Schnarr later visited a doctor who treated his arm, the incident underscored the danger of his work.

About this time the United States started pressuring Canada to tighten up its shipping laws to prevent the illegal entry of liquor. The new laws meant that liquor could not leave directly from a Canadian port. Rumrunners would have to meet ships out in the ocean to pick up their booze. Schnarr knew his boat wasn't designed for the open ocean, so it was time to build yet another boat. The project would have to wait for a while because Schnarr didn't have the money, but he did his best with the boat he had and used a new rendezvous point 100 miles out to sea.

Though the swells were larger and the sea rougher farther out, Schnarr made his first few runs without incident. But each trip used much more gas, and the length of each run was doubled. As many as twelve hours were required for each pickup, then another twelve hours were needed for the delivery and return to Victoria. On top of that, two fast, new Canadian cutters patrolled the Strait of Juan de Fuca, and a more ambitious U.S. Coast Guard had also stepped up its patrols. Schnarr was nearly caught several times, but he always got away. Amazingly, even with all his experience on the sea, Schnarr always got seasick when he was out on the open ocean.

At about this time Schnarr discovered that one of his best friends—Garraro—had cheated him. One of their customers didn't pay them on delivery, so a few days later he sent Garraro to Seattle to collect the money. Garraro returned two days later and told Schnarr the man didn't have the payment. Schnarr figured he'd just have to write off the loss. A couple of months later he ran into the man and asked him about the money. He claimed he had paid Garraro when Garraro had gone to see him. Schnarr confronted Garraro, who admitted taking the money. That was the end of their relationship. After that Tom Colley and Joe Fleming usually accompanied Schnarr on deliveries.

Consolidated Exporters decided to lend Schnarr the money for a new boat. Schnarr put up $7,000 of his own money, and Consolidated loaned him $15,000 more. Schnarr would pay Consolidated 40 percent of every haul to pay off the loan. Less than a year later he had repaid the debt. This boat was 56 feet long with two 860-horsepower Packard airplane engines. For added strength, he built the hull with two layers of cedar planks. He christened it *Revuocnav,* another name that would be hard to remember. (It was actually Vancouver spelled backwards.) Its top speed was 40 knots while fully loaded, but it really sucked down the gas. At a cruising speed of 18 knots it used about 40 gallons per hour. Schnarr had to carry 2,600 gallons of gas onboard, but he could also carry 250 cases of liquor on this boat.

By this time, Schnarr faced steep competition from other rumrunners, a situation that drove the price of liquor down. He had been getting $11 per case, but now he could get only as much as $5. Sometimes Schnarr's share wouldn't even cover operating costs. But he didn't want to be caught, so he kept running the big gas guzzler.

Once he even took liquor up the Columbia River. He made most of the voyage towed behind a large vessel belonging to Consolidated Exporters. He stayed in international waters, 12 miles off the coast of Washington. When the ship reached the mouth of the Columbia, Schnarr cast himself loose. He hauled four loads of 250 cases each. He offloaded the first two batches before the weather became too risky for a return. Two days later he took the last two loads in. The delivery went off without a hitch.

When Prohibition ended on April 4, 1933, Schnarr's rumrunning days were over. In twelve years of full-time rumrunning, Schnarr had made more than 400 runs for at least ten different buyers and delivered to at least thirty-six different locations in Washington. He delivered at least 60,000 cases of liquor and was never caught. He had about $10,000 in the bank and a nice house. After Prohibition, he sold his boat and went back to logging for a short time. Then he worked as a commercial fisherman up until 1969, when he retired at the age of seventy-five. Out of all the rumrunners, Schnarr may have been the most elusive and the most successful in Washington State.

Jake Terry

The Terror of Puget Sound

Jake Terry was hanging around Sumas, Washington, waiting for his next scheduled delivery when he ran into customs inspector Lawrence J. Flanigan, who was trying to catch him in the act of smuggling. He bragged to Flanigan that he would be crossing the border between Washington and British Columbia with illegal Chinese immigrants that night and that there was no way Flanigan would catch him. He was so sure of this fact that he even told Flanigan where he was planning to cross the border.

This attitude made Flanigan ever more determined to catch him. He deputized A. Schumaker to help him, and the two men borrowed a railroad speeder, a hand-driven railroad car, and rode to the spot where "Terrible Terry" had said he would cross. They left the speeder parked on the track, where it would be in Terry's way, and hid out of sight to wait for Terry's arrival.

Meanwhile, Terry picked up his contraband—four Chinese illegal aliens. The Chinese Exclusion Act of 1882 barred Chinese immigrants from entering the United States. Only those who had immigrated before November 17, 1880, could remain in America. Demand for their cheap labor was still very high, however, and Washington State was in an advantageous location for a lucrative smuggling trade. Human contraband could be smuggled in by land and by water. Terry was one of many who profited from transporting Chinese immigrants. Terry and the four Chinese immigrants boarded a railroad handcar in Canada, and Terry propelled them down the line.

About two o'clock the next morning, Terry arrived at the speeder blocking his way. The Chinese men began to panic, but Terry kept his cool. Before he could think of a plan, however, Flanigan and Schumaker, the customs men, jumped out of their hiding place and demanded his surrender. Terry did as he was told. He didn't even get a chance to draw his own gun. The jig was up.

Flanigan marched him into town and threw him in the city jail. He was held on bail of $2,000. He did not have the money, so he had to stay in jail until his trial. Originally the trial was set for March 9, but Terry waived his right to a speedy trial, choosing instead to go to the district court in Seattle. His trial began on June 5. He pled guilty to the charge of smuggling and was sentenced to one year in prison and a $1,000 fine.

Born in Missouri in 1853, Terry had come to Washington sometime in the 1870s. He committed his first crime on July 19, 1873, when he had an argument with Delbert Wright, proprietor of the Fashion Saloon in Seattle. Terry did not want to pay for his drinks. Wright insisted that Terry pay his bill. Terry left the saloon but came right back with a gun and wounded Wright in the chest.

Two days later Terry was arrested for assault. On August 5 he was found guilty. He appealed the conviction, but the decision was upheld. He was sentenced to five years at the territorial penitentiary in Steilacoom. He was released in August 1878.

He left the state for the next few years and worked as a railroad engineer. Perhaps Terry meant to stay out of trouble, but while running a train across the Canadian border, he realized he had a lucrative opportunity to smuggle illegal Chinese immigrants into the United States. After several successful runs, he started attracting too much attention, so he decided to move on. On his way back west, he stopped in Montana. He met a woman there named Annie, whom he brought back to Washington with him. They moved to Island County in 1883 or 1884 and lived together for five years before they split up. What Terry did for a living during that time is unknown, but presumably he kept on smuggling.

He moved to Seattle after his breakup with Annie, and for a while he drove a stage between Cherry Street and Ravenna Park, making one trip every hour. After that he worked as pound master of the city. He also served a short stint as a police officer but was fired because his bosses didn't like the company he kept—or perhaps the activities he engaged in, such as counterfeiting. He left Seattle proper and settled in Kellytown, a small town outside of Seattle.

Soon Terry returned to smuggling. In July 1891 he made plans to smuggle some Chinese across the border near Sumas. He traveled on foot from his home to Sedro. From there he sent a telegram to Zachary Holden, an unscrupulous customs inspector from Seattle. Holden and Deputy Marshal George Poor met Terry at Sedro. Terry knew from experience on the Seattle police force that he could count on both men to assist him in his scheme.

Meanwhile, two other customs inspectors had heard rumors of the plan, so they met near Sedro to try to intercept the smugglers and their contraband. On about July 26, the customs inspectors ran into Holden and Poor in Sedro. To avert suspicion, Holden told them that he and Poor had heard that illegal Chinese immigrants were in the area and that he was looking for them.

Something in his remarks or attitude told one of the customs inspectors that all was not right, so he followed Poor until he met with Terry, who was leading about fifteen Chinese men. The customs inspector saw them and ordered them to surrender, but Poor declared he was a U.S. marshal and had come to arrest Terry himself. The customs inspector didn't believe him and ordered both men to raise their hands. No one knows who went for their gun first, but Poor was soon dead and Terry was injured. The immigrants scattered and were never found.

The customs men carried Terry to town, where a doctor examined him. The doctor predicted that Terry didn't have long to live, so officers took what they thought would be a deathbed statement. Terry stated that he warned King County Sheriff Woolery about some Chinese being smuggled and stated he could capture them if Woolery sent help. Poor and Holden were the men Woolery sent. They had simply been taking the Chinese to the authorities, he claimed.

Terry was charged with smuggling Chinese laborers into the United States and held on $1,500 bail. His trial was scheduled for December. While awaiting trial he was sent to the McNeil Island Penitentiary. He tried to escape with four others on October 11, but they were captured the next day.

Terry went to trial on December 15, and the jury found him guilty of smuggling Chinese laborers into the United States. He was sentenced to ten months at McNeil Island and required to pay court costs. Because he had no money, the court ordered that his personal possessions be sold to pay the court costs of $550.60. After discovering that Terry had nothing to sell, the judge added thirty days to his sentence.

Initially the two customs inspectors were also arrested for killing Poor. They were tried and convicted for manslaughter but were later released because both had acted "in good faith." Terry testified at their hearings that the officers had fired first and that he had had no gun with which to defend himself. Terry's statement was largely ignored.

On December 23, 1891, Terry was taken to McNeil Island to serve his sentence. For good behavior he was released early on September 30, 1892. But Terry had not learned his lesson; he went back to smuggling immediately. He set up his headquarters at Sumas, a perfect location for getting men across the border easily and quickly under cover of night. On May 30, 1893, he smuggled three men across the border and put them on the Whatcom train with no questions asked.

Terry enjoyed playing jokes on his pursuers. He played a particularly memorable trick on customs inspector Flanigan. One day Flanigan boarded the train at Sumas after receiving a tip that opium would be smuggled on that train. He spotted a package taped underneath one of the railroad cars. He ripped the box off the railroad car and took it to the station agent. After some struggle, he finally got the box open. His mouth fell open in shock when he saw its contents—horse manure! No doubt Terry himself was the source of the opium rumor!

In October 1893 customs inspectors discovered that Terry was working for a Chinese man named Leong Youk Tong, a brothel owner in Portland, Oregon. He was also likely working for Tong when he was caught sneaking men over the border. Terry again served time at McNeil Island Penitentiary before being released early on May 24, 1895.

Yet another prison term did not set him straight. He did realize that he would probably be watched closely for a while, so he tried his hand at the less visible crime of counterfeiting. He and his partner, Dave Dixon, set up shop on Camano Island, where they made fake silver ten-cent coins. Terry gave thirty of the coins to a woman on the island. Shortly afterward he was arrested by U.S. Deputy Marshal James M. Quilter, who took him to Everett for a preliminary hearing. Bail was set at $2,500. Terry had no money, so he had to stay at the King County jail until his trial in December.

As bad luck would have it, the same judge presided over this trial as his earlier one. Judge Hanford labeled him a career criminal and this time sentenced him to ten years of hard labor at McNeil Island.

On December 26, 1895, Terry and five others were transferred to the infamous San Quentin prison in California after U.S. Marshal James C. Drake petitioned the attorney general to allow transfer of some convicts to a more secure prison. Again Terry behaved himself while in prison and was released early on June 2, 1902. While behind bars he met someone who would become his next partner in crime—Bill Miner.

Miner had been in prison almost twenty years when he was released a year before Terry. Miner was living in Bellingham with his sister when Terry was released in 1902, and Terry joined Miner there.

In 1904 Terry and Miner decided to rob a train in British Columbia. Neither had robbed a train before, but Terry's experience as a railroad engineer came in handy. Terry found out that a gold shipment was on its way to Seattle, and Shorty Dunn recruited the two men to help them with the robbery. In September, Miner and Dunn left Miner's home in Princeton, British Columbia, telling townspeople they were off on a hunting trip. A short while later they met up with Terry near the Canadian border.

At about half past nine on the night of September 10, 1904, the three men boarded the Canadian Pacific Railway Transcontinental Express Number 1 at Mission Junction, about 40 miles east of Vancouver, British Columbia. They hid until the train gathered speed, then they crawled over the roofs of the railroad cars until they reached the engine. They held Engineer Nathaniel J. Scott and Fireman Harry Freeman at gunpoint and told them to stop the train.

Miner ordered Freeman to uncouple the express car from the rest of the train, then he ordered the engineer to pull the train forward to the Whonock milepost and stop. Terry guarded the fireman while Miner and Dunn led Scott back to the express car. Opening the safe should have been a piece of cake. Earlier in the day Terry had sent a telegraph to the train station pretending to be a railroad official. He claimed that the combination to the safe had been lost and asked that the safe be left open. But when Terry checked the safe, nothing was in it. All was not lost, however—there was another safe. Miner commanded the express messenger, Herb Mitchell, to open it. Mitchell did as he was told. In it was $6,000 in gold dust and $1,000 in cash. Miner also took $50,000 in U.S. bonds and about $250,000 in Australian securities from the registered mail.

The crime was the first train robbery in Canadian history, so British Columbia police had no experience to guide their investigations. They asked the Pinkerton Detective Agency for help. The Pinkertons were sure that Bill Miner was involved, but they couldn't prove it. After a short investigation, they gave up the hunt.

Terry and Miner found out that Miner was the chief suspect. They also knew that as soon as they cashed the bonds their trail could be traced. The wisest course of action was to part ways. Terry returned to

Bellingham, where he supposedly spent October 2, 1905, the night of the Great Northern train robbery, in Seattle. A reward of $1,000 was offered for the capture of the bandits, but the perpetrators were never caught. Even so, the robbery was always attributed to Terry, Miner, and Dunn.

After that Terry moved his headquarters to Port Townsend. He started smuggling again, but in December of 1905 he returned to Sumas for Christmas. He just happened to walk into a notions store and found that the proprietor was none other than his ex-wife Annie.

After her breakup with Terry back in 1889, Annie had stayed on in Sumas and opened the store, where she sold cigars, candy, and writing materials. Annie was very popular, and every man in town wanted to court her. Finally she had accepted the attentions of a man named Gus Linday, a telegraph lineman. When he asked her to marry him, she said yes. They set up a home in the back rooms of her shop.

Terry was overjoyed to see her, but he did not realize that she was married. While Terry talked to her, the very jealous Gus Linday walked in and let Terry know how things stood. Terry backed off but noted that Annie didn't seem to be in overwhelming agreement with her husband. Her hesitation encouraged Terry to pursue the issue right then and there. Soon the two men were throwing punches. Finally Terry had the upper hand and threw Linday out of the house. Linday returned the next day, but Terry threw him out again.

Linday went across the street and drowned his sorrows with a few drinks. Two days later he led some men to the store intending to reclaim his wife. Before they could approach the door, Terry fired at the group from inside. Linday and everybody else scattered. Terry strolled down the street after them, firing shots over their heads. For nearly a week Terry terrorized the town, shooting at anyone in his way.

Terry was arrested a few days later. The sheriff escorted him to the county seat at Bellingham. He was held on $250 bail, but Annie paid the bond almost immediately. Terry didn't wait around for his hearing. Because Sumas was so close to the Canadian border, Terry skedaddled over the line and set up new smuggling operations in the Huntington Hotel. By crossing the border, Terry forfeited his bail. A warrant was immediately issued for his arrest, but as long as he stayed in Canada he was beyond the reach of American lawmen.

Terry began smuggling opium across the border. The drug was in high demand by the Chinese immigrants already living in the United

States. Though lawmen dogged him at every step, they were not able to catch him. They even set traps for him, to no avail. When he needed money, Terry would work as a logger or an engineer. George Manning, an immigration guard, passed notes back and forth across the border for Terry and Annie, and Terry gave Annie money, probably part of the booty from the train robberies. It was only a matter of time before Terry had another showdown with Gus Linday.

On July 5, 1907, Terry snuck back across the border. After having a few drinks at the Sumas saloon, he walked down the block to Annie's store. He confronted Linday, who ordered him to leave their house. Terry refused. Annie saw trouble brewing and ran for the sheriff. By the time she returned, Terry was dead from two gunshot wounds to his head and side.

Immediately Gus ran down the street to the judge's office and turned himself in. Linday had attracted so much sympathy among the townspeople that Sumas merchants practically fought one another to post Linday's bail of $7,000. George Bocking, Frank Hayworth, C. E. Moulton, D. B. Lucas, and William Gerstberger put up the money, and Linday was released. He returned to his job on the telegraph line and divorced Annie, who left Sumas and was never seen again.

On the day of the murder, Terry's body was taken to the Gillies Hardware Store. People came to gawk, and, incredibly, his autopsy was performed right there in the store window, where anyone could watch. After the formalities were over, Terry's body was shipped to Bellingham and buried in a potter's field.

Over the course of fifteen years, Terry was the terror of Puget Sound. Whether he was robbing trains, smuggling Chinese men or opium, or counterfeiting, he led police officers on quite a chase. In the end, the law couldn't catch up with him, but a jealous husband did. Gus Linday ended Terrible Terry's reign as king of the smugglers with two well-placed shots from his gun.

Lou Blonger, Overlord of the Underworld

Con Man, Swindler, and Schemer

It was the year 1922 when Harry Tammen, called the "Little Dutchman," who co-published the *Denver Post*, said to one of his reporters: "You know, son, I'm sure sorry we had to print old Lou's name, but the story got so damn big we simply couldn't hold it out any longer."

Tammen was referring to one of the biggest stories in the news business and in Denver history. Lou Blonger had been arrested that day, and his crimes were finally exposed and out in the open. Up until then Lou had managed to befriend all the "right" people in Denver, and he kept his name separate from his underworld activities. Apparently even the *Denver Post* had not felt the need to make too much of Blonger's "business" because it seemed harmless enough. Except to the victims. Blonger had spent years doing one thing very well, and that was to "catch a sucker." But on this day his underworld and con game racket finally "caught" him.

Lou Blonger was short, rotund, and likeable. His main physical characteristics were his large, bulbous nose and protruding lower lip. At the theater and other public events he enjoyed wearing full formal dress, which drew attention in a crowd.

His working life in Denver started in the saloon business in 1880. He was a French-Canadian who had previously operated a few illegal activities in New Orleans and Salt Lake City. He had also run a Denver dance hall.

Blonger branched out into the gambling business with the policy shop racket. "Policy" was considered the poor man's gambling game because it made the poor even poorer. It was similar to the numbers racket, which paid off for picking the winning number. Like all numbers games, the odds were highly stacked against the bettor, but the reward for winning was very enticing. A "day number" paid five to one if any number up to seventy-eight was among the first fifteen numbers drawn. Or a bettor could win thirty-two to one if his two selected numbers, called a "saddle," appeared anywhere on the list.

A "station number" paid sixty to one if the winning number was in a specific position on the list. Blonger soon became the kingpin of Denver's policy shop racket.

When Lou Blonger arrived in Denver, Doc Baggs was already operating a con scheme that swindled men out of thousands of dollars at a time. Baggs donned a glossy stovepipe hat and carried a silk umbrella wherever he went. He could never understand why another Denver con-game newcomer, Soapy Smith, settled for cheating a sucker out of five dollars when he could have conned him for so much more.

Doc Baggs was growing old and Soapy Smith had begun to dominate Denver's confidence racket, forcing Doc to join his gang. Soapy was interested in fast profits in mass volume. Lou Blonger was soon forced to join with Soapy too, if he wanted to run his schemes in Denver.

Lou would eventually take Doc's technique and develop it into a multimillion-dollar racket. Soapy later left Denver, and when he returned a few years later, it would be Blonger who demanded and received a percentage of Soapy's profits. Lou Blonger had become the leader of Denver's underworld, and every other con man had to report to him.

Blonger had learned a lot from Soapy in the early days. Just as Soapy had done, he and the members of his growing underworld group preyed only on visitors to Denver, not the local residents. Blonger also maintained protection from local law enforcement by contributing heavily to both parties during election time. His payroll included many highly ranked officials in the police department, district attorney's office, and the local office of the U.S. Department of Justice.

The summer tourist season was one of the best times for Blonger to operate his new scheme. He had learned it from Doc Baggs, who liked to make thousands of dollars off of each "sucker." One of Blonger's men, called a "steerer," would stand near the newsstands waiting for a prosperous looking man to buy an out-of-town newspaper. He would then follow the man back to his hotel lobby and wait for an opportunity to sit next to him for a moment. Then the steerer would get up and walk away, leaving a wallet on his vacated seat.

The out-of-town stranger, seeing the wallet, would pick it up and look inside for information about the owner so that the wallet could be returned. The stranger would find a ten-dollar bill, a newspaper clipping, and a document. The clipping told of a huge profit made in a stock-market transaction by a man whose picture was shown. There was also a $100,000 bond, which guaranteed his ability to provide this service. The clipping and bond were both forgeries.

Usually the stranger would turn in the wallet at the hotel's front desk. The next day the steerer would come to the hotel to claim the "lost" wallet. He would be accompanied by another man, called the "spieler." The grateful owner of the wallet would ask the hotel clerk where he might find the person who had returned it. He and the spieler would then meet the out-of-town stranger to thank him. The stranger, now dubbed the "sucker" by the con men, would immediately recognize the owner of the wallet as the man whose picture was in the newspaper clipping.

The steerer would graciously thank the sucker and expound on the importance of the bond in his market transactions. He would then offer the sucker a reward for finding the wallet and its contents. The spieler would then go into action by interrupting this offer saying: "From his appearance, this gentleman obviously is not the type who would accept a cash reward. Why don't you show your appreciation by giving him a tip on the market? Give him a chance to make some money."

The steerer would mildly object to this idea, saying he wasn't supposed to give out tips, but, on the other hand, he was indebted to this man who had returned his bond. The spieler would then take over by lauding the abilities of the stock market operator. He would relate how he'd seen him make thousands of dollars in the last thirty days. He said that he had cleaned up on a couple thousand as the result of a tip he'd been given by this talented man. The clincher in the spiel was when he told the sucker that he was sending for more money from his relatives back in his hometown so that he could get into the next big deal. It was expected to bring a huge return within the next few weeks. This suggestion was to encourage the sucker to think about what a "sure thing" this must be if the man would do that.

The sucker usually showed interest since he had seen for himself the newspaper clipping and the $100,000 bond to back up the stock operator's abilities. He was offered an opportunity to go with the two men the next day to visit the stock exchange. The sucker had nothing to lose by taking a look, so he would agree to meet them. Little did the sucker know that the "stock exchange" was a complete fake, created specifically to lure him in for the kill.

The stock exchange looked entirely real to the sucker, and he would overhear the stock operator say that he had just made a profit that morning. He had earned thousands of dollars when his stock had gone up two points. Then he predicted that it was likely to double in a few weeks, so he decided to leave his money in this stock a while longer rather than cash out his profit.

The spieler, who also overheard this remark, would lean toward the sucker and start talking to him in a low voice. He would say: "This is too good a chance to lose. Let's go in together and make a killing."

The spieler would then buy a few thousand dollars of stock while the sucker watched. No further pressure was put on him, and they would all leave the stock exchange, inviting the sucker to accompany them again the next day. The next day their visit would be rewarded by more good news that the stock had gone up again. With this good news as encouragement, the sucker would then place a minimal buying order, putting up no cash. Each day they would come back to find the stock had continued to rise. When the stock appeared to have tripled, the spieler would suggest they sell and take their winnings. The cashier would actually place a huge stack of cash in the sucker's hands before realizing that the customer had not originally made a payment. The cash was pulled back by the cashier, who would say: "Our customers must either establish a line of credit or put up the actual cash." He would add, "It's merely a formality; as soon as you produce the cash as evidence of good faith, we'll settle the account."

The sucker had seen the money in his hands and would believe he only needed to come up with the cash to be rewarded with triple that amount. The spieler, who had also supposedly bought a large amount of stock, then suggested that the sucker go back home to get the needed cash. He was even encouraged to mortgage his house if necessary to get the money. The sucker would go home to raise the cash and return to meet the spieler. Then they both would go together to the stock exchange and the sucker would present the cash. The cashier would say that everything was now in order and that they should return the next day to receive their winnings.

Unfortunately they would be told the next day that the stock price had plummeted overnight and they had both lost all their money. The spieler would be outraged over this information and would start a fight with the cashier, even taking a swing at him with his fist. The brawl would be broken up, and the spieler and the sucker would leave empty handed. The spieler would try to console the sucker, who would believe they both had been big losers.

Usually the sucker was never aware that he had been a victim of a confidence game. The spieler's final task was to get the sucker out of town. He would be advised to go home and wait while the spieler promised he would try to get their money back somehow. Nothing would ever come of it, though, and the sucker would often be too ashamed to admit his loss. If he did suspect the scam, his pride usually prevented him from admitting he had been such a sucker. Either way, the con men were rarely reported.

If the ruse was reported by a victim, the police first tipped off Blonger, who would vacate the stock exchange location before the police arrived. The victim was then victimized once again by being made to look like a fool when he led the police to an empty office.

Lou Blonger's gang is said to have swindled countless men out of a total of $645,720 in one season. Another account suggests the figure was as high as $1 million. The typical victim was suckered for around $5,000, but it could range as high as $100,000, depending on his wealth. By 1920 only one gang member was ever tried and convicted for this crime.

Blonger, in his early seventies, had enjoyed decades of success in maintaining a stronghold over his Denver operations. He was said to have had additional branches of his racket operating in Florida, California, and Havana.

He planned to continue to run his operation in Denver with the blessings of the corrupt officials. His mob did all the work, and he maintained the relationship with politicians by paying them off handsomely. A direct phone line was said to have been installed between Blonger and the chief of police.

What Blonger hadn't counted on was an honest district attorney. Philip S. Van Cise ran for the office in 1920. He had been a colonel in World War I and he was a popular candidate among Denver citizens. Blonger tried his usual approach and offered Van Cise a $25,000 campaign donation. If elected, all Blonger wanted in return was for Van Cise to fix the bonds at $1,000 for any of his mob who might be arrested.

Not only did Van Cise turn down the offer, he won the election, and immediately began to lay plans to bring down Blonger. It would take fifteen months of preparation while he used special investigators, hidden dictaphones, and records gathered from victims of the gang from across the country. In one neatly planned operation, a surprise raid was about to end Lou Blonger's criminal career.

It began at dawn on August 14, 1922, when Van Cise gave the signal to begin the ambush of the entire Blonger gang, numbering sixty-three members. Deputies, special deputies, and members of the state ranger force began their carefully designed actions.

One by one and in twos and threes, the gang members were quietly rounded up by the various deputies and rangers. Many were found at their homes, apartments, and other lodgings. Others were eating breakfast at local cafes and some had just emerged onto the streets. They were not taken to the local city and county jails. If they had been, the whole operation would have been given away as soon as the first prisoner entered. Van Cise had thought of this in advance and obtained permission to use the Universalist Church as a temporary holding place. Lou Blonger was among the first to be brought in, and all of the men were stripped and searched.

One startling side event almost undermined the whole scheme that Van Cise led that day. He had been painstakingly precise in every part of his strategy to get Blonger and his mob. However, he could not have accounted for an overzealous *Denver Post* reporter who had picked up a tip the night before the raid. The lucky part for Van Cise is that the reporter didn't know for whom the raid was intended. The reporter's information suggested it would take place at the statehouse, so he showed up at the capitol building at daybreak. He ran across various deputies who were leaving to get into their cars, but none of them would talk to him. He had overheard an earlier conversation among the officers that mentioned a church. He repeated this about a "church" to see if it got any attention. One of the officers heard him and feared that the reporter knew far more than he really did and offered to take him there, hoping to detain him. At the Universalist Church the reporter still did not realize what was happening until he recognized Lou Blonger being led into the building. Immediately he ran for a phone but was blocked by a guard. Events were soon happening so quickly that the guard left the reporter unattended. He got away and was able to phone in the story to the *Post*.

Another lucky break for Van Cise came when the reporter returned and shamelessly announced he had called the *Post*. The district attorney had just enough time to call the managing editor to convince him to hold the story. The editor agreed to hold it rather than ruin the raid. Although the young reporter lost his big scoop, the story was printed and ran the next day. Lou Blonger had always managed to keep his name out of the newspapers, but this time Harry Tammen said they had to run it.

About thirty-four gang members were captured that day. Of those, twenty actually went to trial in Denver. A few were turned over to officials in other states. Six jumped bond, and one was declared insane.

Lou Blonger and his chief assistant, Adolph W. Duff, alias "Kid Duffy," spent large parts of their fortunes to defend themselves. Legions of attorneys were hired to contend that the state could not prove its case against them. The two men were confident that they would be acquitted when the trial began in February of 1923.

Van Cise had done his homework, however, and the time spent on investigating Blonger, Duff, and the other con men paid off when all the evidence was presented to the jury. It took the jury four days to reach a guilty verdict. Blonger and Duff were sent to prison for seven years each. The other defendants received three years. Since Lou Blonger was already seventy-three years old, seven years turned out to be longer than he could survive. He died in prison, and so did an era of organized crime in Denver.

STELLA AND BENNIE DICKSON

South Dakota's Own Bonnie and Clyde

For her sixteenth birthday Stella Dickson robbed a bank. For her seventeenth birthday she was sent to a federal prison.

Little Stella Redenbaugh fell for the older, tousle-headed Bennie Dickson during the worst of the Great Depression. He was a promising boxer and former Boy Scout who one day hoped to be a lawyer. In 1918 he and his brother Spencer had even rescued a woman when she attempted to drown herself in a local pond. The heroic act led the Kansas governor to nominate the boys, who lived in Kansas at the time, for the Carnegie Medal. But somewhere along his life's journey, those who knew him said Bennie had proceeded down a wayward path.

When Bennie married Stella, she wasn't yet sixteen. Money was scarce, jobs were nonexistent, and very few in the Midwest had an easy go of it. Undeterred by conventional wisdom, the starry-eyed couple vacationed at a family cabin on Lake Preston in eastern South Dakota. As Stella's special birthday approached, they apparently didn't think much about cake and candles. They thought about cash.

At about 2:30 p.m. on August 25, 1938—just a half hour before the Elkton Corn Exchange Bank's scheduled summer closing—Bennie marched into the foyer and saw the bank's two employees on duty, cashier R. F. Petschow and bookkeeper Elaine Lovley, engaged at the main business counter. Bennie approached, leveled his revolver at the pair, and calmly said, "This is a holdup. Do exactly as I say, and there will be no trouble and nobody hurt."

Should a patron enter the bank, Bennie instructed Petschow to lead him or her to the floor behind the counter. When informed by the cashier that the delayed time lock to the bank's vault would not open until 3:00 p.m., the composed criminal said he'd wait, which he did—for thirty-five minutes.

During the period no less than twenty individuals entered the bank, including the institution's president, L. C. Foreman. All were scrutinized and quietly led to their holding place on the floor behind the teller's counter. As each customer entered the bank, "the bandit had them hand over their currency, but with an apparent desire not to take money from private individuals, except in instances where indications were that the loss could be well afforded, [and] he had Mr. Petschow look up the balances of each individual customer, to whom in most instances he casually returned their money," the *Elkton Record* reported a week later.

"Mrs. Koehn in the excitement incident to the proceedings dropped a $20 bill for which she had come in to get change, and the robber in a gentlemanly manner picked it up and handed it back to her," the newspaper added. "Roy Kramer had $240 in currency, and after ascertaining that this was his private money and not the property of the Standard Oil Co., and the records showing only a small credit balance, this currency was returned to him."

When Bennie had acquired sufficient resources with which to secure a birthday present for his newlywed wife as well as finance his imminent departure, he herded the bank officials and their customers into the vault, closed the heavy door, and made his getaway. A short time later, the bankers flipped an emergency switch within the vault intended for just such a purpose. The switch activated a warning light in Elkton's Dressel Store, and the captives were soon released.

Within minutes, bank officials telephoned news of the brazen daylight robbery to Sioux Falls, and within two hours of the holdup, investigators with the state and federal departments of justice were on the scene. Bennie had been wearing gloves, so efforts to find his fingerprints proved futile. But officials were aware that Bennie had an accomplice, even though they didn't have a clue who either of them was or where they had gone.

With the help of Sheriff Hank Claussen, law enforcement authorities spent the next few days securing evidence they hoped would lead to the apprehension of the desperados. The *Elkton Record* pronounced, "One fact which may be of value in tracing the pair by checking the circulation of the stolen money is that a shipment of new currency had been received on the day of the holdup, and the serial numbers of these bills will be a matter of record."

A week after the crime, Bennie and Stella were leading a life on the lam with as much as $2,500 in cash. But after lying low for two months, their financial reserves began to dwindle. It was time to hit another bank. On the eve of Halloween, they arrived in Brookings, a modest college town in extreme eastern South Dakota that was just recovering from its annual hell-raising Hobo Day. Bennie and Stella would bring life back to the party.

When officials of Northwestern Security National Bank opened the doors for business at 8:30 a.m. on Monday, October 31, they were greeted by a handsome young couple equipped with a machine gun and a sawed-off shotgun. The dynamic duo calmly waited for the delayed time lock to open at 11:00 a.m.

The previous Saturday's celebration of Hobo Day had ensured a brisk Monday morning business at the bank, the *Elkton Record* reported three days after the robbery, in a story adjacent to the newspaper's near-breathless announcement that *Boys Town* starring Spencer Tracy would soon come to the Elks Theatre. When Bennie and Stella arrived in Brookings, a tree-lined bastion of academia, they may have sensed easy pickings. In the two and a half hours that the heavily armed pair stood vigil, more than 100 people walked in and out of the bank, making their weekend deposits and loan payments, getting change, and conducting other transactions. None of them was ever aware that they stood one misstep from two desperate fugitives in the midst of pulling off a most daring raid.

At 11:00 a.m. the time lock opened, allowing access to the vault. Bennie and Stella quickly stuffed as much of the available cash as they could into bank bags and chose Northwestern Security officials R. M. DePuy and Jon Torsey as hostages. Coolly, the four left the institution unnoticed and began their getaway. Bennie and Stella got in the front seat of their black Buick while DePuy and Torsey were instructed to stand on the running boards on the outside of the vehicle. Then the car bolted forward. A few blocks later, when it appeared they had not been pursued, "Bennie slowed the sedan and his petite blond-haired accomplice dismissed the bankers with a smile and a good-bye."

A short time later, authorities received reports of the vehicle traveling at a high rate of speed southwest of Elkton. Officials quickly responded but were unable to apprehend the pair.

As they sped down gravel back roads in a cloud of dust, the Depression-era outlaws must have thought themselves another Bonnie and Clyde. Just four years earlier, Bonnie Parker and Clyde Barrow had terrorized the Midwest with a series of bold bank heists and epic gun battles with authorities. After four years of outrunning law officers and capturing the imagination of an entire nation, Bonnie and Clyde died on

May 23, 1934, in a hail of gunfire near their Bienville Parish, Louisiana, hideout, struck down by a posse of heavily armed Texas and Louisiana lawmen.

As immortal as only youth can imagine themselves to be, Bennie and Stella didn't likely dwell on Bonnie and Clyde's tragic fate. In their black Buick the newlyweds carried $47,233 in cash and bonds from the Halloween holdup at the Brookings bank, and they were intent on putting as much ground between themselves and pursuing posses as they could.

But the police had all the time in the world. When they eventually tracked Bennie and Stella to a tourist campground in Topeka, Kansas, on November 24, authorities closed in on the pair. After a brief gunfight Bennie and Stella separated, both making good their escape. Bennie fled in his Buick to South Clinton, Iowa, stole another vehicle, then doubled back to Topeka to retrieve his bride at a prearranged rendezvous point one day after the shootout.

As the couple traveled to Michigan, authorities made several attempts to capture the fugitives. In one incident, while being pursued by a patrol car, Stella grabbed a gun and shot out the cruiser's tires, earning her the nickname "Sure Shot" Stella. During the shootout a cop's bullet grazed Stella's forehead, leaving a scar she would carry for a lifetime. In a series of confrontations, the bank robbers took three men hostage, stole getaway cars in Michigan and Indiana, and eluded capture on country back roads.

Now far from home and aggressively pursued by lawmen from several states, the young couple reached St. Louis and tried to blend in. When Bennie was lured to a hamburger stand by a female informant on April 6, 1939, he discovered too late that the FBI was closing in. As he attempted to flee, a young federal agent put at least four holes in Bennie's back, creating a sixteen-year-old widow and putting an end to Bennie's short lifetime of regrets.

Apparently alerted to her husband's death, Stella fled 250 miles west to Kansas City. When authorities caught up with her the next day, she was unarmed, carried $70, and was wearing three rings, including the wedding set with seven diamonds that Bennie had provided. With the fight knocked out of her and the romance gone, little Stella Dickson was apprehended without any resistance. When arrested, she also possessed a key to a New Orleans apartment and a poem Bennie had penned. It read,

"In the eyes of men I am not just/But in your eyes, O life, I see justification/ You have taught me that my path is right if I am true to you."

Returned to South Dakota for trial on bank robbery charges in federal district court in Deadwood, Stella reportedly listened to the proceedings while clutching a doll in her arms. Whether she did so to emphasize her youth to the jury or merely because the doll gave her comfort was never determined. The *Mitchell Daily Republic* claimed she looked "more like a schoolgirl than a gun moll awaiting the proceedings of the court on charges of bank robbery including the taking of hostages, a possible capital offense."

But Judge Lee A. Wyman did determine that Stella was guilty of taking other people's money at gunpoint. Citing her youth and the corrupting influence of her older, now-dead husband, the judge sentenced Stella to two ten-year sentences to be served concurrently. On the day she walked into the West Virginia federal prison for women, she turned seventeen.

While the shock of confinement and the loss of Bennie must have case-hardened her heart, Stella spent her time in prison taking vocational technical courses and thinking about freedom. When she was paroled in 1946, she was just twenty-four years old.

Following her release, she served a stint as a flight attendant, fixed her own plumbing and built her own fence, cared for her disabled brother, and had a lengthy career as a clerk at Kmart. She remarried twice over the course of years, but later in life admitted to a Kansas City neighbor that she had only ever truly loved one man.

As she aged, Stella became increasingly reclusive, adopting more than a half dozen pets from the animal shelter at which she volunteered. She led a quiet life with few friends save the furry ones she rescued from a hell she had personally known. Her austere lifestyle eventually earned her a pardon for her youthful crimes from President Nixon, but few who knew her in the last decades of her life remotely suspected that little Stella had ever been in trouble with the law.

When she died on September 10, 1995, following an extended illness, no obituary marked the passing of "Sure Shot" Stella, one of the youngest and prettiest outlaws to ever plague the Plains.

Helen Sieler

The Woman with Ten Lives

It was New Year's Eve 1936 when the sensational powder-house explosion rocked Sioux Falls. Fueled by three and a half tons of black powder and 3,300 pounds of dynamite, the force of the detonation was felt more than 50 miles away. The flash was visible for 15 miles, and the crater it created was 25 feet deep. The explosion shattered $20,000 in windowpanes in the immediate vicinity, and several nearby farms were damaged.

And when the dust settled, there wasn't enough left of the man it was meant to kill to fill a baby-food jar.

The story of this Sioux Falls saga, unsurprisingly, did not start with a tale of innocence. Each of those involved was no stranger to crime and conspiracy. Each had a record, and even the victim was a paroled convict.

In 1936 South Dakota and much of the Midwest was in the midst of its Dust Bowl days. Yellowish brown hazes alternated with black blizzards to blanket the Great Plains in misery. Children donned dust masks for school, homemakers did what they could to deal with the incessant filth and grime that permeated every part of their lives, and thousands of farmers simply watched as their crops dried up and blew away.

In South Dakota the lingering drought coupled with high winds and barren fields yielded skies that were darkened for days. In many places dust and dirt drifted like snow, killing what few cows remained and covering everything that didn't move. In the middle of the Great Depression, President Franklin Roosevelt would tell the American people, "I see one-third of the nation ill-housed, ill-clad, ill-nourished . . . [T]he test of our progress is not whether we add more to the abundance of those who have much; it is whether we provide enough for those who have too little." And by all accounts one downtrodden gang of heavies and hoodlums had finally decided they had far too little.

Three days before Christmas 1936, a gang and its moll conspired with a Sioux City, Iowa, jewelry store owner to relieve him of some excess merchandise. He'd pocket a handsome insurance settlement, and they'd each bag a grand in mad money. At least, that was the plan.

The gang consisted of a forty-five-year-old Sioux Falls bank robber and ex-convict named Lee Bradley; William Nesbeth, thirty-seven, a Sioux City bartender; Harry "Slim" Reeves, described as a thirty-six-year-old Sioux City desperado; Harold Baker, fifty-one; and his sweetheart, the pretty, dark-haired Helen Sieler, twenty-five, of Sioux City.

Sieler was no stranger to struggle or red-light districts, but she was out of her element. Three weeks before the crime she had left her husband, Edward Sieler, and taken up with the wild Harold Baker, a parolee who had spent time in a California prison. It was later learned that Baker's real name was Floyd H. Parker. Baker and Sieler were living on a quiet residential street in Omaha, under the names Mr. and Mrs. Roy Johnson. In late December the couple was visited by Bradley, Nesbeth, and Reeves, who were planning a robbery in Sioux City, just 100 miles north of Omaha.

On the night of December 23, 1936, the four gangsters robbed the Ehlermann Wholesale Jewelry Company in Sioux City. When the group blew the safe on the second story of the Orpheum Building, the blast showered glass down on the crowd standing in line in front of the theater below. Reported stolen was $36,000 in miscellaneous jewelry and $1,000 in cash.

Police suspected an inside job from the beginning, particularly when they noted the acetylene tanks and torches conveniently stored in the jewelry firm's vault. A couple of weeks later, the *Daily Argus-Leader* in nearby Sioux Falls would report, "peculiar details of the crime are still under investigation."

Meanwhile, following the heist, the gangsters fled first to Omaha, then to Norfolk, Nebraska, and Yankton, South Dakota, before holing up in separate hotels in Sioux Falls. When their promised payoff didn't immediately materialize due to the ongoing police investigation of the robbery, they began to turn on one another. Baker and Mrs. Sieler talked of returning to Sioux City and turning themselves in. The suggestion was not met with enthusiasm by the couple's accomplices, who were afraid that Baker and Sieler would implicate them in the crime. To protect themselves, the other members of the gang began to conspire against Baker and Sieler.

On New Year's Eve, Bradley, Nesbeth, and Reeves suggested to Baker and Sieler that they steal some more dynamite—the key ingredient to their successful safecracking. The nearby powder house operated by the Larson Hardware Company had ample supplies, and so the group headed to the site five miles southeast of Sioux Falls shortly after sunset. Mrs. Sieler waited in the car while the men set about breaking into the depot.

Baker, dressed nattily in a tan camel-hair overcoat, black hat, deep tan shirt with figured brown necktie, a dark mixed suit, black oxfords, and gray socks, probably looked more a mobster than a burglar as he sauntered toward the powder house. As he reached the structure, Nesbeth hit Baker over the head with a hammer so hard, it flew out of his hand. Baker fought back, but he was quickly subdued.

The three assailants then went after his girlfriend, dragging her into the dark depot. Nesbeth hit her on the head with his hammer. Another of her assailants kicked her in the face. Then the trio fired eight gunshots into her body and dragged her to a position next to the prone body of her boyfriend in the dynamite shack.

While Reeves ran back to start the getaway car, Nesbeth and Bradley fashioned a fuse long enough to give them ample time to get clear. Even they weren't sure what would happen when the cache of 300 twenty-five-pound cans of powder and 3,300 pounds of dynamite went off. As the fuse burned and the gangsters fled eastward toward the Minnesota border, Mrs. Sieler regained consciousness and saw the inevitable fate that awaited her if she didn't move quickly. Dazed, with head wounds from the beating and eight bullets in her body, she crawled toward the doorway of the magazine and dragged herself out into the wintry night as far away as time would allow.

At 9:35 p.m., with the getaway car five to six miles away and Mrs. Sieler crawling through a snow-and-ice-filled ditch a couple of hundred yards from the powder house, the fuse completed its fateful mission.

The tremendous blast shook structures for miles around Sioux Falls, causing plaster walls to crack. Hundreds of windows in area businesses shattered from the concussion, which was heard and felt in Pipestone, Minnesota, over fifty miles away.

Police would later say that Mrs. Sieler had been hurled in the air 200 feet by the explosion. The terrific detonation blew away the lower portions of the coat she was wearing and officers found two pieces of matching fabric 300 feet away from where she landed. Already suffering from a beating and bullet wounds, she was taken to nearby Moe Hospital in serious condition and in severe shock.

When Mrs. Sieler awakened in her hospital room an hour after the blast, she first asked about her boyfriend and then started telling anyone who would listen about how her sad state of affairs had originated and who was responsible. By the next morning authorities had launched one of the most intense and far-flung manhunts in the region's history.

As police scoured the scene of the blast for any evidence of Baker, Sioux Falls salesman J. D. Higgins stopped by police headquarters to turn in a piece of flesh he had found about 200 feet east of the powder house. Police believed it to be a remnant of Baker's shattered body, and they turned it over to a physician for examination.

The next morning Sieler told the *Daily Argus-Leader* that the trouble between Baker and his three killers began over a disagreement about the division of loot from the Sioux Falls robbery. Sieler said the band had burglarized a Nebraska store, stealing clothing, while she remained in the car. She also described in detail how Reeves, Nesbeth, and Bradley had assaulted her, shot her full of holes, and then left her to die beside her boyfriend in the dynamite shack.

"They first shot me once in the arm and then slugged me with a hammer," she told police. "They dragged me inside but I don't remember when they fired the other shots at me." That afternoon, doctors planned to "take X-ray pictures," the newspaper said. No slugs had been removed from her body, and a bandage covered one eye where she was hit by a bullet. "It felt like my head was blown off when that one hit," she was quoted as saying.

After she gave police a full statement, the newspaper reported what would be the first of many surprises in the ensuing investigation of the powder-house blast. "It appeared unlikely she would face any charges. Police said she might be held as a material witness. She is under heavy guard of police and deputy sheriffs, fearful the gang might yet attempt to kill her."

As doctors began to treat Sieler's extensive injuries, they informed media outlets that she had been shot twice in the back, twice in the thigh, three times in the hip, and once in the face below the eye with a revolver of undetermined caliber.

When the dust and smoke had cleared the site of the explosion the next morning, officers measured a crater 25 feet wide, 35 feet long, and 25 feet deep. Scraps of iron and concrete had been hurled hundreds of yards in all directions. Warrants were issued, and law enforcement agencies began issuing bulletins throughout South Dakota, Nebraska, and Iowa telling officers to be on the lookout for the three men they variously described as "a convicted bank robber, an underworld character, and a bartender." Regardless of their previous experience, they were all now sought on murder charges.

On January 2, 1937, as Sieler started her second day as the most notorious patient in Moe Hospital, her estranged husband walked through the door and into her room. Mr. Edward Sieler told a reporter that his wife had left him three weeks before this unfortunate series of events and that he had traveled all the way to Sioux Falls because he was still in love with her. Witnesses said Mrs. Sieler felt otherwise.

The seriousness of Sieler's injuries became more apparent when Dr. A. J. Moe gave her less than a fifty-fifty chance of survival. In addition to the injuries previously described, her doctor disclosed that her right leg had been frozen and was worsening, and that a bullet imbedded behind her right eye had caused the loss of sight in that eye.

While police continued their manhunt, health-department laboratory technician Harry Falconer examined what little remained of Harold Baker. Scouring the area of the blast, searchers had been disappointed to find only the bit of flesh, a bone fragment, and a small piece of cloth that appeared to be part of a man's trousers. Sieler had given police a detailed description of what Baker had been wearing when he was killed, right down to his pink silk underwear.

Murder warrants issued by Sioux Falls judge Lewis Larson named "Lee Bradley, alias Tom Tobin, South Dakota bank robber, and former convict; William Nesbeth, also know as Bill Nesbeth, Sioux City bartender; and Harry "Slim" Reeves, Sioux City underworld character."

As Mrs. Sieler struggled against death in the hospital three days after the explosion, Sioux Falls police chief Henry Morstad discounted a statement attributed to him that the powder-house blast "had been felt in San Francisco." He told the local newspaper that "he had not made any such comment, neither had he heard any reports that seismograph instruments on the West Coast had recorded the blast."

When fugitive warrants were issued on January 4, federal agents joined the search for the three desperados who had crossed state lines after committing a felony. The same day, fearing reprisals from the gang, Chief Morstad doubled the guard around the hospital room of

Mrs. Sieler after officers received reports that three men armed with pistols and a submachine gun were seen leaving Ottumwa, Iowa.

Finally the search began to bear fruit. That night, Reeves was captured in a farmer's garage one and a half miles south of Sioux City, after law officers received a tip from an undisclosed source as to the gangster's whereabouts. The capture was without confrontation, according to authorities. When Sheriff W. R. Tice and a deputy knocked on the door of the garage, Reeves reportedly asked, "Is that you, Bill?" When the sheriff responded in the affirmative, Reeves opened the garage door and was greeted by the wrong end of several weapons leveled at him. "All right, I won't give you any trouble," the man said in surrender.

Under intense grilling by law officers, Reeves admitted he had been with the gang that set off the powder-house blast on New Year's Eve, but he denied having taken part in the jewelry store robbery or the murder of Baker and the attempted slaughter of his sweetheart. When informed that Reeves had claimed he tried to save Mrs. Sieler by pulling her away from the powder house, the hospitalized woman said Reeves was lying and that he "was the first to shoot me. I saw him shoot me and he knows it."

Reeves finally admitted to participating in the robbery and was sentenced to 43 years in prison.

As weeks went by Mrs. Sieler's condition gradually improved. Nearly two months passed before officers caught up to William Nesbeth, the thirty-seven-year-old Sioux City hoodlum. Unarmed, Nesbeth offered no resistance when he was arrested in a small hotel in downtown Oklahoma City where he had been staying for three weeks. He was returned to Sioux Falls to face charges of murdering Baker. Investigators reported that, under questioning, Nesbeth had admitted he played a part in the ordeal.

On trial in Sioux Falls three months later, Nesbeth took the stand and denied having played any part in the dynamite blast slaying of Baker or the attempted murder of Helen Sieler. His claims came after his former partner, Reeves, had testified that it was Nesbeth who had hit both Baker and Sieler with a hammer. Every time prosecutors referred to the small glass jar that held the remains of Baker, Helen Sieler wept uncontrollably.

As his wife and mother watched him testify, Nesbeth put the blame for the murder on Reeves and the still-uncaptured Bradley.

But the jury didn't buy his story and, after just ninety minutes of deliberation, convicted Nesbeth of murder. The conviction carried a mandatory life sentence.

As Nesbeth was led away to begin his long term behind bars, E. D. Barron, the state's attorney, told reporters that Sieler, who had been held in the county jail as a material witness since being discharged from the hospital, would be released and allowed to go home to live with her mother in Sioux City. The twenty-six-year-old woman still carried eight bullets in her body from the ordeal, he noted.

Two months after the judge sentenced Nesbeth to life in prison, the last fugitive in the crime was caught while working in a hay field near Yakima, Washington. The arrest of Lee Bradley, forty-five, was triggered by a tip from an unidentified reader of detective-story magazines, police said. Extradited to South Dakota to stand trial, Bradley pleaded guilty to first-degree murder charges and was sentenced to life in prison, his third prison term in twenty years of crime.

Handcuffed to the local sheriff, Bradley replied to every question the judge asked with a mix of candor and humor. "No, I'm not proud of my record," he told Judge John T. Medin. "Money gained through crime comes much harder than when it is honestly earned." He told the judge that he had never been in trouble as a young man, when his father's guidance precluded consideration of crime.

In his conversation with the judge before sentencing, Bradley admitted that he had lit the fuse at the powder house while in a daze from consuming alcohol and marijuana. When the judge suggested that they had traveled to the site with the express purpose of murdering Baker and Sieler, Bradley objected."We did not," he replied emphatically. "You know marijuana and liquor combined can create an awful mess. It just happened on the spur of the moment." Following the lengthy discussion, Judge Medin sentenced Bradley to the South Dakota penitentiary for the rest of Bradley's natural life.

With the last of the three murderers caught, tried, and sentenced to long terms, it might have ended the news coverage of the trio and the dynamite blast that had ushered in 1937 for Sioux Falls. However, seven years after Bradley began his prison term, Nesbeth walked away from the state penitentiary while serving as a trustee, just three years before he was eligible for parole. He remained free for three and a half years, before two grade-school boys found him living in a cave near St. Paul and alerted police. Recaptured, Nesbeth was returned to prison and served four more years before being released in May 1954.

Helen Sieler, who had survived being beaten and shot eight times, who had escaped all criminal charges, and who was once branded by a newspaper as "the woman with ten lives," was never heard from again.

Caleb Lyon

The Opportunist

Caleb Lyon was not an unfamiliar sight at the territorial Indian Affairs office—as governor of the territory, he was also the Indian Affairs commissioner. With his elegant suits, his perfectly coiffed goatee, and his poetic if patrician manner, he was as unmistakable as he was familiar—to a great many Idahoans, altogether too familiar. But on this day his smooth patter and deft assurances still didn't entirely satisfy the clerk, who was unsure why the governor needed to personally withdraw $50,000 in cash from the federal receipts.

"The tribes have to be paid," he said. "They are getting impatient."

This didn't sound right, as Lyon usually preferred that tribal leaders come to him, not the other way around. Not only that, Lyon had dispensed money before, and this was not the procedure he had used.

The clerk resisted and suggested that Lyon's successor take care of it. Even in this remote place, hundreds of miles from the nearest telegraph, word had arrived that Lyon was soon to be replaced by a political appointee named David Ballard.

"Who knows when Ballard will get here," Lyon insisted and then walked out with $50,000.

Days later he took the stage south and made his way to San Francisco. He stayed there several months, through the winter, then boarded a ship for the long journey around the Americas. By the time he arrived in New York, Ballard and others had checked over the books at Indian Affairs and had questions for Lyon.

Soon after he disembarked at New York, federal inspectors tracked him down and began the interrogation. Lyon told them he had never seen the money. His patter was smooth enough that they went on their way, thinking someone must have been mistaken.

Agents eventually caught up with Lyon in Washington, D.C., and questioned him further. Lyon's new story was that he had taken the best care of the money. He watched it day and night. On the train from New York to Washington, he took a sleeper car and kept the money under his pillow. And the night before he arrived in Washington—it was stolen. Somebody had robbed him.

It was a story not many eastern government officials were inclined to believe. Something about the western territories seemed to bring out the worst in political appointees with sticky fingers. For many years Nevada was called the "rotten borough" for its corruption in the 1800s, but to its north the Idaho Territory matched Nevada's reputation. The few government officials Idaho Territory had in its earliest days were given little money either from the federal government or from local taxpayers, but what little there was managed to find its way mostly into the pockets of shady dealers.

One of them was Alfred Slocum, who became treasurer of Boise County (which did not include Boise but was based around the busy mining towns northeast of there). In 1864 his office managed to collect $14,000 in property taxes. The next year the territorial government demanded he turn most of it over, as the law required. Slocum refused, offering one excuse after another. For one thing, he said, money was needed to run the county jail; but that didn't amount to much, since the "jail" was a barnlike building that held no one who chose to leave.

Furthermore, he noted that two men were each claiming to be the treasurer of Idaho Territory, so he didn't know whom to pay. Slocum said he wanted the matter settled in court. Actually he wanted it to go away, since (as territorial officials learned later) Slocum had embezzled the money and already spent most of it. When he was found out, a long legal battle ensued covering two trials, one hung jury, and an attempt to escape to Oregon. Eventually Slocum served prison time.

Caleb Lyon, who liked to call himself "Caleb Lyon of Lyonsdale," never served time in prison, but that seems to have been not for want of effort but because he was just slippery enough and he had a gift for talking his way out of problems.

He came from money and prominence; "Lyonsdale" actually was an estate in northern New York, and the Lyon family had some inherited money along with political and business contacts. Caleb was given the appropriate advantages, was sent to boarding school in Montreal and university in Vermont, and went off for several years to complete his real-world education in Europe. He began writing, with mixed results, an almost baroque poetry and an odd novel about a British traveler who fell into the hands of the Aborigines of Tasmania. He occasionally lectured around the eastern states as well. Lyon made no great waves but he cut an unusual figure, dressing atypically for the day; for a while he was best known for his velvet coat, red cravat, and shoulder-length hair—definitely not in style in the 1840s.

With family money at his back, he might have stayed in those circles, but apparently he was given the impression from family members that he should at least make a show of entering a career. With his gift for speaking and making connections, he soon made his way to politics.

The opening came from his father, who was active in Democratic politics and a personal friend of William Marcy, who was secretary of state in the Polk administration. In 1844 a treaty was signed with China providing, among other things, that an American consul would be stationed at the Chinese city of Shanghai. Marcy gave the job to his friend's son Caleb. What Caleb Lyon did with the job is unclear; the available records seem to suggest that he never crossed the Pacific and that when he resigned in 1849 at the end of the Polk administration, he had never set foot in Shanghai. Maybe it was just as well; Lyon considered himself a Whig, not a Democrat.

Two decades later, just before he was to become governor of Idaho, Lyon claimed he had spent the mid-1840s as an Army officer, traveling with General Winfield Scott in the Mexican War. Searches of military records from that period found no reference to him, and he seems to have made up the story.

When he surfaced in 1849 to turn in his resignation as consul, he was in California. The next year, in Sacramento, he talked his way into the job of secretary of the constitutional convention of the state-to-be; he apparently executed that job. But when he presented to the convention a proposed state seal, which a grateful convention paid him $1,000 for designing, he apparently failed to mention that he'd plagiarized it: It was actually designed by someone else.

Returning to New York, Lyon leveraged his gift for self-promotion first into a term in the state Senate and then two terms in the U.S. House. After he lost the House seat in 1856, his family's mansion burned and money became tighter, and Lyon migrated to Washington to look for another appointed job.

After Abraham Lincoln's election in 1860, the politics were right for Lyon—he had made the transition from Whig to Independent to

Republican, much as Lincoln had—but he had to wait his turn. Over the next couple of years, as the Civil War intensified, stories circulated about Lyon as a Union military leader (some of them suggesting he had enriched himself in the position), but he never wore a uniform in this war, either.

Courtesy of a connection to Lincoln's interior secretary, Lyon got the appointment in early 1864 as governor of Idaho Territory, a jurisdiction created less than a year before and which Lyon had never visited. There was opposition. The outgoing (and first) governor, William Wallace, who had resigned to become Idaho's delegate in Congress, advised Lincoln to appoint someone else. And word from back in New York, notably from influential Republican Roscoe Conkling, was less than supportive; Conkling specifically questioned Lyon's "moral character." But Lyon was confirmed by the Senate in February 1864.

He did not speed his way west. He stayed in New York until June. Then, having hired the interior secretary's son as a personal assistant, he sailed around South America to Portland and arrived in Lewiston, the territorial capital of Idaho, in August. He hired the services of Wells Fargo to move his books and other major supplies, and told them to bill the federal government—which refused to pay. Wells Fargo apparently was never compensated.

In his first report back, Lyon wrote, "I commence the administration of this Department under difficulties of the gravest description." This time Lyon told the literal truth. The territory, little more than a year old, was already $44,000 in debt, and no sources of financial help were obvious. Lyon had no law enforcement and no territory marshal to call upon. The territory was flooded with antiwar Democrats who had no use for any kind of Republican. As governor, Lyon was superintendent of Indian Affairs, and the Indian tribes in the territory, mainly the Nez Perce and the Shoshone, were complaining that federal treaty obligations for money, supplies, and more had not been fulfilled. Lyon did learn, however, a little about the Nez Perce treaty lands. He sent a confidential letter to the interior secretary urging that the treaty with the tribe be amended to exclude a specific tract of land with valuable minerals on it—so that he and the secretary could swoop in and buy it.

There were more problems. Many of the residents wanted to split the territory between north and south, and those in the south wanted the capital moved to the new town of Boise. In the fall of 1864, Lyon traveled south to the Boise area and the new mining territory there, and concluded the obvious: This would be the site of most new population and economic growth. He publicly backed moving the territorial capital from Lewiston to Boise, and when the legislature convened in December at Lewiston and passed a bill to do just that, Lyon signed it.

Lewistonians didn't take the news well. The next February they filed a lawsuit seeking to throw out all of the actions of the last legislative session and got a court order to require Lyon to stay at Lewiston. He wanted to leave, fast, fearing that Lewiston was becoming a dangerous place for him. So he told people he was heading to the Snake River to hunt ducks, but instead, once out of sight, crossed to the other side, joined a buggy he'd sent ahead, and raced for his life to Walla Walla, not stopping for long until he had crossed the continent completely the other way and returned in the spring to Washington, D.C.

In the months that followed, the territorial capital was moved south to Boise, but the work of the territory slowed to a crawl, except for one thing. Early in 1865, about the time Lyon was hightailing out of the territory, Congress finally agreed to send money west for the operation of Idaho Territory—$33,000 for salaries and other expenses. More money to meet the terms of the Indian treaties would soon be coming and thus was awaiting recovery by a proper Idaho official.

The highest official in the territory at the moment was a private secretary. Lyon's territorial assistant, DeWitt Smith—who had been left holding the bag at Lewiston—had died, and his secretary, a former San Francisco bartender named Horace Gilson, was more or less in charge. After raiding the accounts of his now-dead boss, he made friends with territorial businessmen and looked for other funds. When he heard about the $33,000 at Oregon City, he arranged the necessary paperwork to pick it up. A few months later, he said that he needed to go to San Francisco to negotiate a printing contract for the territory. Neither Gilson nor the $33,000 was ever seen again.

When officials back in Washington found out the money they had sent for the tribes was gone, they were furious, and the seeds of investigation were planted. But one of the first things they did was to pull out more money from the federal treasury and send it west to Idaho.

Using his smooth-talking ways, Lyon turned back several efforts in Washington to fire him from the governor's office. Lyon returned to Idaho, arriving just a few weeks ahead of the second round of federal payments. While in Washington, he had interested investors in a railroad scheme to connect the Portland area with the East, and pushed a special bill through the territorial legislature.

But by then much of his attention, and the territory's, was focused on the increasing anger and discontent among the Indian tribes, which still were not receiving the annuities they had been promised. In the fall of 1865, Oregon senator James Nesmith began looking into the Indian bureau's accounts. With the turn of the New Year, he accused Lyon of having "shamefully neglected" his work with the tribes and having failed to keep many of the accounting records for the money.

The investigation continued, and general criticism from within Idaho continued to reach Washington. After Lincoln was assassinated and Andrew Johnson, a Democrat, took over as president, Lyon lost his source of political support. In April 1866 Johnson sent word that Lyon was dismissed, his place to be taken by an Oregonian, David Ballard. Lyon headed back to San Francisco, but his Idaho story was not over.

Nesmith advised Ballard to keep looking into the records of the Indian Affairs office, and soon that summer they found what they had suspected—a $50,000 discrepancy between the amounts Lyon said he had received and the amounts he said he had given to the tribes. His first response was that he'd never had the money.

Communication was slow in those days, and the federal department heads threatened to take Lyon to court to squeeze the money out of him. Lyon took his time in San Francisco and finally returned to New York in the spring of 1867. Asked what happened to the $50,000, Lyon coolly replied that he'd had it with him when he left Idaho, and that he'd planned to turn it in to the appropriate federal officials. He had it with him, he said, on a train headed to Washington. He said he had kept it under his pillow. But from under his pillow, he said, someone had stolen it while he slept.

Lyon was never prosecuted; his trial probably would have been a big embarrassment to too many prominent people. The money was mostly recovered from the bonding company that had insured Lyon. But Lyon's political fortunes never recovered; he retired quietly in New York, where he died in 1875.

On hearing of that news, the *Idaho Statesman* in Boise remarked that he ought to have died in prison.

Ferd Patterson

A Civil War Reenactment

The summer Sunday was bright and almost glaring at Idaho City, and about a mile south of Main Street on the road to Boise, the afternoon had turned sultry. The warm springs just south of town—an easier, more relaxing bath than the hotter springs to the north—had drawn only a few people so far this day, though the saloon in front, between the Boise Road and the pools, was about half full.

The drinkers within had felt surly for weeks. Some of them were Southerners, expatriates from the now-beaten Confederacy, surrendered at Appomattox three months before. Nearly all the rest of the clientele sympathized with them. Just about all were glad Abe Lincoln was no more. This was a Democratic mining town, and Republicans were not welcome.

So they were startled when they heard a clear, strong voice outside, a couple of clomping horses bringing it ever closer, ever louder, singing the hated tune (to the music of "The Battle Hymn of the Republic"):

The stars in Heaven are looking kindly down,
The stars in Heaven are looking kindly down,
The stars in Heaven are looking kindly down,
On the grave of old John Brown.

The singing paused, and then the singer strolled in—a big, confident, cocky smile on his face. They all knew him. It was Ol' Pink himself—Sumner Pinkham—til recently a U.S. marshal and more recently a candidate for sheriff. He was a Unionist, and a Republican, and he was rubbing it in.

He got to the bar, ordered a drink, smiled to his friend, and kept right on singing.

We'll hang Jeff Davis to a sour apple tree,
We'll hang Jeff Davis to a sour apple tree,
We'll hang Jeff Davis to a sour apple tree,
As we go marching on.

Pinkham smiled again and looked around. But he drew little reaction. The bar's patrons weren't going to give him the satisfaction.

He and his friend sat down with their drinks. They sat there a while and chatted, but the glares from all around got to be too much for them, even for Pinkham, a man known to enjoy infuriating everyone else in a room. So they stood up and headed for the door, the idea being to finish their drinks on the front porch.

As they hit the door, they came face to face with Ferd Patterson.

The silence went from uneasy to deadly.

The two men had a history. It went back to Pinkham's days as a marshal, when some of his most energetic work had to do with Patterson. It also had to do with the political polarities of Boise: Patterson was as ardent a Democrat and Confederate as Pinkham was a Republican and Unionist.

When they met at the door, they looked each other in the eye and ran through the quick inventory—he's armed, I'm armed. (Some people later said Patterson had arrived at the warm springs unarmed.) By some unspoken agreement, it seemed, the rivals determined this was not the time or place. They made their way past each other, Pinkham to drink on the front veranda with his friend, Patterson to do likewise in the saloon.

After some drinks in the saloon, Patterson walked out back to the swimming pools. He sat around there for a while, talking with friends, probably enjoying the late afternoon weather. And the drinking continued, steadily.

He would say later that he was trying to forget who was on the front porch and was trying to outwait him—hoping Pinkham would leave first. But every so often, that big singing voice would erupt again, and Patterson would know he was still there.

The fury increased.

Patterson had another drink. Then, finally, he'd had enough.

He was not alone, as the crowd in the saloon badly wanted to smack that smirk off Sumner Pinkham's face, and who better to do it than Ferd Patterson?

The saloonkeeper waved him over to the bar and reached down behind it. He pulled out a rifle. "Here," he said, "you can use this."

The saloonkeeper had a secret. He wanted no fighting or killing on his premises, and the powder keg he saw before him needed only the tiniest spark. The gun, he knew, wouldn't work. He had left the rifle out in the elements, out in the snow, all winter—had forgotten it was there—and it was ruined now. He had inspected it not long ago, and it was spoiled—choked with rust, pieces almost falling apart.

Patterson, who was skilled with guns and knew something about rifles, had had enough drinks that he didn't notice.

He ambled to the front door, pushed through, and peered out onto the front porch. Sumner Pinkham was still there, talking with his friend. He paused to look over at Patterson. His right hand moved south, toward his gun belt—he certainly was armed.

Ferdinand Patterson, a little shakily, rose to his full six feet, stalked to within a man's height of Pinkham and spat out at him: "You will draw on me, will you?"

He pulled up his rifle, aimed it, and pulled the rusty trigger.

And it fired.

Pinkham's body, probably dead before it hit solid ground, flew off the front of the porch, twelve feet down into Warm Creek, which ran in front of the porch.

The next thing the people at the saloon saw was a small cloud of dust to the north—Patterson was riding off, as fast as he could go.

The shooting of Sumner Pinkham by Ferdinand Patterson at the Idaho City warm springs on July 23, 1865, was not a surprise. People around Idaho City had expected it for some time; the issue was when and where, not if. But who was right and what it meant—there was the rub, a rub touchy enough to bring two mobs face to face, just short of starting a small civil war in the largest city in Idaho.

The storm had been building for two years. Or longer.

Ferd Patterson grew up in Alabama—we do not know if he was born there—and took his social cues from the southern aristocracy of the place. He grew tall, probably more than six feet, and wore a curved mustache that gave him a distinguished look. He had an impressive, serious mien; he might have managed a career in politics but instead latched onto gambling. Two other things came with him out of Alabama: a deep attachment to the states' rights and Democratic politics of his home, and a hair-trigger, sometimes lethal, temper. Drinking was said to worsen his temper, and most of his violent incidents happened in or around saloons.

He left Alabama for Texas and then left Texas for California. He was drawn, along with so many others, to the California gold fields of the Sacramento area. Soon enough, he plied his gambling skill at separating overconfident miners from their finds and became moderately prosperous. He dressed stylishly, wore a gold watch and chain, and walked with a trendy cane.

When the Civil War cracked open, California turned sharply from a Democratic state with some sympathy for the South to a Republican, pro-Union place. That may have been part of the reason that in late 1862, Patterson booked one-way passage on a ship headed north to Portland for himself and his mistress, a long-haired blonde beauty who instantly attracted plenty of attention. On arriving in Portland, he learned that the captain of the ship, staying in the same hotel he was, had taken notice of the couple and, in loud barroom talk, was denouncing him as a Southern traitor. That pulled the hair trigger; Patterson grabbed the pistol from his room, ran down the stairs, and shot and killed the captain.

Patterson was arrested and jailed. He managed to clear himself by claiming he had shot the captain in self-defense. But then his hair trigger was pulled again when he found his mistress, back at the hotel, with another man. This time he put down his pistol and grabbed a bowie knife, and started hacking the blonde tresses from his mistress. In the process, he became overeager: He explained later in an Idaho saloon, "My knife slipped, and the blade, I reckon, cut a little too deep."

He was arrested again, and immediately posted the $500 bail. And then, as the *Idaho Tri-Weekly Statesman* would soon put it, he "left for some other city where there is no penitentiary"—but where, it might also have noted, there were plenty of Southern sympathizers.

He could hardly have chosen better than the new mining boomtowns of Idaho.

First stop was a city less than eighteen months old that would be, within a few years, a ghost town: Florence, in north-central Idaho northeast of what is now Riggins. There he found an environment much like that of the mining communities of northern California, with two differences. It was more rugged and temporary. But, offsetting that, the miners were overwhelmingly Southerners or Southern sympathizers, and by the time Patterson arrived they had already heard tales about how he had defended the cause back in Portland.

Patterson became cockier in Florence. With some Southern friends, he decided to take over a new local brewery, and not through arm's-length negotiations. The aggrieved owner and others in town called on the U.S. marshal to do something, and the marshal did—he threw Patterson in jail. That marked the first run-in between Patterson and the marshal, whose name was Sumner Pinkham.

Pinkham and Patterson saw in each other everything they each loathed. Patterson was slippery, corrupt, and crooked by nature, and liked living that way; Pinkham tended to self-righteousness. Patterson organized crime; Pinkham did what he could to break it up. Most especially, Pinkham was a Northerner—a native of Maine, raised in Wisconsin—and an ardent Unionist Republican. Their meetings were especially combustible because of what they had in common. They were both powerfully built men, and both skillful with firearms. Both liked to dominate a room, and both reacted swiftly to a challenge. Pinkham was a little older, and his thick white beard seemed to add still more years. Pinkham had some background as a gambler, but he had moved on to throw in with law enforcement. And he had a temper that easily matched Patterson's.

Both of them liked to be provocative.

That summer of 1863, the gold mines of Florence were dying out, and the mining community there began to scatter. Idaho also became a territory, and law enforcement was about to be increased. Pinkham left Florence for Idaho City to the south, there to become the Boise County sheriff, at least until an election to be held the next year. Patterson, hearing about the next big mining town forming at Idaho City, took the same route. Organizing his fellow Southerners, he helped defeat Pinkham when the office of sheriff came up for election.

As the last of the ballots were being counted, as Patterson was celebrating on the main street of Idaho City, he came face to face with Sumner Pinkham, who was worked up into a rage. There was no discussion; there was nothing to say. Pinkham simply twisted a bit to the side and swung, a legendarily powerful, smashing blow to the jaw, throwing Ferd Patterson almost off the street and into the gutter on the side. The audience, quickly grown in the space of a minute, was silenced and did not interfere as Sumner Pinkham walked off. Patterson's friends discouraged him from giving chase and helped him back to his rooms.

Patterson had the rest of the night to recuperate and consider. When the next day he emerged on the street, he did not do what many in Idaho City expected, which was to hunt down and kill Sumner Pinkham. Instead he emerged coatless, in his shirtsleeves, showing that he was unarmed and not seeking a fight. He stayed that way for a few more days.

And then, saying he had to visit his dying mother in Illinois, Sumner Pinkham rode out of town.

In the year that followed, Idaho City prospered, and so did Ferd Patterson. He became a popular leader in town among the Southern sympathizers, a role that did not diminish even as word reached Idaho that the Confederacy's days were over. For a time about 20,000 miners packed into the Boise River basin mountains near Idaho City and, briefly, the gold mining was good. Patterson's ways had not changed, but they fit smoothly into the scene.

Then one day in July of 1865, a few months after Appomattox, as Southern sensitivities reached their peak, Sumner Pinkham returned to Idaho City.

Word spread from one end of Idaho City to the other. A low buzz ran through the town, and the message was consistent. Sometime in the days ahead, Ferd Patterson and Sumner Pinkham were going to have it out.

The first words anyone heard from Ferd Patterson after he had shot Pinkham were spoken about fourteen miles southwest of Idaho City on the road to Boise, at the small Star Road House run by Frank and Hester Davis. Patterson had not had sufficient time to calm himself. He was tearing up the road as he jumped off his horse and approached Frank Davis. From a distance he hollered, "Frank—Frank—I shot Pinkham at Warm Springs. Quick—give me a blanket and something to eat. I must cut off into the hills."

Hester Davis said later (in a signed statement) that her husband promptly brought a blanket while she prepared a lunch for Patterson to take along in his saddlebag. He rode off, but only minutes later "we saw five or six men coming on horseback, not in the road but over the hills. They hollered, 'Got any fresh horses?' and 'How long since Ferd came?'" They were led by the sheriff—Jack Gorman, whom Patterson had helped elect—and Deputy Rube Robbins.

Orlando "Rube" Robbins would go on to become one of the legendary lawmen of Idaho Territory. He had been all around the mining camps, gradually moving himself into law enforcement, and had some experience by the time of the Pinkham shooting. But this was his first big capture. That same evening he led the final surround of the road house, still shy of Boise, where the sheriff's posse finally caught up with Patterson. They started back to Idaho City, intending to lock Patterson in the Boise County jail. Charged with the murder of a former sheriff, he seemed unlikely to escape easily this time.

That was where Idaho's own civil war almost began.

Gorman and his deputies got advance word that the road back to Idaho City was lined with people, most of whom, for one reason or another, had come to hate Patterson or befriend Pinkham. Taking a back trail through the mountains, they made their way into Idaho City from behind, slipped into the courthouse, and barricaded themselves inside their offices and jailhouse. Not that the jail offered much protection; it was only a rough stockade, located next door to the Buena Vista saloon.

Soon word spread, and the people from the road gathered in the Idaho City cemetery, only about a block from the courthouse. By most accounts, there were more than 900 of them, some of them members of the local vigilante organization based out of Payette. Mob mentality quickly took over. They were determined to lynch Patterson, and for several days they kept vigil. The town's "fighting parson," Elder Kingsley, offered prayer for the success of the lynching.

On the second day they chose a leader. William McConnell, a future Idaho governor and senator, was the leader of the Payette vigilantes and was well respected in the region. The mob asked him to take over. McConnell was sympathetic; Pinkham had been a friend of his (and McConnell, too, was a Union Republican). Reconnoitering the situation, he told the group, "We can take that jail." There was a roar in favor, but then he poured cold water on it: If they tried, he said, "It will be at the cost of many lives. I cannot see the sense of sacrificing forty or fifty good men's lives for the purpose of hanging one murderer."

That seemed to end it, and as the group began to break up, McConnell started to ride out of the mountains. He was accompanied by Rube Robbins. Then a breathless horseman dashed up behind them with news. About a hundred of the most angry members of the mob had collected at Gilkie's smith shop, and the sheriff had approached them and ordered them to disperse. This only infuriated them. In minutes they had changed their minds and were planning to storm the courthouse. The sheriff in turn collected a crowd of a hundred or more—many of them Patterson's friends—and prepared for battle.

When McConnell and Robbins arrived, both sides were ready to shoot, and a single bullet would have begun an extended battle. McConnell moved out between the groups and negotiated a settlement.

Somehow the peace held, for month after month, until the trial in November. Newspapers across the West did their best to keep things inflamed, taking either Patterson's or Pinkham's side, depending on their partisan leaning. The *Idaho World* in Idaho City was in Patterson's corner; the *Idaho Tri-Weekly Statesman* in Boise wanted him hanged.

The trial lasted six days, and testimony regarding many details of the shooting conflicted. The most skilled lawyer was defense attorney Frank Ganahl, who argued that Pinkham was simply waiting for a chance to shoot Patterson. One report said "men and women alike were crying when Ganahl finished his impassioned plea."

It apparently worked. The jury was out for an hour and a half and returned with a verdict of not guilty.

Calculating the odds for survival, Ferd Patterson split town as soon as he was released.

But he failed to calculate well enough.

Patterson fled west, to Walla Walla, pausing there to rest. We don't know where he was headed next, because his journey ended at a barber shop at Walla Walla. He was in the chair, his face under a hot towel prior to shaving, when another man entered the shop and pulled a gun.

It's been said that Patterson was fast enough on the draw to yank the towel from his head and actually pull his gun from the holster in the moments between the firing of the shots and his almost instant death from them. But the stories vary.

The way Ferd Patterson lived his life, he left open many possibilities for suspects: No lack of people wanted him dead.

Henry MacDonald

The Storyteller

Henry McDonald knew George Myers from the hauling business, though not well. Based on what he did know, he thought that in Myers he could see his own future. He had no notion that he was also seeing his end.

McDonald was a piecework hauler in the Wood River Valley, carrying supplies from one town to another in the still-booming mining district, usually accompanied only by his dog. He occasionally veered south out of the valley over some low hills and into the Snake River plain. There he would bump into an older and better-used trail, between the Boise and Boise Basin settlements to the west and the Salt Lake City area to the southeast. Haulers took that road often as the best way to get from one set of settlements to the other; there was none to speak of in between.

McDonald had some ambition. He wanted to buy an outfit—horses, a wagon, the equipment he needed to haul longer distances running his own business; he'd had it with being a wage slave. He put out the word on the road, when he ran into other haulers, that he was interested in buying, though he was unclear about how much money he had to spend. After a few months a reply came back to him. George Myers, a veteran of the trade, was looking to cash out. Communications, slow but direct for the era, were sent out. McDonald wanted to buy, Myers was willing to sell. Across the sagebrush desert routes, secondhand and thirdhand word went about that a business deal seemed to be in the works.

The two arranged to meet at a spot called Soul's Rest, on the Boise–Salt Lake trail. McDonald joined Myers on his run, hired on to begin with as an employee, with the idea of taking over before long, bringing his dog along for the ride. The two of them headed west through the desert south of Hailey. It was not an especially rigorous journey. But in the days ahead, they got no rest.

Myers was a cranky old man, a heavy drinker—and he was drinking on this trip—efficient enough at his business but not especially likable. McDonald was utterly unfamiliar with the realities of business, especially of buying or selling one. We don't know exactly for how much Myers was willing to sell his established operation with an established clientele, but a figure of around $2,000 to $3,000, or maybe more, seems likely.

McDonald had nowhere near that kind of money. He had little more than pocket change. He was hoping he could pay Myers over time. The negotiations fell apart quickly, and that set the tone for their relationship. The arguments were only the beginning.

They argued about everything. When in early September a group of freighters passed them, they overheard Myers and McDonald yelling at each other about McDonald's dog, which kept falling out of the wagon. Myers threatened to shoot the dog, McDonald would recall later.

The exact circumstances of Myers's death were never made clear. He and McDonald probably came to blows, and Myers fell to the ground and was run over by the wagon—either accidentally or on purpose. That much would at least be consistent with the facts police eventually unearthed.

The truth has been buried in the almost impenetrable web of lies McDonald began telling as soon as he encountered the next road traveler—and picked up as soon as he hit town.

Today the word "teamster" is associated with the international labor union, but decades ago, and in the old West, it had a different meaning, implicit in the word itself. A teamster was the driver of a team—sometimes of a mule train, sometimes of a half-dozen oxen, or sometimes several horses. In conversation at the time, any of these would usually be called an "outfit."

Henry McDonald, who drove teams for the purpose of delivering supplies between the mines of Utah and Idaho, was a teamster for hire; he did not own his own outfit. His desire to become an independent businessman was what led him to the gallows and resulted in the only legal execution in Idaho's most rugged area and still among its most lightly populated, Owyhee County.

The few surviving pictures of McDonald suggest a wiry man, tall, thin, with a thick, bushy mustache, but, by frontier standards, carefully groomed. He gave off no sense of the hardened desperado. But the look in his eyes is a bit like those of a deer in the headlights, a man perpetually caught by surprise with the reality around him and never quite able to catch up. Although his job of driving teams from one town to another would not seem especially stressful, apart from the normal hazards of the road, he often seemed a man in over his head.

We do not know much about McDonald's early life. As much as he liked to talk and write, he never had much to say about his early years—not that we would necessarily believe him if he had. Probably he emigrated from an eastern or southern state in the 1870s, looking for work in the western mines. As of 1880, when he was driving teams between Kelton, Utah, and the Idaho mines in the Wood River Valley and in the Silver City area, he said that his mother was still alive and he had a wife and two children. He gave the impression that they were still living in the Salt Lake City area, just south of Kelton, but few Idahoans ever heard much more about them than that, and Henry McDonald spoke of them only toward the very end of his life, when he was facing the death penalty.

In the summer of 1880 he quit his job hauling goods around the Wood River area to pick up on a new opportunity. He hired on with George Myers, a long-timer on the Utah–Idaho route who owned an outfit and was said to be interested in selling out. They both told people in Idaho that McDonald planned to buy, and at Soul's Rest, McDonald joined the haul with Myers.

One day in September McDonald showed up in Boise with a load and the outfit, pulling through that place on his way to Silver City. Freighters familiar with everyone's horses and wagons—they were distinctive identifiers—noticed that while Myers's outfit was pulling into town, someone else was driving it, and Myers was nowhere around.

McDonald stopped only briefly in Boise; he had a load bound for the Silver City mining district. But the questions and concerns were enough to prompt the Ada County sheriff, Joe Oldham, to mount up, ride out of town, and catch up with him on the route. Somewhere out in the desert flats near the town of Mayfield, he stopped McDonald and began to ask questions.

"These are Myers's wagon and horses," the sheriff said. "Where is Myers?"

McDonald said they weren't Myers's anymore, that he had sold him the outfit for $600 down, which he had paid, and $800 in regular payments to be paid later. After they had concluded their business out on the trail, he said, Myers had taken off.

Oldham pressed him. "Where did Myers go?"

"Oh, I remember now," Myers said. "There had been a horse Myers had lost in the war with the Bannock Indians, and someone we passed told him he had heard it was spotted somewhere in Oregon. And then Myers rode off to try to find it."

The sheriff found none of this very convincing. McDonald had admitted wanting Myers's outfit and he didn't look to Oldham like the sort to be able to buy it outright, or even with $600 down—he didn't seem the type who was able to put that much money together in one place at one time. Figuring McDonald for a liar, Oldham hauled him back to Boise and jailed him at the courthouse while he pondered a search for the body. McDonald insisted that wasn't necessary. I'll be proven innocent, he insisted. You'll see the evidence. Before the pair had split up, he said, Myers had posted a letter to the Boise area that would prove McDonald's innocence.

But Sheriff Oldham held him behind bars. Then, several weeks later, William Morlatt, a freighter on the road to Idaho City, dropped by the sheriff's office with a letter bearing the signature of George Myers, dated in October, quite a while after McDonald had been jailed. Addressed to Morlatt, it advised him, "I have sold me team too Henry McDonald, and have got track of that horse of mine and am going to find him."

It sounded just like the letter McDonald had told the sheriff to expect. Maybe a little too much like it.

There was just one problem, Morlatt said. He'd gotten letters from Myers before, had done business with the man, and he knew his signature. And this wasn't it.

The sheriff discussed the situation with Tom Calahan, the prosecutor. Avoiding any mention of the letter, Calahan grilled McDonald, who repeated that a letter should be coming. Calahan said he didn't believe it. McDonald told him that Myers must have been held up by robbers on the road. The lonesome trails were dangerous places, after all.

McDonald's comments probably did spark a new line of inquiry, though, among the people at stage stops and out on the road. Sheriff Oldham and territorial officials sent out inquires and got some responses. They found a group of freighters who remembered seeing Myers and McDonald together in early September, and not getting along well: Apparently they had been arguing about McDonald's dog. At another stop, one of them heard a new story from McDonald, who was traveling alone now. According to this story, their arguments had gotten worse; Myers had reached for a gun but slipped under a wagon wheel and was badly injured, with bones broken. McDonald said he was trying to fix his wounds when three other riders, apparently immigrants from a

European country, appeared and said they would take care of Myers, so McDonald rode off.

McDonald was held in jail for an appearance before the grand jury.

Oldham and Calahan were frustrated. The case was far from airtight, and they knew it. McDonald was obviously a liar, but they had no body and no solid evidence—only possibilities. They knew they needed more, so they tried a trick.

Bill Glines, a short-time offender, was installed in the cell next to McDonald's. Unlike McDonald, he had some education, and since McDonald was only marginally literate, he called Glines over and asked for help in writing a few letters.

Glines did, not writing them personally but holding a candle and advising McDonald on how to write and improve his grammar and spelling.

The main cover letter, addressed to a bartender friend at Kelton, Utah, said this:

> *Dear George, I am in a tite place. If I have to stay for the grand jury I am gone for good. Now doo mee a favor, for this does depend on my life and I will make it all rite with you when I see you. George, be sure and see some of Myers hand rite and sine his name as near like it as you can. George now dont fail and don't write anything but the affair between me and Myers because the sheriff opens letters and reads them.*

The inmates also wrote a couple of enclosures, letters dated in November that purported to be from Myers and addressed to McDonald—suggesting he was still alive.

As soon as they were done, Glines grabbed the letters and handed them over to the sheriff, to McDonald's roaring fury. Prosecutors now had another lie on record, and samples of McDonald's handwriting to match the earlier letters, but they still had no body.

However, a man named Lewis was traveling near what is now Glenns Ferry when he noticed clothes, boots, and rope off the trail. Looking more closely, he found bones. There was no certain identification, but it all fit the description of George Myers.

The location was believed to be in Owyhee County, so the sheriff and prosecutor moved their prisoner to Silver City, the county seat.

McDonald had tried to tunnel his way out of the Ada County jail, an effort that failed early, but he soon saw he had no hope at Silver City. There, the cells were built into a cave on the mountainside.

By the time of his trial in the spring of 1881, McDonald had said that Myers had lit out for Oregon, that he had been killed by robbers, that he had been injured on the road and hauled off by travelers, even—in his last letters—that he had taken ill. At his trial he took the witness stand and delivered what he said was the real, complete story. It could not have been told before, he said, because he feared for his life from two other men.

He said that he had heard Myers wanted to sell his outfit, and he—McDonald—wanted to buy. He hopped another wagon headed for Kelton, the same direction Myers was taking, and caught up with him. They agreed to the sale of the outfit, he said, and signed papers to that effect at Salmon Falls, south of present-day Twin Falls.

Myers was not, McDonald said, an easy traveling companion. He drank heavily and turned into a mean drunk, berating McDonald and abusing his dog. Finally, as they were riding back through southern Idaho, they argued about the dog, and Myers reached for his pistol in the wagon's jockey box, saying he was going to shoot the dog. Instead, he fell out of the wagon and slipped under one of the axles, and then a wheel ran over part of his body. The horses kept on and the wagon dragged him a few feet before McDonald could get full control and grind the outfit to a halt.

He was struggling to pull Myers, who was probably already dead, out from under the wagon, he said, when two men, Len Lewis—the uncle of the man who had found Myers's body—and Frank Kellet, rode by. They pulled Myers's body to the side, but they would not help him load it for the trip to Salmon Falls, the nearest community. As McDonald explained it, they had been looking for a crime to blame on a man named Gus Glenn, and they would set up the evidence to frame him. And, McDonald said, they warned him on pain of death to say nothing about the plot.

And, he suggested, that explains how it was that Lewis's nephew was the finder of Myers's body.

It was McDonald's first detailed story, and it caused a big stir. It established his creativity, at least, since it seemed on the surface to tie up most of the loose ends in his many earlier stories.

But the prosecution was well prepared, as usual. Territorial officials had located Len Lewis and established that he was hundreds of miles away from Idaho when the incident occurred. Kellet was never found, and McDonald was unable to find anyone who would say they even knew him, including Lewis. Nor could anyone find out anything about the mysterious Glenn.

The jury concluded McDonald was lying again, and he was sentenced to hang in August. The event was delayed for two months with appeals to the territorial supreme court. But it would not be delayed long: The court set a hanging date in October.

On that day, McDonald was escorted in a wagon from his cave jail to the nearby mining town of Ruby City, then out beyond that small town to a cemetery where the gallows had been constructed. Though the day was overcast and, by the time of the hanging, raining as well, hundreds of people showed up to watch—McDonald had been big news across Idaho for months.

The man who had told so many stories that didn't pan out, however, did get it right in his last reported statement. A few miles out from the place of execution, seeing some people hurrying along beside the wagon carrying him to the gallows, McDonald is said to have remarked:

"Take your time. There won't be much going on before I get there."

JOHN "BADEYE" SANTAMARAZZO

The Weston County Poisoner

In the 1814 book *Traité de Toxicologie,* Mathew J. B. Orfila wrote:

> *Revolted by the odious crime of homicide, the chemist's aim is to perfect the means of establishing proof so that the heinous crime (of poisoning) will be brought to light and proved to the magistrate, who must punish the criminal.*

In the Old West, deadly weapons of all types were readily available to anyone who wanted them. The most common weapons included rifles, shotguns, pistols, axes, and knives. Other dangerous weapons were available based upon a man's occupation, and miners had access to picks, shovels, sledges, and all sorts of tools and materials that could be used to kill another person. Therefore, with all of these readily available weapons, it was surprising when a man resorted to poison as a means of bringing about another man's death.

Nonetheless, this seemed to occur about once every ten years between 1887 and 1906. In 1887 Frederick Hopt from Utah asked a druggist to supply him with strychnine "to kill the rats which are eating my grain at camp." The druggist refused to supply him with the poison, and so Hopt returned to camp and bludgeoned John F. Turner to death. Twenty years later in Montana, Miles Fuller put strychnine in Henry Callahan's sugar bowl in the hope that he would eat the poison and die, leaving his land vacant for Fuller to occupy. Callahan must have noticed the tampering and did not eat the poison. In his defense, Fuller would later claim, "I know too much about poison for that purpose and recommend arsenic." In another incident John Santamarazzo tried to use strychnine to kill a man with whom he had a dispute. Like the others, he too failed to kill his victim with poison.

John Santamarazzo was born in Italy in 1843. He came to America as a youth and traveled west, settling in Wyoming by the mid-1890s. He had been a miner all his life and found work in the coalmines of Weston County in northeast Wyoming. In August 1895 he was fifty-three years old. He was "married but without children" and described as "poorly educated, about five feet eight inches tall and weighing one hundred and sixty pounds, with long black hair and black eyes, 'white' but with a very dark complexion," according to Elnora L. Frye's work on the prisoners at Wyoming's Territorial Prison.

Santamarazzo's appearance was rugged, and he looked like a true outlaw. He had been injured in a mine explosion during his earlier mining days and it had left him with powder burn discoloration on the left side of his face and ear. His left eyelid drooped over a blind eye, earning him the sobriquet "Badeye." He had led a somewhat violent life as evidenced by a cut scar in the middle of his forehead, another on his left arm, another large cut on his "short ribs," and an "ax mark" on his left arm.

In April 1895 Santamarazzo was working for the Cambria Mine. There he met Mike Dancy (sometimes spelled Dacy, Dacey, and Darcy), who was a teamster at the mine. Dancy and Santamarazzo had a heated argument on August 13, but it failed to escalate to violence; still, the ill-tempered and vindictive Italian swore he would kill Dancy.

The following afternoon Dancy took his dinner break with Santamarazzo, Theodore Shaw, Freeman Fossler, Charles Isem, and Henry Sulzner. He opened his meal bucket and took a large bite of bread, and then remarked to his companions that it had a "strong bitter taste to the first mouthful." Immediately, Dancy's neck began to stiffen in an awkward position. Before he could speak another word, he collapsed and was immediately overcome by violent spasms. His body jack-knifed back and forth, and he groaned in agony. The slightest noise or vibration on the floor aggravated the symptoms and caused the convulsions to become even more severe.

Once summoned, Dr. George Garrison Verbryck rushed Dancy to the nearby hospital for treatment. Dancy's dinner bucket was also collected and turned over to the doctor because there appeared to be foul play. Upon examination Verbryck found a colorless crystalline powder sprinkled throughout the food. The doctor identified the substance as strychnine and determined there was enough of the poison present to kill a hundred men.

Fortunately for Dancy, the bitter taste had caused him to pause in eating his meal and have a conversation with his fellow workers. This had prevented him from ingesting a fatal dose. The doctor managed to pump his stomach and administer activated charcoal, which soon revived the patient. Still, it took a short while before the victim could talk. When he was able to speak, he stated that he did not know who could have tried to kill him. He knew of no enemy who would want to take his life, "unless it was that Italian who I argued with yesterday. He said he would kill me."

Sulzner, who was at the meal table that day, would later testify that he observed Santamarazzo "when Dancy first took ill and saw actions and expressions of the Itallion [*sic*] . . . and believed M. Dancy received poison at the hands of Santamarazzo." Others said they had seen Santamarazzo lurking around the meal buckets earlier in the day.

On the afternoon of August 14, 1895, Weston County Sheriff John Owens filed a criminal complaint before Justice of the Peace P. J. Welsh. The complaint charged that "J. Santamarazzo . . . [tried] to take the life of Mike Daucey [*sic*] by distributing poison in his lunch and victuals with the intention of poisoning the same." Dancy also filed a criminal complaint charging that Santamarazzo " . . . did willfully, maliciously, and unlawfully administer poison with the intent to kill the said Mike Dancy." The judge issued a warrant based upon the complaints, and upon receiving it the sheriff immediately served it on the suspected poisoner, arresting him and lodging him in the Weston County Jail in Newcastle.

On April 4, 1896, Sheriff Owens took Santamarazzo from jail to the court, where counsel was appointed. Since the defendant could not adequately speak or understand the English language, the court provided an interpreter. On April 20, 1896, Wyoming's Fourth Judicial District Court convened and heard the testimony of several witnesses, including the four men that were present and Dr. Verbryck.

Theodore Shaw testified, "I was present and witnessed the condition of M. Dacey [*sic*] and saw that he had spasms and that I examined the dinner pail and contents and could see something resembling strychnine in the bread, and Dr. Verbryck made an examination of the food and found strychnine freely distributed in the food." Freeman Fossler testified next, stating that Dancy "had spasms resembling that of a man having taken poison" and saying he believed it was "administered by the hands of the accused prisoner." Charles Isem swore that "I was present . . . and saw the condition and action of M. Dancy after he had eaten his dinner and saw the food containing strychnine." Lastly, Henry Sulzner testified to the same and to the guilty aspect of Santamarazzo's countenance and demeanor. The doctor testified to the type of poison, its presence in the food, Dancy's symptoms, and the treatment for strychnine poisoning that had successfully revived the victim.

An indictment charged the defendant with two counts. The first stating that: "Santamarazzo . . . unlawfully, willfully, maliciously, and feloniously . . . administered poison—to wit: strychnine—to one Mike Dacy [*sic*], with intent to kill him . . . death not ensuing there from, contrary to the form upon the Statute in such case made and provided, and against the peace and dignity of the State of Wyoming." The indictment's second count read, " . . . and the said L. T. Griggs, County and prosecuting attorney . . . informs the Court and gives the Court to understand, that the same (Santamarazzo) did unlawfully, willfully, maliciously, feloniously . . . mingle poison—to wit: strychnine—with food of one Mike Dacy [*sic*], with intent to kill him . . . death not ensuing there from."

Santamarazzo was arraigned and a jury was quickly empanelled. The same counsel that had represented him at the arraignment was appointed to represent him at trial. The case began before noon on April 19, and the presentation of evidence occupied the remainder of that day and the next. The case went to the jury shortly before 9:00 p.m. The jury could not arrive at a verdict and remained in the jury room overnight, but in the morning the foreman told the judge that it was hopelessly deadlocked—eight for conviction and four for acquittal. The jury was dismissed and a second jury empanelled.

Santamarazzo was then arraigned on a charge of "the crime of attempt to kill with poison," which was a slight change in the wording from the first trial. The testimony was again taken on April 21, and the case went to the jury late on the second day, but again this jury could not arrive at a swift verdict and spent the night in the jury room. Deliberations continued throughout the following day. At 4:00 p.m. John P. Ost, jury foreman, announced, "We the jury . . . do find the defendant . . . guilty as charged in the Information." The prisoner was then remanded to the county sheriff to be held in the jail until sentence was passed.

Within a few days, on April 28, 1896, the prisoner was brought into court again. The former coalminer was sentenced to serve nine years in the penitentiary near Laramie. On May 5, 1896, the prisoner was delivered from the Newcastle jail to the prison by Weston County's Sheriff John Owens. He was registered in the Bertillon Book as convict #258.

Santamarazzo was at the Laramie prison, known as the Territorial Prison, when the new state prison, called the Frontier Prison, was opened in Rawlins. He was in the fourth group of convicts transferred there on December 21, 1901. On June 23, 1904, by reason of "expiration of sentence," authorities released Santamarazzo on his earliest release date, having awarded him 460 days of good time credit as required under the Goodwin Act. His release date would have been April 27, 1905, without the credit for good time.

Good police work and the willingness of witnesses to testify led to the arrest, trial, and conviction of John Santamarazzo before he could commit another crime. His disdain for the life of another man suggests that if he had succeeded in killing Mike Dancy, he would not have hesitated to commit another crime. He may have again chosen the diabolical and unique method of poisoning.

GEORGE A. BLACK

A "Black Day" for Ol' Tanglefoot

George A. Black was born in Indiana in 1862. When but a boy he moved with his parents and five siblings to Ryan County, Missouri. After his father died, the family moved to Davis County. He was a sickly child and unable to attend school. When he turned eighteen, he left home for Laramie, Wyoming. There his health improved and he married a fifty-three-year-old widow with several children. The marriage lasted only four years, and after that Black moved onto a small piece of land not far from Laramie, located next to the far superior claim of Robert Burnett.

Robert Burnett, who was known as "Ol' Tanglefoot," had lived near Meridian, Missouri, during the Civil War, where he lost everything, including his wife. After the war he started westward, settling at several places for a while. After a decade of wandering, he finally settled in Wyoming. Though quite peculiar he was a likeable sort. His friends described him as an "eccentric." He wore gunnysacks, tied with wire, on his feet. He ate only with his hands and threw the scraps on the floor of his cabin, and had not been known to bathe in many years.

Burnett was feeble-minded and terribly superstitious, but he was also a litigious old man. Burnett sued his neighbor, George A. Black, for harvesting the old man's hay. Burnett won the suit, and when Black could not pay the judgment, the plaintiff was awarded Black's buildings, some hay land, and a few cows. With no place to live, and the better part of his poor land gone, Black had no choice but to vacate his property.

Black wanted Burnett's land and held a grudge when he lost his property. He tried to drive the old man off the land and played upon Burnett's superstitious nature by posting White Cap notices—crude drawings of skulls, crossbones, and coffins—on his cabin door. Once he hid in a clump of sagebrush and fired on Burnett, but missed his mark. The old man, instead of turning and running, charged and captured Black. Black insisted that he had mistaken Burnett for an elk, so the old man released him without charges being filed.

When Black failed to drive Burnett off the property, he moved to Medicine Bow but soon returned to the Pole Mountain area near

Laramie to live with his brother Benjamin. There Black found a willing accomplice to help him in his ongoing battles with Burnett. Black first met twenty-eight-year-old Dwight "Roxy" Rockwell at the JD Ranch in Wyoming's Silver Crown mining district. Black and Rockwell became reacquainted in Laramie, where Black explained how Burnett had "stolen" his land. Rockwell agreed to go with Black to Burnett's land to help him reclaim "his" property. Black filed a mining claim on Burnett's property in Laramie, and then the two men stocked their wagon with supplies and started out.

They arrived at Burnett's cabin on May 28, 1889, and found the old man seated on an overturned pail cutting seed potatoes inside his cabin. Rockwell stood nearby while Black talked with Burnett. Black asserted that the land belonged to him and asked, then commanded, that Burnett vacate the property, but the old man refused. Suddenly Black pulled his six-shooter and shot Burnett in the back. When Burnett reached for his rifle, Black shot him in the head and then fired one more ball into the dead body.

The two men wrapped the head and then the entire body of Burnett, hauled it up a remote canyon, and placed it at the end of a huge log. They piled pitch pine onto Burnett's remains and set it afire before returning to the cabin to sleep. In the morning they scrubbed the wagon and smeared grease on the tarp to cover the bloodstains before returning to the body. They raked what remained of Burnett into a pile and, with a new pile of tinder, again set it afire. Then they returned to the cabin and replaced the blood-stained floorboards. That night they returned to Burnett's remains, gathered up the larger bones and remnants, and buried them in a gopher hole. Black and Rockwell took possession of the cabin, but Rockwell soon left for North Park, Colorado.

Burnett was not missed for several weeks. When friends finally noticed his absence, Black explained that the old man had sold out to him and gone east to spend his final days with his daughter. That story was soon discredited, but there was no evidence of foul play, so no action could be taken. There was talk of organizing a search, but this was abandoned when Black threatened to kill any organizer of an investigative committee.

The Pullman family, Charles, Mattie, and teenage daughter Mary, had recently arrived from Missouri. On August 6, 1889, Mattie and Mary were berry picking when they saw a strange pile of ashes covering an area nearly 8 feet in diameter, certainly no campfire. They investigated and found small human bones, bits of wire, and small remnants of clothing. They hurried home and told Charles. The next day the three returned to the site. Charles Pullman examined the remains, gathered every bit of evidence he could find into two pails, and carried them to Laramie.

Pullman gave the pails to the Albany County attorney, who called in Dr. John W. Harris. The doctor and his associate identified the remains as human finger bones, part of a skull, teeth, and a rib bone. They also found rivets from overalls (like those always worn by Burnett), hobnails, and bits of baling wire. Coroner Dr. J. H. Hayford convened a jury and over five days of testimony and investigation found the remains to be Burnett's. The Black brothers and Rockwell were charged with the murder.

George Black and his brother Benjamin were arrested and jailed. At the preliminary hearing before Justice Charles E. Carpenter on August 22, George was held and Benjamin was released. The evidence against Black, though circumstantial, was very strong. Two weeks after the discovery of Burnett's remains, Sheriff Charles Yund learned that a check payable to Burnett had been endorsed by Rockwell and cashed in North Park, Colorado. Yund deputized J. J. Moore, and the two men went in search of the fugitive. Rockwell was working in a field on George Fletcher's ranch when the two officers found and arrested him. He willingly returned to Wyoming and confessed all the details, first to officers and then under oath at Black's trial.

In mid-October Black was indicted for first-degree murder while Rockwell was indicted as an accessory after the fact. The trial in the district court commenced on Saturday, November 2. Five days later Black was found guilty. On November 16 Judge M. C. Saufley sentenced Black to hang on January 15, 1890.

Rockwell was tried after Black and received a light sentence, in consideration of turning state's evidence, and two years later was living in Montana. The appeals process, financed by his brother Benjamin, began for Black. The execution was stayed while the state's supreme court considered the matter, but the respite was only six weeks in duration. The supreme court denied the bill of exemption and upheld the lower court's decision. Governor Francis E. Warren quickly denied the petition for commutation of sentence, and the date for Black's execution was rescheduled for February 26, 1890.

Black had been a Baptist, but a week before the hanging he was baptized into the Catholic faith. On Tuesday evening, February 25, the prisoner was talking with his deathwatch guards when the reporter from the *Leader* was escorted to his cell by the sheriff. In the cell were papers and books read to him by the guards, a bouquet of flowers, and a potted plant. The reporter offered to print whatever the condemned man wanted to disclose and encouraged him to confess, but he professed his innocence and persisted in saying Rockwell committed the crime and that he was denied a fair trial. Just before the visitor left at 9:50 p.m., Black ordered his last meal of fried chicken.

Black retired at 12:50 a.m. and spent a restless night. He arose at 6:00 a.m., when he was awakened by the changing of the guard. Father Hugh Cummiskey arrived next and was with Black a good part of the morning, and Benjamin Black and their three sisters joined them for a while. Deputy Sheriff Alex McKay visited and pleaded with Black, for the sake of his soul, to tell the truth, but the condemned man continued to insist that he was innocent. The prisoner had his breakfast at 9:30 a.m., and this seemed to brace him for the ordeal. He dressed in a new black suit and kept his derby hat at hand. Special deputies were then admitted in small groups, and Black's last visitors, three women, came and went.

The scaffold had been erected within a 20-by-20-foot shed at the rear of the jail. At 11:00 a.m. Father Cummiskey started from the cell with the prisoner, a metal cross firmly gripped in Black's right hand, and Sheriff Yund followed closely behind. The distance to the trap was only 100 feet. The procession ascended but stopped a few feet from the trapdoor, where the priest offered a prayer, shook hands with Black, presented a cross for him to kiss, and then quickly retired. Fifty people watched as Black stepped onto the trapdoor, unassisted, and then Deputy McKay pinioned his arms and legs with straps. The sheriff placed, cinched, and adjusted the noose. He asked the prisoner if he had anything to say to the witnesses, but Black declined except to say, "I am not the one who did it." Sheriff Yund pulled the black cap from his pocket and placed it over the prisoner's head at 11:12 a.m. and in the next moment turned toward the release, gave the twine a firm tug, and the trap fell. The body dropped 8 feet, breaking the prisoner's neck.

Dr. T. Getty Ricketts of Carbon and Drs. J. H. Finfrock and Henry L. Stevens of Laramie stood on chairs; one monitoring the heartbeat while the other two each held a wrist and counted the pulse of the hanging figure. The condemned man's pulse ceased at six minutes, and life was pronounced extinct. Black's body was cut down at 11:39 a.m., twenty-seven minutes after he fell. Black's remains were placed in a cheap coffin provided by the county and slid into a one-horse hearse. He was buried in a potter's field at county expense that afternoon.

Black had tried for months to murder Robert Burnett or drive him off his land, and he finally succeeded in committing one of the most cold-blooded murders in Wyoming history. He coveted another man's land and was willing to do anything to get it.

George Cooke

He Had His Man for Thanksgiving

Mary Ann Cooke (sometimes spelled Cook) gave birth to son George in Worcestershire, England, on October 18, 1854. Four years later her husband died, and Mary Ann spent the next eighteen years raising her seven children—four boys and three girls. One son, upon reaching adulthood, found employment in the East Indies, but the remaining six children emigrated to America with their mother in 1876. The family settled in Laramie, Wyoming.

George's brother Albert and sister Mary Ann, named for her mother, settled in Laramie, while his brother James moved to Rock Creek. One sister moved to Fort Russell and the other sister moved to Denver, Colorado. In 1883 Mary Ann married James Blount, a large, forty-year-old man who spent a good deal of his time in the many saloons of Laramie. He worked as a janitor at a public school building but relied upon his wife for a substantial portion of their income. They had a son they named Samuel, and on November 25, 1883, Mary Ann gave birth to a second child, a daughter.

George, who had little education, first found work as a cowpuncher at various ranches near town. Later he found more permanent employment as an ostler and coal-heaver with the Union Pacific Railroad at its Medicine Bow roundhouse. George was considered a good worker, but it was obvious that he had a wild streak.

On the evening of Wednesday, November 28, 1883, George hopped a freight train from Medicine Bow to Laramie. His purpose was to see his new niece and spend Thanksgiving with his family. The train arrived before daybreak. It was too early to disturb his family, so Cooke, who had developed a fondness for liquor while a cowpuncher, went to a nearby saloon for a few beers. From there he moved on to another saloon and had several drinks while waiting for the gunsmith to open his shop, then picked up the .45 caliber six-shooter he had left for repair during a previous visit to town. George continued his rounds of the saloons and by mid-morning had crossed paths with his brother-in-law and brother Albert. The three men continued their drinking at one place after another with no further thought of family or Thanksgiving dinner.

George was an inoffensive man when not indulging but became rude and contentious when under the influence of liquor. His brother-in-law Blount was always a bully, but especially so when he was drunk. During the course of the day, Blount threatened several times to pummel George, who had never hidden his displeasure at his sister's choice of a mate. George threatened to kill Blount if he tried.

The three men parted company about noon, before any trouble developed, with George and Blount continuing their sprees in separate saloons while Albert went his own way. After nearly a dozen hours of hard drinking, George was ready to initiate, rather than fend off, trouble. He went to the railroad's oil room and robbed the workers of their loose change, then went to another saloon to spend his windfall.

At 6:30 p.m. George was in Cleveland's Saloon, where he announced that he would kill Blount the next time he saw him. A half hour later he was in J. Fred Hesse's Saloon on Front Street. He left the saloon with two men to eat dinner. George stepped onto Front Street and nearly collided with Blount, who was coming out of Abrams' Saloon two doors away. George loudly insulted and threatened Blount, who tried his best to calm the situation and offered to buy George a drink, but finally threatened to beat George if he continued his harangue. Without warning or further provocation, George drew his pistol and pointed it at Blount's head, then fired a single shot. The ball entered Blount's left cheek just below his eye, the blast burning and blackening the skin around the wound. The ball ranged through Blount's brain and lodged against the back of his skull. He died instantly.

George fled west on Front Street, threatening pedestrians as he went, and vanished into the darkness. A posse was organized and went out in every direction in search of the murderer. After 8:00 p.m. George was seen near the rolling mills at the foot of North B Street. There he went inside and tried to sleep, but he was too restless and had moved on before he could be arrested. He made his way to the railroad tracks and threw away his pistol, which was later found by the city marshal during the night. At 7:30 a.m. George was found skulking around the railroad tracks trying to find a boxcar in which to hide.

He was arrested by Harry Smith, a railroad worker, and Cooke said that if he could have made it to Medicine Bow he would have gotten a horse, never to be seen again. He was lodged in an eight-by-ten-foot cage in the Albany County jail.

On December 1, 1883, an inquest was held, and George Cooke was charged with murder. On December 3 he was indicted, and four days later his trial commenced. He did not deny the killing but said he could remember nothing. As his defense he stated that he was too intoxicated to have formed "malice aforethought" or to premeditate the murder, as required for a finding of murder in the first degree. Nevertheless, the jury found him guilty of first-degree murder, and within a few days Justice Jacob B. Blair sentenced him to hang.

An appeal followed, which delayed the execution, and during that period George spent his time in jail singing, telling obscene stories, and reading every newspaper and periodical he could obtain. During the early days of his confinement he made one feeble attempt to escape but then settled in to await the outcome of his appeal. The supreme court spent nearly a year considering the request for a new trial before upholding the lower court's decision to deny one. The date of George's execution was then scheduled for December 12, 1884. An application for commutation of sentence to life in prison was submitted and just as quickly denied.

George's mother, infirm and unable to bear up, returned to England. Three days before his execution George wrote to Blount's widow, his sister Mary Ann, to ask her forgiveness. At first she refused but then reconsidered and forgave him. However, she would not visit him.

The night before his execution George spent time conversing with his deathwatch guard William Tatham before retiring after 11:00 p.m. He slept soundly even though a bright light burned in his cell all night. Upon arising he made his toilet and then dressed in his burial clothes—a white, collarless shirt, blue suit pants, and new shoes, but set aside his suit jacket. He ate a hearty breakfast and then received Reverend Father Hugh Cummiskey, who heard his confession and blessed him. After the priest left, the doors of the jail were flung open and more than 200 curious people filed through to have a last look at the condemned man and bid him farewell.

George was described as five foot ten, 160 pounds, with sandy hair and a light sandy beard he had grown since being incarcerated. His time in jail had left him pale, but he had gained a little weight during the previous year. The doors to the jail were closed when Father

Cummiskey returned at 10:00 a.m., and the priest spent those last hours with Cooke.

A temporary board structure had been attached to the rear of the courthouse building to house the gallows and obstruct public view of the execution. At 11:00 a.m. Sheriff Louis Miller called together the five reporters and escorted them into the execution building. A photographer was already in place with his camera set up. The priest, wearing a cassock and stole, led the procession to the scaffold a few minutes later, with the prisoner at his side. Sheriff Miller and Deputy James Sterling followed closely behind, and then came the jurors and witnesses walking two by two. In all, fifty men assembled within the execution building.

Father Cummiskey continued his prayers for two minutes after the condemned man was upon the trap. The prisoner had taken his position facing the scaffold. The priest turned him to face the crowd, took his hand and said, "Good-bye, George," and the prisoner responded in kind.

As soon as the priest left the platform, the sheriff stepped forward and asked, "George Cooke, have you anything to say why the sentence of the law should not be passed upon you?" George replied, "Nothing." The prisoner's hands were tied behind his back with a piece of rope; one strap was tightly bound about his chest to hold his arms, another was buckled just below his hips to secure his wrists, and a third strap was secured about his ankles. The sheriff produced a black velvet bag. The rope was put over Cooke's head, cinched and positioned, and the black bag was pulled over his head. Both lawmen stepped back, and at 11:20 a.m. the supporting post was jerked out and the trap was sprung.

City physician Dr. J. H. Finfrock, and Drs. Newell K. Foster, P. F. Guenster, and Lewis S. Barnes monitored Cooke's pulse. Just before the drop his pulse was at 200 beats per minute; at one minute after, it was eighteen; at two minutes, thirty-two; at three, forty; at four, twenty-five; at five, eighteen; at six, sixteen; at seven and eight, fifteen; at nine, ten; and at ten minutes after the drop, George Cooke's heart ceased to beat. He was pronounced dead.

The coroner's jury of six men was summoned, and they delivered a verdict in accordance with the circumstances. The body hung a total of fifteen minutes before being cut down and placed in its coffin. Examination of the body revealed that the deceased's neck had been broken in the fall, but he never lost his grip on the crucifix in his right hand. The black bag was removed, and Cooke appeared more asleep than dead, except for a deep red contusion about his neck. The lid was fastened on the coffin, and just after noon he was buried in the city cemetery at the county's expense.

And this is where George Cooke's story ends. He participated in activities of robbery and murder with no remorse. A cold-blooded killer, Cooke chose to become an outlaw. Perhaps most characteristic of how bad to the bone this outlaw was is that he perpetrated his worst crimes on Thanksgiving Day, a day set aside for peaceful family gatherings.

The Gangs of St. Louis

Prohibition-Era Gangsters

The young thief cursed as he held a bloody handkerchief up to the bullet wound on his face. His friends had carried him to a dingy little backroom in the "Kerry Patch" neighborhood of St. Louis, reassuring him that the doctor would soon arrive, but the Irish-American thug didn't care. His eyes glittered with hatred and determination. No copper's bullet was going to stop Tom Egan. He would rule this neighborhood, him and his gang. He was already the best thief in the area, feared by all. Everyone knew Tom Egan was mean.

And that policeman's bullet had just made him a whole lot meaner.

As the nineteenth century turned into the twentieth, American cities witnessed an unprecedented expansion. The tide of immigrants who had created the country now turned into a flood as faster and cheaper sea transport made it possible for all but the poorest people to save up enough money for a passage on a steamer. St. Louis and Kansas City, already expanding in the last two decades of the 1800s, boomed as thousands of immigrants, mostly Italian and Irish, came looking for a new life.

Hardworking men and women got jobs as laborers, opened shops, and helped build Missouri into what it is today, but unfortunately these groups brought with them a seedy undercurrent of organized crime. From Ireland came hard-drinking brawlers who banded together to form tough gangs. From Sicily came the Mafia, with its rigid codes of silence and vendetta. In Irish and Italian neighborhoods, crime soon became organized, but the fight over who would run it created bloody feuds that lasted for decades.

For the first thirty years of the twentieth century, four gangs dominated St. Louis, two Irish and two Italian, fighting over the stakes in their own neighborhoods but, interestingly enough, rarely facing off against each other—occasionally even cooperating. Organized crime fell along ethnic lines, and their territories encompassed those same lines.

The most notorious of the Irish-American gangs, Egan's Rats, got their name from a policeman (who supplied the "rat" part) and one of their cofounders, Thomas Egan, a hoodlum who grew up in the tough,

Irish-American waterfront Kerry Patch neighborhood. He and his friend Thomas "Snake" Kinney first formed the gang in the 1890s, picking pockets and committing small-time robberies.

Snake Kinney was a pool hustler who decided to get ahead by going into politics. He got elected to the St. Louis Democratic City Committee, helped in no small part by Egan's thugs, who strong-armed people into voting for him and scared opposition voters away. Kinney began moving up the political ladder, losing his rather impolitic nickname in the process, and Egan ended up running the gang all by himself. Kinney became Missouri state senator in 1904 but never cut his ties with his old gangster friend. On the contrary, they remained close all their lives; Kinney even married Tom Egan's sister.

Egan, too, played a role in the rough-and-tumble politics of the era—first using his gang to convince voters to back their favorite candidates for the "Bloody Fourth" ward—and ended up heading the Democratic City Committee. Tom Egan looked every bit as tough as he was. The bullet from that early shootout had left a livid scar on his jaw. Later, in a move that was bold even for him, Egan served as city constable. He kept the peace in his own way, viciously gunning down rivals who tried to operate in his territory and ruling his gang through a mixture of rich rewards and abject terror. Nobody betrayed the Rats while Tom Egan lived.

By the first years of the twentieth century, Egan's Rats had become the most feared gang in the city, killing with impunity, although Egan reassured frightened citizens in an interview with the *St. Louis Post-Dispatch* that "we never shoot unless we know who is present." When one of their members was gunned down and the killer brought to trial, the Rats sought justice in their own fashion by shooting him in the courthouse.

While Egan's Rats were predominantly an Irish-American gang, it was an early equal-opportunity employer. Some Italian immigrants and Jews joined up. If you were vicious enough, you could be a Rat.

Amazingly, Tom Egan died of natural causes in 1919, a rare fate for a St. Louis gangster. His younger brother William took over the gang. "Willie," as most people called him, inherited a complex operation with hundreds of followers. He also inherited a distribution network for liquor. Tom Egan's political savvy made him realize that Prohibition would eventually become the law of the land, so he started building up an underground network of distilleries and distribution centers while alcohol was still legal. Thus when the government banned liquor the year after Tom's death, Egan's Rats could step in and supply the demand.

Prohibition was a godsend to the underworld in St. Louis and the rest of the country. Suddenly something a large percentage of the population enjoyed doing had become illegal. Like the prohibition of drugs, the prohibition of alcohol provided a ready and lucrative market for dealers. Hundreds of "speakeasies," as illegal bars were called, opened up overnight, run and supplied by criminal syndicates.

Willie Egan turned out not to be as tough as his big brother and had trouble keeping the Rats together. Soon "Big Maxie" Greenberg, one of the gang's few Jewish members, decided to keep a shipment of bootleg whiskey so he could sell it himself. Willie found out and ordered one of his gunmen to go kill him, but Greenberg was only wounded. He joined an up-and-coming group called the Hogan Gang, run by Edward "Jelly Roll" Hogan, the son of a policeman. Jelly Roll became a big name in St. Louis bootlegging operations despite holding the post of Missouri State Beverage Inspector. With the large number of gangsters in positions of authority, it's not surprising the law did little to stop bootlegging in particular and gangsterism in general. Only when the body count began to rise and included a growing number of innocent citizens did public outrage grow strong enough to force the government into action. But even the weak attempts to arrest those responsible for the shootings usually came to nothing. There was a conspiracy of silence among gangsters, even when it came to incriminating the other side.

This was eloquently demonstrated by some of Willie Egan's last words. He continued in his attempts to kill Greenberg, but it was Willie who ended up getting gunned down in front of his saloon in 1921. As he lay dying in the hospital, he was asked to identify his killers, but all he said was, "I'm a good sport."

Leadership of the Rats now passed to William "Dint" Colbeck, who was made of tougher stuff than Willie. He had been a member of the Rats since he was old enough to fight, and had served in the Eighty-Ninth Infantry Division during World War I, taking part in the bloody Meuse-Argonne offensive in France. Colbeck had survived poison gas attacks, machine gun fire, and artillery barrages and wasn't about to be intimidated by the Hogan Gang. He went after them with a vengeance, murdering more than a dozen members and shooting up Hogan's home. After one grand shootout on Lindell Boulevard, in which everyone got away miraculously unscathed, there was a huge public outcry. The gun battles had become too public, too numerous. Colbeck tried to calm the good citizens of St. Louis by telling the *Post-Dispatch:*

> *We are not insensitive to the fact that the public is aroused over what the newspapers have consistently characterized as the violence attending the fights between the Hogan and Egan factions. Our men are not trying to disturb peaceful citizens and it is unfair every time violence occurs in St. Louis to attribute it to myself, my men or the rival gang.*

This rather self-righteous statement sounds much like the one Tom Egan gave the same paper several years before. What's remarkable about the two interviews is their blatant honesty. The leaders of the Rats had no qualms about admitting they were gangsters or even that they fought running battles with a rival gang. Everyone knew it anyway, so why lie?

Although Jelly Roll Hogan survived the several attempts on his life, he lost too many men and was forced to negotiate a truce with the Rats in 1924. Hogan moved on to the greener (and safer) pastures of politics and served four terms in the Missouri state senate. Egan's Rats were now firmly on top.

Greenberg, slippery as ever, managed to survive the slaughter, making it all the way to 1933 before being found shot dead in a New Jersey hotel.

Whoever Greenberg's killer was, it probably wasn't a member of Egan's Rats. Colbeck, not satisfied with the profits from bootlegging, had started organizing armed robberies. He often went along for the fun, toting a machine gun he had learned to use on German soldiers. It turned out to be just as effective on bank guards. In one famous case, the gang robbed a registered armored mail truck in St. Louis, kidnapping the driver and guard and driving the vehicle to a back alley before emptying the mail pouches. They stole 327 letters containing an undisclosed amount of money. The post office initially claimed that the amount was less than $2,000, but the next day admitted it was more than $70,000 in cash and negotiable bonds. The actual sum turned out to be $2.4 million. The gangsters turned out to be more honest with reporters than the post office was. This and other heists netted the Rats an estimated $4 million.

But this string of armed robberies would be their downfall. Trading in liquor was all well and good, but stealing rich people's money was not something the powers in St. Louis were going to tolerate. State prosecutors got an imprisoned Rat to rat on his fellow Rats. On the basis of his testimony, the courts found Colbeck and eight other gang members guilty of robbing the mail, a federal offense, and gave them twenty-five years each. As Colbeck swapped stories with cellmate Al Capone, the remnants of his gang hid or fled to other cities to join other gangs. Considering their credentials, they had no trouble finding work in the underworld.

Colbeck got out of jail in 1940, having served only sixteen years. He told his parole officer that he had taken a job as a plumber, a trade he learned in his early years, but apparently he once again got embroiled in the politics of the St. Louis mob. Someone shot him dead with a machine gun in 1943.

Prohibition didn't just help Egan's Rats and other Irish-American gangsters. In the Italian neighborhood of the Hill, the men prided themselves on the quantity and quality of the produce from their private stills. Home brewing was an old Italian tradition, and when Prohibition came into force that hobby became quite profitable. Brewers paid off the cops with cash or free product, and some even got them to help out with the brewing. A few enterprising residents of the Hill lined their cellars with concrete and turned their entire basements into giant vats. When the St. Ambrose Church burned down in 1921, the rumor went around that the fire started because a vat of moonshine exploded in the rectory.

To keep up appearances, the authorities did conduct a fair number of raids, stopping a tiny percentage of operations by destroying stills and dumping the contents onto the street. Back then it was common for immigrants to keep farm animals to help keep the grocery bill down, and one old-time resident of the Hill recalls that when the booze washed down the street, chickens would drink it up and go wobbling off drunk. Nobody thought to arrest the chickens for consumption of an illegal substance.

While the Hill was rife with bootlegging, it didn't become a center for organized crime like the city's other Italian neighborhood, Little Italy. The Hill was populated mostly by people from Lombardy and east Sicily, regions not known for large amounts of Mafia activity. Little Italy, however, acted as a meeting point for immigrants from West Sicily, the birthplace of the Mafia. It was a cornerstone of West Sicilian society, and it would have been impossible for it not to have been replicated in any West Sicilian neighborhood. While the residents of the Hill were content to brew their own booze and pay off policemen, the gangsters of Little Italy organized into rival operations to run the local liquor trade and extort money from more honest West Sicilians. The Mafia acted like a parasite, living off hardworking Sicilian immigrants who gained their region's bad reputation while seeing none of its rewards.

Organized crime in the Italian neighborhoods of St. Louis had existed as long as there had been a sizeable Italian population there, but things really started getting going when a small group of Mafiosi decided to leave Italy in pursuit of their own version of the American Dream. Junior members of the "Green Ones" faction, they had tired of getting the most dangerous jobs while getting the least amount of loot, so they held up a rich theater owner in Palermo to pay their way on a tramp steamer to the New World.

They moved to Little Italy in St. Louis and started their own "Green Ones" away from their old bosses in Sicily. It was a new country, but the same old business. The Green Ones made their living by operating a protection racket, with "clients" given the choice between an informal insurance policy or the wrong end of a shotgun, and when Prohibition passed they added bootlegging to their operations.

In 1923 two police officers named John Balke and Ohmer Hockett discovered one of the Green Ones' stills and decided to make a little extra cash by extorting money from the owner. The bootlegger offered $200, a fair amount at the time, but the police held out for more, so the man told them to wait until his boss arrived. At this point the two cops should have realized they were about to get more than they had bargained for, but they waited patiently until four of the Green Ones showed up. The gangsters proceeded to beat the policemen unconscious, drag them to the woods, dig their graves as they watched, and shoot them.

Profits from bootlegging, however, proved too tempting, and soon the Green Ones had competition from another gang, the Cuckoos, who had worked with Egan's Rats to plan the mail truck robbery. The Cuckoos would roar around Little Italy in their cars, each man carrying a Tommy gun. They perfected an early form of drive-by shooting, practicing on leading members of the Green Ones. The gang fought back, and over the next few years dozens would be killed or wounded.

The Green Ones began to fracture under the pressure. Tony Russo, the leader of one of the factions, worried about both the Cuckoos and rival groups among the Green Ones. Russo needed allies. In desperation he turned to Joseph Aiello, a Chicago gangster and rival to Al Capone. The famous gangster still ruled Chicago and had not yet become Colbeck's cellmate after being found guilty of tax evasion. Aiello offered reinforcements for the battle for St. Louis in return for the killing of one man—Al Capone himself.

Russo went to Chicago with one of his most trusted killers to take care of his end of the bargain, but they got in over their heads. Russo and his henchman were found riddled with bullets.

The war continued and more men on both sides died. In 1928 Tony Russo's brother James was found dead in a vacant lot, alongside the corpse of his henchman Mike Longo. This brought the total number of dead in the war up to twenty-one in a single year. One of the Cuckoos was arrested as a suspect.

James Russo and Mike Longo were buried in Little Italy amidst a throng of mourners and onlookers. Armed policemen walked through the crowd, eyes open to any potential trouble. Patrolmen toting Tommy guns cruised the neighborhood. They even raided the house next door to where Russo lay in an open casket surrounded by $2,000 worth of flowers and wreaths. They had received a tip that some gunmen were plotting to murder the remaining Russos, and they arrested four Italians they found inside. All of them were armed.

That same night the Carr Street police station received a call from Willie Russo, the remaining leader of the Russo faction. He asked the precinct captain for an escort to the train station.

"What for?" the policeman asked.

"I'm leaving town," Willie Russo replied.

"Leaving for good?"

"Yes, for good."

That must have been music to the policeman's ears. He ordered two carloads of heavily armed detectives to escort Willie and his family to the station, where they boarded a train and took off into the night. When speaking with reporters that evening, the police claimed they had no idea what train the Russos had boarded or where they were headed. This was certainly a lie, but while the police may have preferred to see the Russos hunted down and killed, they had offered safe passage out of town and perhaps hoped that if they honored that promise, more gangsters would take them up on it.

Few did. The gang wars abated for a time, then flared up periodically in the following decades. The Green Ones and Cuckoos had almost wiped each other out in the bid to control the liquor trade, only to lose it in 1933 when alcohol became legal again. But even after that Irish and, increasingly, Italian gangs continued to operate in St. Louis, consuming one another and themselves in a relentless bid for power that continues to this day. But while telling the tales of Prohibition-era gangsters is history, writing about contemporary gangsters is suicide.

The Pendergasts

Running a City Ran in Their Family

It was Election Day in Kansas City in the year 1900. A new century had dawned. For more than 100 years America's great experiment in democracy had flourished, and now voters once again prepared to freely and fairly elect someone who would honestly reflect the will of the people.

Long lines snaked toward the polling stations, proof of the thriving democratic spirit of the century's first election. But a shrewd observer, or even one not so shrewd, would notice that the lines moved awfully slowly, and that men carried chairs up and down the line, asking people what candidates they intended to vote for. If the answer was acceptable, they got a chair to relax in while they waited. Voters who answered incorrectly had to stand and often ended up leaving in disgust.

And then there were the homeless people, crowded around polling stations in the worst neighborhoods. They seemed content, as if they had just eaten their first big meal in a long time, and they proudly went up to vote for the same slate of candidates the men with chairs supported. When they were done voting, they returned to the back of the line to vote again.

All across the working-class neighborhood of the West Bottoms, drunken mobs poured out of saloons and stumbled to polling stations, convinced by several rounds of free drinks that the saloon owner's candidates were the best men for the job. Not surprisingly, these were the same candidates the homeless people voted for, and the same ones the men with chairs supported. Now if only the drunks could remember the candidates' names . . .

No fear on that score; the saloon owner had men working the polling stations to remind them.

And who was this man? He started life as a nobody, just another working-class Irish-American coming to the big city with the hope of becoming rich and famous.

He became both, but not in the usual manner. Like the heroes of other American success stories, he was a shrewd, hardworking businessman who built up a network of important connections, but he was more than that. He was a huckster who rigged elections and virtually ran the Kansas City Democratic Party for decades.

His name was James Pendergast, and he built one of the most successful political machines this country has ever known.

James Pendergast was born in 1856 and grew up in a working-class neighborhood of St. Joseph. Many of his neighbors were Irish Americans like him, but there were also Germans, English, and some African Americans. This eclectic upbringing made him comfortable with a wide variety of people, a skill that would help him in his political career.

In 1876 James, who usually went by "Jim," headed to Kansas City to seek his fortune. Kansas City was a boomtown, acting as the industrial center of the west, and had huge milling and meatpacking operations. The railroad had arrived less than a decade before, and steamboats still chugged down the Missouri River bringing the city's products to the rest of the world. Pendergast rented a room in a boardinghouse in the crowded West Bottoms, on the Missouri side of the state line. In this raucous neighborhood, working-class families of all ethnicities labored, played, and drank together in crowded but exciting streets lined with saloons and illegal gambling houses. People called the area the "Bottoms" because it sat below a tall bluff called Quality Hill, where the rich lived in giant mansions and frequented the grandiose opera house, the singers doing their best to drown out the sound of the carousing drinkers and churning factories in the Bottoms below.

Pendergast was a muscular, stocky man weighing 200 pounds, and he had no problem finding a job. At first he worked as a meatpacker in one of the many plants that processed the huge herds that came from as far away as Texas. Then he got a better-paying position as a smelter in an iron foundry before being promoted to the position of puddler, the highly skilled task of pouring molten metal into molds. He made good money, but not enough to satisfy his burning ambition. People didn't come to Kansas City to do well; they came to get rich, and the fine houses on Quality Hill showed him what he could have if he could just figure out how.

Local legend says that he got his first break through sheer luck. Jim had always been a gambling man, and he put a stake down on a long-shot horse named Climax who pulled ahead and won him a pile of money. With it he bought the American House saloon in 1881, in the West

Bottoms near the old location for Union Station. A more prosaic theory is that he hoarded his money, working long hours until he could earn enough to make a down payment. Whatever the truth, he had made an excellent choice of businesses. Even though Kansas City had no shortage of saloons, the people never seemed to get enough of them.

The American House also had a boardinghouse and hotel in the same building, which added to his income. The location was good too, right in the center of the red-light "tenderloin" district where men flocked to gamble and meet prostitutes. Jim opened a gaming room in the back of the American House and rented rooms by the hour for any "couples" who didn't need to stay the whole night. He soon had enough money to expand into the building next door. He also set up a banking service to give loans to workers and cash checks. Since many working-class people, especially immigrants, didn't have bank accounts, this earned him a lot of gratitude. Of course he took a small percentage, but that was only to be expected, and his winning personality made people think of him as a friend, not a business owner. Soon everyone knew him as "Big Jim."

Jim now looked set to become one of Kansas City's leading men, but he had other ideas. The snobbish circle of aristocrats and nouveau riche held no interest for him. He stayed in the West Bottoms, where people knew and liked him. He decided a big house on Quality Hill wasn't what he was after. What he really wanted was power.

As an Irish American, the obvious choice was to join the Democratic Party. In 1884 he attended the Democratic City Convention and became one of eleven delegates to represent the Sixth Ward of the West Bottoms.

A bit of political power earned him even more customers as everyone wanted to get on his good side. Soon his saloon gobbled up more buildings on the 1300 block of St. Louis Avenue, and he brought in many of his younger brothers and sisters to work for him. His brother Tom started coming up from St. Joseph in 1881 when he was only seventeen. Tom liked the excitement and easy money of the big city, and when he was twenty-two he moved there permanently. Tom was much like his brother, a burly man who would be friendly until crossed, and then snapped into a dangerous rage. He worked for Jim as a bartender and was the man to come to if you couldn't see Jim.

Around 1890 Jim bought another saloon, a high-class place right downtown at 520 Main Street. As always, his businesses weren't just for making money but for gaining influence. The new saloon happened to be right near the city hall and the courts, so when influential lawyers or politicians came in to get a drink or engage in a little backroom card playing, Jim would be there with a ready smile and an attentive ear. The savvy lawmakers were probably not fooled by this, but they recognized political talent and ambition when they saw it and made sure to be friendly to him.

From 1887 to 1892, Jim served as a First Ward Democratic committeeman. The First Ward included most of the West Bottoms and pulled a lot of political weight because of all the businesses there. He became well known within the party (and soon across the entire city) for how he handled elections. At this time primaries were done informally by getting people together and having a voice vote. Jim would tell only his friends the time and place for the vote, usually by throwing a free party at his saloon and then getting the drunken crowd to show up at the polling place and scream at the top of their lungs for the candidate of his choice. Whoever got elected knew to whom he owed his office. When more modern techniques were introduced, with supposedly secret ballots, he found that the drunks could be relied upon to do the right thing, and he always had a few other tricks to make sure his candidates won.

Pulling the strings behind his favorite politicians whetted Jim's appetite for more direct power, and he got his large personal following to elect him alderman for the First Ward. Nobody dared oppose him in the primary, and he soundly defeated his Republican opponent in the general election.

Once in office, Jim ran the First Ward much as he ran his saloon—anyone friendly to him and his goals would be treated like gold, and everyone else had better leave. He would get drunks out of jail quickly so they wouldn't lose their jobs, helped policemen who were in trouble with their superiors, gave coal and turkeys to the poor, and basically lent a hand to anyone so that on Election Day he could call in those favors.

High finance in Kansas City at the time was dominated by the small group of white, Anglo-Saxon Protestant businessmen who ran the Commercial Club. This club had no interest in having some grubby Irish saloon owner as one of its members, so Jim merely sidestepped its influence and built a power base of his own. He noticed the club never did any charity work, so he made a name for himself, and made lots of friends, by giving assistance to those in need. Someone who needed a job or some food for their family could always turn to Big Jim.

He became known as "King of the First" and easily won re-election. He kept his Republican rivals from clamping down on gambling, which was his political cashbox and the main source of income for many of his friends. Although gambling was actually illegal, Jim's friends in the police department gave him protection. They also ran rival operations out of town, making it appear to the public that they were doing something about illegal gambling.

An important aspect of Jim's political job was patronage. Since he got to appoint some posts and had influence over other politicians who did the same, he could put his own men in the jobs or give contracts to businesses he had invested in. The beneficiaries, of course, would know to whom they owed their allegiance. Patronage was, and still is, one of the ways politicians create a power base.

His little brother Tom worked out well as a bouncer and barkeep, so in 1894 Jim got him a job as a deputy constable in a First Ward city court. Two years later he became deputy marshal in county court. This job paid $100 a month, a lot in those days, but still left Tom with plenty of time to be on committees where he could assert his big brother's interests. Soon Tom became precinct captain, helping Jim cheat on Election Day.

Jim also had another brother, Mike, who helped rig elections but was a bit crazy. He once entered an opposition saloon, bought everyone beer, then threw his own drink in their faces. His political rivals piled onto him and although he got pummeled in the fight, he enjoyed himself thoroughly.

Jim wasn't the only political boss in town, or even in the local Democratic Party. Joseph Shannon moved to Kansas City and had crawled up the ladder of power in a similar fashion to Pendergast. An Irish-American Democrat like Big Jim, he had his base of support in the Ninth Ward, southeast of downtown.

Pendergast and Shannon started running opposing candidates, and sometimes even allied themselves with the Republicans to beat each other. The origin of their rivalry is unclear; perhaps it was as simple as each not wanting to share the lucrative patronage that came with the jobs.

In the 1900 elections, their greed got the best of them and they spent so much energy fighting each other that the Republicans won several important offices. After this they made a truce such that they fought in the primaries but cooperated in general elections. Their "fifty-fifty" agreement dictated that whoever won, patronage would be split between both factions equally, but of course both sides cheated any chance they could.

One of Jim's best political investments was James A. Reed, a lawyer he and Tom chose to be county counselor, equivalent to the county prosecutor of the modern era. In 1898, backed by Jim's gambling money, Reed won the race for prosecuting attorney in Jackson County. He became mayor in 1900, got re-elected 1902, and went on to become senator in 1910.

With such a powerful politician in their pocket, the Pendergasts reaped huge rewards. Reed made Tom Pendergast superintendent of streets, an important job earning $2,000 a year and coming with 250 jobs to hand out as patronage. Jim got to fill 123 police jobs, which made his gambling ring safe from any pesky raids by do-good policemen who actually wanted to enforce the law.

Tom worked out well as superintendent, greatly improving the city streets and gaining public support in the process. He had learned from his big brother that the best way to keep power was to give people what they wanted. He listened to complaints about potholes and litter and treated black neighborhoods and workers the same as white ones, something blacks in Kansas City, or anywhere else in the country for that matter, weren't accustomed to enjoying. In 1902 Tom became county marshal, earning twice his previous salary.

With money rolling in from big government contracts and a wide range of businesses, Jim worked on several charitable projects to improve the quality of life in Kansas City. He organized the building of parks and pedestrian boulevards, assisted by William Rockhill Nelson, a powerful real estate magnate and owner of the *Kansas City Star.* Nelson's paper usually railed against the corruption of the Pendergast family, but Nelson realized that property values would go up with the addition of parks and sidewalks. His paper managed to look the other way while Jim's companies and followers gobbled up the lion's share of building contracts. Apparently Nelson learned something from the Pendergasts about doing well while doing good.

While most of Jim Pendergast's "charitable" projects had ulterior motives, he did seem to have a genuine concern for the people of Kansas City. When the Missouri River overflowed its banks in 1903, displacing hundreds of citizens, Jim provided food and shelter. The good press this generated surely helped him, but in this case at least he probably spent far more than he earned. He also supported the relocation of Union Station away from the West Bottoms. While this would hurt his saloon business, he saw the new location as more central to the expanded city and in the best interest of the city as a whole.

By the first decade of the twentieth century, Jim's power was at an all-time high, but his health had begun to fail. His beloved wife Mary died in 1905, and Jim lost much of his spirit after that. He left his city council seat in 1910, a position he had held for eighteen years, and gave it to Tom, who easily won the "election." Jim died the next year.

In the years to follow, Tom Pendergast built up the political machine his brother had founded until he practically ruled Kansas City. He could make or break politicians, and even helped get a young judge named Harry Truman elected Eastern District judge of the county court, the first step in a political career that would lead to the White House. While Truman tried to distance himself from the Kansas City political machine, in his private papers he referred to Tom Pendergast as "the Boss." When Truman got elected to the senate, many referred to him as "the senator from Pendergast." Not even someone as ambitious as Jim Pendergast could have dreamed that the machine he built would one day reach so high.

But it all came crashing down in 1939 because Tom got too blatant with his election rigging. Times had changed, and the federal government was clamping down on political machines all over the country. Many members of the Missouri Democratic Party saw the Pendergast machine as an embarrassment, opening up the party to accusations of corruption. While nobody could pin any specific corruption on Tom Pendergast, the Treasury Department discovered he had cheated on his taxes and sent him to prison. He only stayed behind bars for fifteen months, but that was long enough for the political machine his brother had built to disintegrate.

In a fitting epitaph, the *Kansas City Times* published an interview with Jim Pendergast on November 11, 1911. Big Jim, in his last months of life, confided, "I've been called a boss. All there is to it is having friends, doing things for people, and later on they'll do things for you . . . You can't coerce people into doing things for you—you can't make them vote for you. Wherever you see a man bulldozing anybody he don't last long."

While his claim that you can't make people vote a certain way isn't exactly borne out by the facts of his career, Jim Pendergast was right about one thing—one of the only ways to live a life of crime and die a free man is to make more friends than enemies.

The Union Station Massacre

The Shooting Spree That Transformed the FBI

On Saturday morning, June 17, 1933, Union Station was bustling with early morning travelers. People hurried in and out of the station, coming off the trains to visit family or do business in Kansas City, or entering the cavernous waiting hall before heading out to the platform to catch the next train out of town.

Some passengers looked at their watches and frowned. The 7:00 a.m. from Fort Smith, Arkansas, was late, and didn't arrive until 7:15. The train had chugged all night along the Missouri Pacific line through Oklahoma and along the Missouri-Kansas border. As it pulled to a stop, people who wanted to board suddenly had to make way for a tight group of grim-faced men who pushed through the crowd. A worried-looking fellow walked in the center of the group, his wrists handcuffed in front of him. One of the others gripped his belt.

The prisoner was Frank Nash, a convicted bank robber who had escaped from Leavenworth three years before. Guarding him was Joe Lackey, an agent with the relatively new U.S. Department of Justice's Bureau of Investigation, which would later be called the Federal Bureau of Investigation. Frank Smith, another Bureau agent, was with him, along with Otto Reed, a police chief from McAlester, Oklahoma.

Nash himself was nothing remarkable to look at, being a bald, forty-six-year-old man who sported a bright red wig. He'd spent the previous six years in Leavenworth acting like a model prisoner, working his way up through various prison jobs while avidly reading a one-volume set of the complete works of William Shakespeare in the prison library. He became so trusted that he got a job as the deputy warden's chef and handyman. One day the warden sent Nash on an errand outside the prison, and Nash never returned. The complete works of Shakespeare disappeared too.

Just nineteen hours before arriving at Union Station, the trio had swooped down on the unsuspecting fugitive at a store in Hot Springs, Arkansas, hustled him into a car at gunpoint, and sped off. The reason for the style of arrest, which seemed more like a kidnapping, was that Hot Springs was a notorious outlaw hideout where fugitives from the law enjoyed protection by the local underworld. The lawmen had barely gotten out of town before word spread to contacts in the underground network all over the country that one of their own had been taken from their favorite vacation spot.

Local gangsters soon had the agents traced. They had been spotted with Nash at the Fort Smith depot boarding the train to Kansas City. A quick check of the schedule showed when they'd arrive. It didn't take long to arrange a welcoming committee.

Waiting at the station was a second group of lawmen headed by Reed Vetterli, another agent with the Bureau of Investigation. The junior agent that day was Ray Caffrey, who waited anxiously for the job to be over so he could get back to his wife and young son. Accompanying them were two Kansas City Police Department detectives, Bill Grooms and Frank Hermanson, who had arrived in Hot Shot, the department's armored car. Usually Hot Shot came equipped with a submachine gun, but for some reason it was missing that morning.

The local men greeted the train at the platform and together the seven officers and agents hustled Nash off the train, hemming him in as a tight group. The group kept close order as they crossed the street to Agent Caffrey's car in the parking lot opposite the station. Caffrey put Nash in front. The convict moved to the driver's side so the passenger's side seat could be pushed forward and Lackey, Smith, and Reed could get in back. Hermanson, Grooms, and Vetterli stood on the passenger side talking as Caffrey moved around the car toward the driver's side door.

Then, just in front and a little to the right of the car, someone shouted "Up! Up!"

The lawmen had only an instant to see a man pointing a machine gun at them when another voice shouted, "Let 'em have it!"

At least three machine guns from three different angles opened up simultaneously. Bullets shattered the windows, popped through the metal of the car, and tore through almost everyone. Nash and Reed died immediately, and Lackey writhed in pain as three bullets lodged in his back.

Outside the car, Hermanson, Caffrey, and Grooms fell dead the instant the guns began to fire. A bullet hit Vetterli in the left arm, and he threw himself down as more whizzed by. He crawled to the rear of the car before leaping up and dashing toward the station doors. One of the attackers fired on him, the bullets stitching a ragged line on the stone wall of the station before Vetterli made it safely inside.

The only one left untouched inside the car was Agent Frank Smith. Ducking down below the window, he heard footsteps approach. He slumped over the seat and played possum.

"They're all dead," he heard a voice say, "Let's get out of here."

The gunmen fled, just as Mike Fanning, a Kansas City police officer assigned to the station, came running out to investigate the shots. He fired several times at the gunmen but missed as they leapt into a car and sped off.

Within moments it was all over. A peaceful, busy train station had become a battlefield, and a stunned calm descended on a scene of carnage that would become known as the Union Station Massacre.

Given the chaos and bloodshed, it's not surprising that eyewitness accounts differ on just about every point. Some people saw two gunmen, some saw up to seven, although most said there were three to five. However many there were, they disappeared into the city. Nobody got a good look at their faces.

J. Edgar Hoover, head of the new Bureau of Investigation, was livid. He took the cold-blooded murder of his agents as a personal affront, and as an opportunity. Eager to give his Bureau additional powers, Hoover used every chance the media gave him to call for tougher federal laws, permission for his agents to carry firearms, and more powers for him and his men. A shocked public and nervous government made sure he got what he wanted.

Hoover told his agents the killers "must be exterminated and they must be exterminated by us."

The Bureau's investigation wasn't helped by the shoddy work done by the police on the scene. Nobody cordoned off the area, and after the initial shock wore off, the parking lot in front of Union Station took on the atmosphere of a carnival. People walked all over the crime scene, smearing the bloodstains and pocketing shell casings as souvenirs while reporters rearranged objects and bodies to take better photographs.

The Bureau scoured the phone records for calls between Hot Springs, Kansas City, and other known gangster hangouts. Soon they had a list of suspects that they slowly narrowed down to three, all of whom the Bureau believed participated in the shooting.

Phone records pointed to Verne Miller, a local hood in Kansas City. When police searched his home, they dusted for fingerprints and came up with a match for Adam Richetti, a known associate of infamous gangster Charles Arthur "Pretty Boy" Floyd, one of the most wanted men in the country. Richetti and Floyd were both in Kansas City at the time and, as friends of Nash and ruthless gunmen, were picked for the job.

After the shooting Richetti and Floyd stayed on the run for a while, but their luck ran out when their car broke down in rural Ohio. Locals thought the men looked suspicious, and when the town's police chief, J. H. Fultz, went to investigate, the men opened up on him. Floyd ran off, but Fultz captured Richetti. He was convicted and went to the gas chamber on October 7, 1938. A posse went after Floyd and gunned him down after a long running battle.

Miller faced a different sort of justice. His body turned up beside a road outside of Detroit on November 29, 1933. He had been beaten and then strangled to death. The FBI believes he died after an altercation with some other gangster, but perhaps the underworld punished him for his part in the Union Station Massacre. Criminals, after all, don't want to give the cops more reasons to hunt them, and the killings shook up the underworld almost as much as they did respectable society.

Four other gangsters were convicted of conspiracy for their part in planning to free Nash and received the maximum sentence—two years in jail and a $10,000 fine.

The above account is the official FBI version, which stood unchallenged for decades until investigative journalist Robert Unger used the Freedom of Information Act to look at the original files. He found numerous inconsistencies between what agents reported to J. Edgar Hoover and what they said during the Richetti trial. He also found that the Bureau had used strong-arm tactics on some of the witnesses and covered up evidence that one of its own agents had accidentally killed three of the people at Union Station.

Unger's account is as follows.

Hermanson and Groom, the two local cops, didn't find the machine gun in the Hot Shot, and Unger hints that it might have been taken out to make them more vulnerable. Most of the other agents and officers only had pistols, but Agent Lackey had borrowed a 12-gauge shotgun from the Oklahoma City Police Department before his trip to Arkansas. Chief Reed had his personal 16-gauge sawed-off shotgun. Sometime during the trip they had accidentally switched shotguns. Reed's was of an unusual type and difficult to handle. If not used correctly, it might not fire at all or it might go off unexpectedly.

As the agents and officers got into the car, Verne Miller and a second machine gunner approached from the south, facing the front of the vehicle. Lackey saw them coming and fumbled with Reed's unfamiliar gun, trying to get it to shoot, and accidentally blew off Nash's head, one ball bearing continuing on to hit Caffrey. He fired again as the mobsters opened up but hit Hermanson and was killed right after that. This idea is supported by the testimony of a cab driver who saw Lackey struggling with a shotgun in the backseat before the firing started.

So some of those dead may have been killed by a fellow lawman. Autopsy reports showed that Ray Caffrey died from a shotgun pellet going through his brain. Doctors found the ball bearing "in or near" his head, and it may have fallen out of the wound as he was dying on the stretcher. In addition, much of Hermanson's skull was torn off as if he, too, had been killed by a shotgun blast. This testimony was ignored to preserve the reputation of the Bureau.

Unger also disagrees with the list of suspects and is especially against the idea that Pretty Boy Floyd participated in the killing.

Not surprisingly, Unger's account has come under criticism, not the least by the FBI itself. We will probably never know who shot who at Union Station that summer morning back in 1933; all we can say is that the gunfight turned a little-known and almost powerless government bureau into the most famous and effective crime-fighting organization in the world. Before the massacre, agents weren't supposed to carry guns and were restricted to investigating prostitution, interstate car theft, and federal bankruptcy violations. Within a year, they had guns and jurisdiction over virtually all types of federal and interstate crime. The public began to think of the newly renamed FBI as the public's defender against organized crime, the heroes who brought infamous outlaws to justice, dead or alive. Whether the right men were named and killed for the crime doesn't change the fact that the FBI became what it is today because of that bloody morning at Union Station.

JOHN WESLEY HARDIN

Family Man

On May 26, 1874, John Wesley Hardin joined his wife, Jane, and their fifteen-month-old daughter Mollie in Comanche, Texas, to celebrate his twenty-first birthday by watching the horse races. The Comanche County sheriff liked Hardin, a light-complected man with blue eyes who was five feet, ten inches tall. They enjoyed playing cards together in the local saloons. Deputy Sheriff Charles Webb of adjoining Brown County was also in Comanche that day, and friends warned Hardin that Webb wanted him dead or alive.

"Do you have papers for my arrest?" Hardin asked Webb.

"I don't know you," Webb lied. He had been studying Hardin's pictures for weeks.

"My name is John Wesley Hardin."

"So I know who you are, but I don't have arrest papers," Webb lied again.

"Then let's go in this saloon and take a drink."

When Hardin turned his back on Webb to enter the saloon, a friend shouted, "Look out, Wes!"

Later, Ranger N. A. Jennings would write that Hardin, with a six-shooter in each hand, could "with lightning rapidity put twelve bullets in a playing card at twenty yards." This time Hardin whirled, cross-drawing his revolvers from the holsters on his chest. Webb's bullet struck first, hitting Hardin in the side, but Hardin's killed Webb instantly with a head shot. Hardin, a careful counter, said Webb was the fortieth man he had killed.

Hardin fled, and irate citizens forgot that the deputy sheriff had tried to shoot Hardin in the back after denying that he had arrest papers. A vigilante mob then hanged Hardin's brother Joe, a completely innocent man.

Texas Rangers, Pinkerton detectives, and assorted gunmen seeking the $4,000 reward combed Texas for Hardin, but three years passed before the Rangers found him in Pensacola, Florida, and brought him back for trial. By that time he and Jane had a son, John Wesley Junior, and another daughter, Jennie, born eight days before the Rangers took her father away. The Comanche County jury found him guilty and the judge gave him twenty-five years. Now Hardin sat in the Travis County jail in Austin, waiting for a decision from the Texas Court of Criminal Appeals.

Jane's brother, Brown Bowen, waited in the same jail for the appellate decision on his murder conviction in Gonzales County. Brown had killed Tom Halderman just before Christmas 1872 in a country store. Hardin was with him shortly before the killing, and he had helped his brother-in-law escape from the Gonzales County jail. The Rangers found Brown about the same time that they found Hardin, and his jury in Gonzales found him guilty at the same time that Hardin was found guilty in Comanche County.

The few meetings of the brothers-in-law, waiting in the Travis County Jail, were not happy ones. First, Brown's carelessness had led to the Texas Rangers finding Hardin in Florida and Brown in Alabama. Jane's brother had betrayed Hardin's whereabouts in a letter to his (and Jane's) father, Neal Bowen, which the Rangers intercepted.

Second, Brown Bowen had the nerve to complain that Hardin only got twenty-five years for killing a sheriff while he got the death penalty for killing a no-account drunk. Halderman had just happened to be in the store that day, he had too much to drink, and he passed out behind the stove when Bowen, out of pure spite, shot him in the back.

Third, it had been Hardin who smuggled the iron file into the jail shortly after Brown's arrest, who pried off his handcuffs after Brown cut through the bars, and who helped him escape to Florida and Alabama where the Bowens had kin. In spite of that assistance, Brown's carelessness had led to Hardin's arrest and Brown's turning against his brother-in-law.

Fourth, and even more insidious, Brown Bowen and his father tried to cast doubt on Brown's conviction by laying the blame on Hardin.

"Why not tell the Rangers you killed Halderman?" Brown asked. "You already got a twenty-five year sentence to serve. One more conviction won't mean much."

"Besides," Neal added, "you've got a lot of friends down in Gonzales. You might get off."

"They had the eyewitness," Hardin said, looking at Brown with contempt. "He saw you shoot the sleeping drunk in the back."

"But don't forget," Brown insisted, "you know how to get out of that poor excuse for a jail in Gonzales. You even escaped from it once yourself."

Hardin tried to conceal his contempt of his brother-in-law. He had never trusted him. But Jane's father had never treated him badly. He'd do his best to keep harmony in the family, but he wasn't going to admit to a killing he had nothing to do with. God knows Texas and some of those other places had enough killings that he did do if they just wanted another one to charge. He looked directly at his father-in-law.

"You can't ask me to make a false statement, Neal. It wouldn't be honorable. They'd see through it. They had the eyewitness, you know."

In his pleas to the governor and to the public through the newspapers, Brown Bowen still claimed innocence and that John Wesley Hardin had shot Halderman.

Later, in answering a question by a newspaper reporter, Hardin was more blunt. "I've never killed a man the way Tom Halderman was killed. He was asleep. He had no chance to defend himself."

Neal, embittered that Hardin wouldn't take the blame for his son's crime, went before the grand jury at Cuero and told about Hardin's 1873 killing of J. B. Morgan. Hardin had never denied that killing, claiming self-defense. He had never been charged, but now, on the complaint of his father-in-law, he was indicted for another murder.

Hardin kept Jane informed of the family struggles, and Jane always stood by him. He wrote, "You can rest assured that Neal Bowen and Brown are not our friends but have done all they can against me. I am sorry for Brown's condition and yet it is only justice. . . . He has tried to lay his foul and disgraceful crimes on me."

Shortly before Brown's scheduled hanging, Neal and another daughter, Matt, visited Hardin in jail.

"Couldn't you make some statement, Wes," Neal pleaded, "something that would save Brown?"

"Not an honorable one. I don't think you'd want me to make a false one."

The day before the hanging, Matt came back to the jail, but Hardin refused to see her. She sent a note, pleading for some helpful statement. He replied: "For your sake, I would do anything honorable. I cannot be made a scapegoat. A true statement would do your brother no good and I won't make a false one."

On May 17, 1878, at the scheduled hour and before thousands of witnesses who packed the streets, Brown Bowen was hanged. Hardin wrote Jane that he had forgiven Brown for "his false and unfounded reports, and may God forgive him. Even after the cap [hood] was taken off, he said he was innocent, but that I had done it. Then he fell 7 feet and lived 7 seconds, witnessed by 4,500 people. May his poor soul be in peace and I hope that God forgives his sins. Kiss those darling babies for me once more and ever remember that I am ever your loving and true husband."

Old Neal Bowen took his son's body and buried it on the family farm in Coon Hollow. He didn't know that he dug the grave under the same oak tree where his daughter and Hardin had pledged their love five years before.

The appellate court affirmed Hardin's conviction and he entered the Texas State Prison on October 5, 1878, to serve twenty-five years.

In spite of his pious statements about only telling the truth, even as a boy John Wesley Hardin had shown a callousness to some people, surprising in the light of his family and background. He was born in Bonham, Texas, on May 26, 1853, the second of eight children born to James and Elizabeth Hardin. His father, a circuit-riding Methodist preacher, named his son after the founder of his denomination. We know of nothing bad about his siblings, including the one killed by vigilantes.

When Hardin was eight his father passed the bar examination and began teaching school and practicing law in Polk County. John Wesley's cold-blooded heartlessness showed up early. In 1868 the fifteen-year-old boy killed his first victim, a former slave. At that time in east Texas the community probably did not consider that the victim was a former slave, but Hardin fled, thinking he could not get a fair trial.

Later Hardin claimed that he had killed three soldiers who tried to arrest him and that neighbors and relatives helped him bury the evidence. Hardin always showed signs of intelligence, education, and fluency in language. His father sent him away in 1869 to teach school in Navarro County where other relatives lived. The sixteen-year-old soon left that for gambling and horse racing. By the end of that year he admitted that he had killed a freedman and four more soldiers.

In 1871 eighteen-year-old Hardin drove cattle to Abilene, Kansas. His cousin, Mannen Clements, was on the trail crew. On the drive up

Hardin killed an Indian who had shot an arrow toward him and five Mexicans who were crowding the herd. When his cousin was jailed for killing two cowboys, Hardin arranged with Wild Bill Hickok for the cousin's escape. Later, after killing a man at his hotel, Hardin fled Abilene, fearing arrest by Hickok.

Eighteen-year-old Hardin married Jane Bowen on February 29, 1872, when he returned to Gonzales after the cattle drive. She would always be loyal to him, even though he was gone much of the time dodging arrest. Later in 1872 Hardin was arrested on a variety of indictments and lodged in the Gonzales County jail. This is when he broke out of jail with the help of Mannen Clements.

Hardin had killed Morgan in April 1873. That killing and the killing of Deputy Sheriff Webb were the only ones for which he was ever convicted.

After the Morgan killing, Hardin became embroiled in the Taylor–Sutton feud in south Texas as a leader in the Taylor faction, many of them his relatives. He helped kill Bill Sutton, the leader of the other side. Two months later came the shooting of Deputy Sheriff Webb in Comanche.

After Hardin's conviction for shooting Webb in October 1877, he was chained into a buggy with thirty pounds of iron around his neck, arms, and legs for transport to Austin. A large crowd followed them out of town. Remembering what had happened to his brother Joe, Hardin was glad the Rangers had an armed escort for the first twenty miles. The crowd disappeared on the second day, and the prisoner breathed easier.

When the rangers reached Brushy Creek, fifty miles north of Austin, one of them rode down to the creek looking for a spring. He found one with a small, dark fortune-teller camped nearby. When the guard carried that news back to camp, Hardin told the Rangers that he believed somewhat in mystic powers and he would like to have his fortune told. They brought the gypsy up to their camp. He gazed into Hardin's eyes, turned Hardin's handcuffed hands up, and studied them carefully.

Finally the gypsy spoke in a low, quavering voice. "You've had a hard life, young man. You are going to the penitentiary for a long time. You will be a good man there and get out."

Then he paused as though finished.

"What then?" Hardin asked.

The dark little man closed his eyes as though not wanting to talk. Soon he continued, "I see grave trouble ahead for you. When you get out you will kill two men. If you are not careful, you will be attacked from the back and killed."

A grim, gray look came to Hardin's eyes.

The Rangers openly admired Hardin and treated him well. He had daring and skill with guns and horses. Many Rangers were not very tamed themselves. Soon after his return to Austin, Hardin wrote Jane, who was now back in Texas, "Dear, I had an ice cream treat today by the Rangers. I thought of our ice cream visits in New Orleans."

Jane hurried to Austin with the children, and for a short time while waiting for the mandatory appeal the family had visits together in the Travis County jail. Jane's cheeks were pale and some sparkle had gone from her eyes, but both she and her husband remembered their pledges to stick together until death. That loyalty was severely tested by the conflict between Jane's husband and her father and brother. But Jane stayed true to her pledge and broke with her father.

Hardin tried several times to escape from prison. He never succeeded and drew severe punishment each time. Eventually he settled down, joined a debating society, began attending Sunday school, and studied law in prison. In 1888, ten years into his prison term, he wrote Jane, "I desire through you once more to make glad the hearts of our precious children by informing them that I, by the grace of God, still live. I still love them with that undying love that belongeth only to a true and devoted brave, but oppressed and exiled, father. I tell you that my deep, anxious solicitude for your welfare and their prosperity is unabating and that my love for you and them is so vast that it is boundless, so deep that it is unfathomable of that tenacious quality that neither time, vicissitudes, nor expatriation can impair, let alone sever. I but faintly outline the love that mellifluently flows from me to them to you that no vocabulary, no symbols, can describe, no sum of words define."

In January 1892 Hardin plea-bargained for a two-year concurrent sentence for the Morgan killing. Jane Hardin died the next November. The children went to live with Fred Duderstadt, a longtime friend of their father's who ranched nearby.

Hardin received a full pardon in February 1894. Although he had only served fourteen years and the early years had been marked with escape attempts and harsh punishments, his pardon recited that he had completed his sentence and was "behaving in an orderly manner." The gypsy on Brushy Creek had proved correct in one prediction: Hardin had been a good man in prison, at least after he gave up trying to escape.

Hardin joined his children in Gonzales, passed his bar examination, and began law practice there in October. He wished that Jane was with him to talk to Mollie when the twenty-one-year-old girl announced that she and Charley Billings were getting married. Hardin tried in vain to get them to wait, thinking that Mollie was in too much haste. In the November 1894 election for sheriff, Hardin supported the man who lost by eight votes out of almost 5,000 cast. The campaign had been bitter, and Hardin decided to leave before he got into trouble.

He moved west to Junction, where his brother Jeff lived. Hardin's son Johnny and daughter Jennie remained with Duderstadt. Hardin opened another law office and in January 1895 he married fifteen-year old Callie Lewis, daughter of a prominent rancher in Junction. Callie, just a few months older than Hardin's Jennie, left him on their wedding night.

In April 1895, after Hardin had given up any hope of reconciliation with Callie, he heard what amounted to a call of the clan from Pecos in West Texas. There, Jim Miller, a close friend and son-in-law of Mannen Clements, who was Hardin's cousin and close friend, had been shot in an unprovoked attack by George Frazer, the former sheriff. Hardin began preparing Miller's defense on rustling charges and was also hired to prosecute a criminal case against the former sheriff for shooting his client. The sheriff's case was moved to El Paso, and Hardin went there to handle the case and finish the autobiography he was writing.

El Paso at that time was a safe harbor for evil. A hunted man could cross the river into Mexico or travel a few miles north to hide in the raw and lawless territory of New Mexico. El Paso was so overloaded with killers that the city hired Jeff Milton—perhaps Texas's greatest lawman—as its police chief.

Hardin had pleaded with his son Johnny to stay away from such places as El Paso, but Hardin opened a law office there. Milton warned his policemen that Hardin was the most dangerous man in America.

As Hardin made the rounds of the saloons, men set up drinks, lost to him in poker, and tried desperately for friendship with such a famous gunman. They knew nothing about his self-education and reform in prison and his later attempts to lead a law-abiding life.

One day, Mrs. Helen Morose called at Hardin's office. The husband of the overpainted woman—a prostitute in her younger days—had fled to Juarez, and Chief Milton sent word that he would be killed or jailed if he tried to return. Mrs. Morose wanted her husband back with protection from the law in El Paso. But she liked the looks of her new lawyer and soon forgot about Morose.

Jeff Milton didn't forget. When Morose tried to return he was shot to death before reaching the Texas bank of the river. Mrs. Morose was soon known as "Wes Hardin's woman."

While Hardin was back in Pecos seeing about Miller's case there, Mrs. Morose went on a binge. Policeman John Selman Jr. arrested her, and she paid a $50 fine. Selman's father, an El Paso constable, had been a gunman in Fort Griffin thirty years before and a close associate of John Larn, another famous Texas outlaw.

When Hardin returned to El Paso and learned of the arrest of his new love, he became irate. "If I'd been here you wouldn't have dared do that," he told the policeman. Brooding about the arrest of the faded blonde, Hardin put her on a train to Phoenix. She sent a telegram from Deming, New Mexico, that she was returning because she had just had a premonition that something terrible was about to happen to Hardin. The premonition troubled Hardin. Perhaps he remembered the prediction of the gypsy on the creek north of Austin.

Early in the evening of August 19, 1895, Hardin told friends that one more day would finish his book. A little later, while walking along San Antonio Street near the Acme Saloon, he saw young Selman and showered him with verbal abuse. The policeman had nerve, but he knew better than to draw against Hardin.

Later, Hardin strolled into the Acme Saloon, which had only a few customers that night. He drank a little and tried a few games. About eleven o'clock, in a good humor, he matched dice with an El Paso grocer. As he rolled the dice, he had his back to the front door.

Old John Selman walked in, drew his revolver, took careful aim, and shot Hardin in the back of the head. One of the West's most dangerous and efficient killers fell to the floor dead.

The Brushy Creek gypsy had missed one of his predictions. Hardin may have wanted to kill the Selmans, father and son, but during his seventeen months as a free man after his pardon, he had killed no one.

Hardin's life was a tragedy from a family point of view. His first wife opposed her own family to stick by him for many years. After she died and he won release from prison, he married a fifteen-year-old beauty, who left him after a few hours. His life ended in a brutal slaying brought on by his relationship with an ex-prostitute. Incidentally, Callie Lewis Hardin later married a physician and won respect from all in Mason and Kimble Counties, but she never wanted to talk about Hardin.

Bill Longley

He Was a Man Before He Was Done Being a Boy

"Believe-It-or-Not" Robert Ripley may have exaggerated in claiming that Bill Longley had been hanged three times. Longley, of course, should have known, and the second time he had a noose around his neck he did say, "Hanging is my favorite way of dying. I'd rather die that way than any other way except a natural death."

When Sheriff J. M. Brown sprung the trap on October 11, 1878, in Giddings, Texas, the noose slipped, and Longley dropped to his knees. He was hoisted up and dropped again, so one can see why Ripley made the claim about three hangings. Nine years before, vigilantes had also tried to hang the man. Longley, finally doing his last dance in the air, was just six days past his twenty-seventh birthday.

Born October 5, 1851, William Preston Longley grew up on the family farm in what would become Lee County, a few miles from Giddings, and learned early to use guns. He would become one of the fastest draws in Texas.

The first of the nation's modern gunslingers, Longley differed from most Texas outlaws in that he was not a robber or cattle rustler, and was never part of a gang. He generally played a lone hand. His distinguishing mark seemed to be his pure enjoyment of the act of killing.

The reconstruction effort after the Civil War included the creation of a state police in Texas, made up mostly of freed slaves. Most Southerners, including Texans from the eastern part of the state, nursed bitterness about the war and hated reconstruction. In December 1866, shortly after his fifteenth birthday, Bill and his father were in town when a black policeman, waving his gun, insulted Bill's father. Perhaps the black man didn't know that Bill's father was a staunch Unionist—a clear minority in east Texas. The elder Longley's sterling record at the Battle of San Jacinto warded off criticism from his white neighbors.

Bill, carrying his usual pistol, stepped forward. "You put that gun down," he said.

The policeman pointed his gun at Bill, and Bill shot him dead. Bill joined other young men and began to terrorize the newly freed slaves.

He was already six feet tall, with curly black hair and a high-cheekboned, angular face, and his small, fierce black eyes smoldered with hate. During 1867 Bill killed at least three and perhaps five black men.

In 1869, near Yorktown, Texas, Bill was mistaken for his brother-in-law and friend, Charley Taylor, one of the leaders in the Sutton–Taylor feud. Black army troops had been ordered into the area to put down violence. Some soldiers, thinking Bill was a Taylor, approached to make an arrest. Bill thought they wanted him for his most recent killing, and he fled. Bill Longley rode like a Comanche, and after six miles he had outdistanced all but the sergeant in charge, who was mounted as well as he. Longley had only one bullet left when the sergeant pulled abreast. He jammed his pistol into the sergeant's side and pulled the trigger. The soldier fell dead from his saddle, and Longley escaped.

Now Longley preyed on freed slaves and Union soldiers in black regiments who were traveling alone. One evening, vigilantes caught him and a horse thief named Tom Johnson, who had joined Longley at his campfire. Believing that birds of a feather flocked together, the vigilantes strung both men up. Longley, just sixteen with five notches already in his pistol, found himself face-to-face with death. But as the vigilantes rode away, they fired their pistols toward their victims in the customary celebration. One of the bullets struck Longley's rope before he died, his heavy body broke the rope, and he recovered from his first hanging. Johnson wasn't so lucky.

By this time Longley was Texas's most wanted outlaw. His aged parents begged him to leave the state. Later that year he joined a trail herd to Abilene, Kansas, bossed by a man named Rector.

After they reached Indian Territory and Rector got his crew to pitch in and buy a keg of liquor, Rector got into a shooting scrape with one of the men, wounding him in the shoulder. The next day Longley remarked that Rector had better not treat him that way or he would regret it. Rector, hearing about the remark, rode up to face Longley.

"I understand, damn you," Rector said, "that you said I had better not run on to you. Is that so?"

"As sure as hell," Longley answered calmly, "I damn sure did say them very words." Rector went for his pistol, but Longley beat him to the draw. Longley had six bullets in Rector's body before the trail boss started to slide out of the saddle, dead.

The trail crew advised Longley to give himself up at Fort Sill, as the authorities would surely let him go on their evidence that Rector had started the fight. But Longley was afraid the authorities would discover that he was wanted in Texas, so he rode on, joined by a cowboy named Davis who volunteered to ride with him.

One night, five Osage Indians tried to steal horses from Longley and Davis. The men killed one Indian; the other four ran. After visiting Abilene for a few days, Longley went on to Fort Leavenworth, where he got into an argument in a saloon with a soldier who had asked him if he was from Texas.

"Yes, I'm from Texas," Longley answered.

"Well, now," the trooper snarled, "if I was from Texas I'd be damned ashamed of it and keep it to myself. I know from firsthand experience that there's not an honest man in Texas nor a virtuous woman either."

Later Longley would say, "Before the words were cold on his lips, I sent a bullet through his heart, and when several of his companions made a move as to interfere, I covered them and informed them that if they did not want to get a quick pass to hell, to keep quiet."

Bill took the train to St. Joseph, where two armed officers grabbed him and said he was under arrest for killing the soldier in the saloon. Three weeks later he bribed the sergeant in charge of the guardhouse with $50 and a violin he had carved out of soft wood, and Bill escaped.

Bill Longley spent the next two years as a miner, mountain man, gambler, and teamster in Wyoming. He killed a man at Camp Brown (later called Fort Washakie) and got a thirty-year sentence in federal prison. Again he escaped and rode south to Colorado, where he lived a year with the Ute Indians.

Lonesome now for Texas, Bill headed for the Kansas trail towns, hoping to find a way to ride back to his home. At Parkerville, Kansas, a small town near the Santa Fe Trail, he shot a man to death in a gambling hall. The victim's father offered a $1,500 reward. Bill and two others, also on the dodge, cooked up a scheme in which the two companions turned Bill in for the reward and then sprung him from the jail. They divided the money evenly and rode their separate ways, Bill going back to Texas.

By this time his parents had moved a short way north to Belton, and Bill spent some time with them. But he learned that a Lee County posse was coming to arrest him for a $1,000 reward, and he again hit the Owl Hoot Trail. Soon a black man who'd gotten drunk and insulted a white woman lay dead with two of Bill's bullets in his head. Bill continued riding west.

Five men caught up with him in the Santa Anna Mountains of Coleman County. After a short battle in which Bill killed one, the other four withdrew. It was now late in 1874, and Bill returned to Central Texas, took the name Jim Patterson, and went to work in a cotton gin. But he got into an argument with a George Thomas and shot him through the heart. He stopped in Bell County long enough to hug his old mother and shake the trembling hand of his father. Deeply conscious of the worry he had caused them, he rode southwest to a lonely ranch in the Frio Canyon of Bandera County. He was just beginning to think about settling down in that beautiful canyon when he learned that a recent friend, Lon Sawyer, was scheming with the sheriff back in Lee County to turn Bill in for half the offered reward.

At first Bill considered just shooting Sawyer, but he learned that a reward had been offered for Sawyer, and Bill decided to turn the tables on him. Bill got himself deputized by the Uvalde County sheriff to bring Sawyer in. Bill, in turn, deputized a youth named Hayes to help him capture Sawyer.

An unsuspecting Sawyer, still waiting to hear from the Lee County sheriff, cantered leisurely down a trail with Longley, Hayes, and a wagon to cut up a steer that Longley and Sawyer had recently stolen and killed. Suddenly Longley leveled his pistol at Sawyer and shouted: "Throw up your hands. You're my prisoner."

"I'll see you in hell, first," Sawyer shouted back, drawing his own weapon and spurring his horse forward.

Longley's first bullet hit Sawyer's shoulder, and Sawyer's bullet missed, as the two men began one of the West's wildest shooting rides. They rode through a cedar brake and burst into a glade about 200 yards long. When they reached the end of the glade, both pistols were empty, Longley was still untouched, and Sawyer had three more bullets in his back. One of the two bullets fired by Longley, which missed Sawyer, disabled Sawyer's horse. Sawyer drew his shotgun, leaped to the ground, and killed Longley's horse. Then Sawyer disappeared into another dense cedar brake.

Bill had a second pistol, but the caps had gotten wet and wouldn't fire. He ran back toward the approaching wagon, where he knew the teamster had a gun. On the way he met Hayes and told him he could follow Sawyer's trail from the blood spurting out of his four back wounds.

Learning that the teamster only had a carbine with three cartridges, Longley unharnessed one of the wagon horses, jumped on its back, and plunged through the cedar brake to cut Sawyer off. In the meantime a pack of hounds, attracted by the noise, were assailing Longley.

Suddenly Sawyer, lying on the ground, fired his shotgun and barely missed Longley. Longley jumped to the ground and fired at Sawyer. He hit the man's shotgun stock and spun around to shoot two of the closest hounds. Then Longley took his time to reload his good pistol.

After Longley fired eight more times and Sawyer six, Sawyer called out that he wanted to talk things over.

"Not unless you throw your pistol out," Longley replied.

Sawyer did that, and Longley walked over to where he lay, weak from loss of blood. But Sawyer had another pistol that Longley didn't know about. He fired it but missed. Longley's shot, fired so simultaneously to his opponent's that they sounded like one roar, hit Sawyer above the eyes, killing him instantly.

Sawyer's last shot had hit Hayes in the leg as he arrived at the battle scene. Sawyer had fired fourteen shots, and only killed Bill's horse. Longley had fired eighteen times, hitting Sawyer thirteen times, besides killing his horse and five dogs. Longley said Sawyer was the bravest man he had ever fought. Longley's short career in Texas law enforcement was over.

Later in 1875, Longley learned that a boyhood friend, Wilson Anderson, had killed Bill's nephew, Cale Longley, in Bastrop County, near where Bill grew up. Joined by his brother James, Longley rode directly to Anderson's farm, found his old friend plowing in the field, and gunned him down with a shotgun. This was the murder that would result in Longley's eventual execution.

After the Anderson killing the Longley brothers fled to Indian Territory and then returned to Texas. James turned himself in and was acquitted of any part in Anderson's murder. Bill Longley stayed on the loose. He was captured in Edwards County by Sheriff Bill Henry. Henry took his prisoner to Austin to collect the reward, but when the governor refused to pay it, Sheriff Henry turned Longley loose.

On February 12, 1876, Bill Longley was riding through Delta County in northeast Texas when he met Louvenia Jack at a small farm near Ben

Franklin. Falling in love for the only time in his life, he introduced himself as William Black of Missouri, saying he had lived in Texas about three years.

"We sat up late that night," Bill would write later from jail. "I never felt such feelings on earth as now seemed to take possession of me. I lay and thought of all my past life, and never before did I realize my true condition. I thought I would give all the wealth in the world, if I had it to give, if I was only a plain, civil, and pious man. I thought I would get up an excuse so I could stop and rest for a day or two, and perhaps in that time I could make up my mind what I should do."

Later Bill got out of bed in the Jack home, retrieved a nail from the fireplace, and hammered it into his horse's hoof. After breakfast he "discovered" that his lame horse could not travel, so Mr. Jack invited him to stay over a day or two. Then sixteen-year-old Louvenia suggested that Bill "Black" talk to a preacher, Roland Lay, who lived a mile away and needed someone to farm his place on shares. Jack thought the idea great, and the arrangements with Preacher Lay soon were worked out.

Bill had always enjoyed working the soil, and now he was only a mile from the love of his life. But he soon learned that the preacher's cousin also had designs on Louvenia. In fact, they had been engaged to be married when Mr. and Mrs. Jack opposed the match.

Bill had taken a great liking to the preacher, and he was shocked to learn that the preacher was the main one encouraging his cousin to resume his attempt to win Louvenia. Three months after he had been living in the preacher's cabin and farming the land, Bill found a note tied to the plow handles, warning him to leave the county. To a cold-blooded killer like Bill Longley, such a note was an invitation to violence. Yet Bill, for the first time in his life, did something noble: He rode away and found work on another farm, ten miles away in Lamar County.

Some days later, while Bill was visiting the Jacks, one of the Lay family killed a Jack dog, and Bill horsewhipped him. Preacher Lay responded by getting a warrant from Lamar County, saying Bill had threatened his life. Bill escaped from the Lamar County jail by burning it down. He reached the Jack cabin just before dawn, grabbed their shotgun from their mantel, rode to Lay's and found the preacher in the cow pen, milking. A double-barreled, heavy load of turkey shot left the community without a preacher. But this time Bill had killed an old, unarmed man, who had an infant daughter asleep in her crib inside the house. Bill knew he had to ride far away.

Bill crossed into Indian Territory, riding past the house where Jim Reed, outlaw husband of Belle Starr, had been killed two years before. He tried to stay away from people; sometimes he didn't see another person for a week at a time. Once, he traded his horse and shotgun to an Indian for the Indian's horse. The Indian changed his mind, caught up with Bill, and attacked him with a knife. Bill shot him in the forehead and again in the chest before the body hit the ground. Then Bill found two improved Colt's cartridge pistols under the Indian's blanket and took them, since they were no use to a dead Indian.

Bill kept thinking of Louvenia back in Ben Franklin, and sometimes cried himself to sleep. He rode through northeast and east Texas, always keeping to himself, and finally reached De Soto Parish, Louisiana. There he made another sharecropping deal, this time as Will Jackson. He became friends with another farmer, June Courtney, who had just been elected town constable. Courtney often asked his new friend to help make arrests. Bill was so efficient as a helper that Courtney began studying wanted posters from Texas. Then Courtney tipped off the Nacogdoches County, Texas, sheriff that he thought he had Bill Longley in his town.

Using a carefully planned approach, the Texas sheriff, his deputy, and the Louisiana constable were able to take Longley into custody on May 11, 1877, without getting hurt.

Longley was tried in Giddings in September for the Anderson killing. On Monday, September 3, 1877, he was arraigned on a grand jury indictment. He pled not guilty and asked for a continuance. The court denied his motion and trial began the next morning at 8:30. Later that day jury foreman J. S. Wade signed a verdict of guilty. The court still had time to take up other matters that day. Longley was removed to Galveston to await the decision on his automatic appeal. While there he complained to the governor that it was unfair to execute him as he had only killed thirty-two men, and John Wesley Hardin received a life sentence for killing many more.

Bill wrote a lot and told a lot to reporters while he was in jail waiting for execution. He had only regretted one of his thirty-two killings. That victim was a cowboy on the trail to Kansas who seemed to be watching Bill too closely.

"I wasn't going to sleep with that fellow watching," Bill said. "So I shot him and then went to sleep. The next day I learned that he was on the dodge, just like me."

Longley came back in court on September 5, 1878, for formal pronouncement of judgment, his execution having been affirmed. The judge ordered "that you be by the sheriff of Lee County hung by the neck until you are dead, dead, dead."

Some detested Bill Longley because he killed for the love of killing. Others saw him as a heroic figure resisting a reconstruction that had been inflicted by an insensitive victor in war. Another judgment is contained in an oft-quoted statement about Longley: He was a man before he was done being a boy.

Longley himself put it this way: "I have always known that I was doing wrong, but I got started when I was a fool boy, led off by older heads, and taught to believe that it was right to kill sassy Negroes, and then to resist military law."

When the noose was dropped over Bill's head in October 1878, just a few miles from where he had started as a fifteen-year-old killer, it was the second time he had felt the noose on his neck. This time, it still took two attempts to succeed.

Jim Miller

Born to Hang

A fair description of John Wesley Hardin would be a juvenile punk who enjoyed killing blacks, Yankee soldiers, Mexicans, and Indians. Jim Miller, Hardin's cousin by marriage, is seldom mentioned in Texas history, but a fair description of him would be worse. He killed his grandparents when he was eight and his brother-in-law when he was seventeen. Eventually he preyed on the world at large, demanding money for his services.

Miller, a slender five feet, ten inches tall and a dapper dresser, never swore, drank, or smoked. He had many friends and attended church so regularly that he was often called "Deacon Jim." He was usually soft-spoken, but his pale-blue cold, unblinking eyes gave some people goose bumps. When he killed his sister's husband John Coop on Sunday, July 30, 1884, he left during an evening worship service and galloped three miles to Coop's house, where his victim was sleeping on an outside porch. Miller crept up and shot Coop in the head and rode back to the church before the service ended. Despite his alibi about being in church at the time, the jury convicted him, and the judge gave him life in prison. But Miller appealed and got a new trial and an acquittal. The bizarre crime and its bizarre result became typical of Texas's leading assassin.

Miller was born in Van Buren, Arkansas, in 1866, one of nine children. His parents moved to Franklin, Robertson County, Texas, when Miller was a baby. When they died he was sent to live with his grandparents in Coryell County. There was no other suspect for their murder in their own home, and Miller was arrested but released as too young to prosecute. Turned over to the custody of his sister, he soon clashed with her husband on their farm at nearby Gatesville.

Three years after Miller killed his brother-in-law he got a cowboy job with Mannen Clements, Hardin's cousin. He married Mannen's daughter, Sally, in February 1888, exactly twelve months after Sally's father had been killed by Ballinger City Marshal Joseph Townsend over a political dispute. Miller later avenged this killing by blasting

Townsend out of his saddle from ambush as the marshal rode home at night.

Miller spent the next two years drifting around southeastern New Mexico Territory. Sometimes he gambled in saloons on the Mexican border; sometimes he rode into West Texas towns. One August afternoon in 1891 he rode into Pecos, seat of Reeves County. Oppressive heat hung heavy above the baked streets, and bystanders wondered why the stranger wore a black broadcloth coat.

Miller swung down in front of Juan's Saloon, and curious heads appeared in windows and doorways to watch. A half dozen cowboys from a rough cow outfit near Toyah and their ramrod, a man named Hearn, studied Miller carefully as he entered the saloon. After Miller ordered a glass of water, Hearn stepped up to the bar next to him.

"That big coat of yours sure makes me sweat," Hearn sneered. His cowboys felt duty bound to challenge someone every time they came to town.

Miller's eyes never changed, but his nose wrinkled in disgust at the dust-covered men with cow dung on their boots. "Your stink makes me sick," he said.

"Take it off," Hearn ordered, pointing with his left hand at Miller's coat.

Hearn's right hand moved too fast to see, and he had it on the butt of his revolver when Miller's revolver seemed to leap from under his coat into his hand, its muzzle against Hearn's belly.

"Drop it," Miller said softly. The room was suddenly silent.

Hearn's half-drawn six-shooter slid back into its holster. "Hell's bells," he muttered, his face suddenly ashen. "I was just a-foolin'."

Miller stepped back, never taking his cold eyes off Hearn. "I like this town and figure to settle here. You have two minutes to get out, and take these jackasses with you." He nodded at the other cowboys. "If you come back to raise more hell, I'll kill you."

When the dust of the departing cowboys had settled, Miller bought drinks for his wide-eyed audience and had another glass of water. The story swept through the small town and its saloon soon filled. Even Sheriff Bud Frazer came in to order a round of drinks.

Other people had declined to ask about the coat, but Frazer inquired, "Would you mind telling me, sir, why you wear such a heavy coat in weather like this?"

The crowd tensed, but Miller smiled softly. "This coat is my life insurance. It belonged to an old friend of mine. He sheriffed on the border for years and never got a scratch." The crowd relaxed and Miller continued. "He gave credit to the coat, and he died in bed with his boots off." Miller stroked his worn coat. "He gave it to me. I figured it must be lucky."

"Well, a man's got a right to his own superstition," the sheriff said. "You say you're going to settle down here?"

"Thought I'd see about working in a hotel. I've done some of that."

"Let's go down to my office. I'd like to propose something you might be interested in."

Miller left the sheriff's office wearing a deputy's badge. Without knowing it, Frazer had deputized Texas's first hired assassin. He would soon become the most dangerous man in Texas, New Mexico, and Oklahoma.

Frazer and Miller worked well together and seemed to like each other. Then suddenly they had a falling out and no one knew why. Some thought Frazer had stumbled onto evidence that Miller was running stolen cattle into Mexico. At any rate, Con Gibson told Frazer that Miller and Mannen Clements had tried to get him to help them kill Frazer. Then a Ranger captain came to town and arrested Miller.

Miller hired two fine lawyers (one would later be a district judge and the other a state senator) and he got an easy acquittal.

Con Gibson, the informer on Miller, left town in a hurry. When he reached Carlsbad, New Mexico, he got into an argument with John Denston, a cousin of Miller's wife. The argument ended with Gibson's funeral, and people considered it a revenge killing, but nothing implicated Miller. Only Bud Frazer seemed to be bitter.

On April 12, 1894, Miller, still wearing his frock coat, was talking to a rancher friend who noticed that Bud Frazer kept walking back and forth near them. Miller, engrossed in the conversation, hadn't noticed.

"I wonder why the sheriff keeps walking by and looking at your back," the friend said.

"Well, I don't know." Miller turned around and stared into the muzzle of the sheriff's six-shooter.

"Jim, you're a cattle rustler and a murderer," Frazer shouted, opening fire. "Here's one for Con Gibson."

Frazer's gun roared, and the first bullet ricocheted off Miller's coat.

Frazer's second shot disabled Miller's gun arm. Miller got his pistol into his left hand and blazed away, but Frazer escaped unhit.

Frazer emptied his gun, but Miller stayed on his feet and kept shooting. When Miller finally fell, Frazer went back to his office, unhurt. By all rights, Deacon Jim Miller should have been dead.

The people who picked Miller up and carried him to his hotel discovered that three of Frazer's bullets had struck directly over Miller's heart. They had flattened against the steel plate he wore over his chest and under his coat. Then, for the first time, Miller's own friends learned why he wore that black coat even in the heat of summer.

When Miller regained consciousness he smiled at his friends and said, "Tell Frazer he can't kill me and he can't run me out. Next time, I'll get him."

Miller took several months getting well, but he repeated his oath that he would kill Frazer if he had to crawl twenty miles on his knees to do it. In the meantime Frazer lost an election and moved to Lordsburg, New Mexico, to visit relatives.

Unfortunately Frazer returned in December. He rode into Pecos the day after Christmas and saw Miller standing in front of the blacksmith shop. Knowing of Miller's oath to kill him, Frazer drew his revolver and began shooting. His first bullet hit Miller's gun arm and the second hit his leg. Then he aimed for the heart. Miller, although again disabled, fired away with his left hand. Frazer again shot Miller over the heart and wondered why the man was still standing. He had never heard about the steel breastplate. Knowing that he was a good shot, the confused attacker turned and fled.

Miller's friends wanted to go after Frazer, but he smiled and said he'd try the legal way first. He swore out a complaint with the new sheriff.

Frazer's trial was moved to El Paso, and Miller hired his cousin, John Wesley Hardin, to assist in the prosecution. But Hardin was killed before it came to trial, and the jury disagreed. The trial was moved to Colorado City in Mitchell County, and Frazer won an acquittal in May 1896.

Miller, disgusted, determined to get Frazer once and for all. It took four months of waiting, while spies from each side reported on the other's movements, but Miller finally heard in September that Frazer was visiting relatives in Toyah, a tiny town eighteen miles from Pecos.

Knowing that Frazer would be advised of his every step, Miller got a friend, Bill Earhart, to wait outside Pecos with two horses. Then he sauntered out of town on foot to meet Earhart and the two rode to Toyah.

Earhart rented a hotel room across the street from the saloon on the night of September 13, and Miller slipped into the room by the back way.

The next morning, Frazer went to the saloon as usual and started playing cards with friends. Earhart signaled that all was clear, and Miller walked rapidly across the street with his shotgun. He pushed the swinging door open and fired both barrels. The double-barreled charge practically blew Frazer's head from his body.

One witness reported: "All of a sudden the room exploded like dynamite had hit the floor. I happened to be looking at Bud, and like to have fainted when I saw his whole head disappear in a clot of splashing blood and bone. That's all I took time to see. I dived through the window, taking glass and all with me. Next thing I remember I was under my bed three blocks away, shivering like hell."

Frazer's sister borrowed a gun and, with her mother, set out for Pecos. She confronted Miller when he arrived, covering him with the pistol.

"If you try to use that gun," Miller said softly, "I'll give you what your brother got. I'll shoot you right in the face."

She lowered the gun but gave Miller a vicious tongue-lashing. One of Frazer's friends, Barney Riggs, caught up with Earhart and killed him along with another of Miller's friends.

Miller's trial for murdering Frazer was transferred to Eastland, between Abilene and Fort Worth. Miller moved to Eastland well in advance of trial, went into business as a hotel operator, transferred his church membership, contributed to local charities, and did everything he could to make a good impression. Also, he had his wife and two sons—five and two years old—with him.

The three-week trial started in June 1897. Dozens of people came from Pecos to testify. One said Miller's conduct was as "exemplary as that of a minister of the gospel." Nevertheless, eleven jurors voted to convict. The one holdout made a second trial necessary. At the second trial Miller was acquitted on grounds of self-defense.

After keeping a saloon in Memphis in the Texas Panhandle, and even working for a time as a Texas Ranger, Miller went to Monahans, back in the Pecos area, where he apparently became a deputy United States marshal. For the next eight years he killed sheepmen and farmers, both classes despised by some West Texas ranchers. His standard price was $150 per man. Once Miller said with pride, "I have killed eleven men that I know about; I've lost my notch stick on sheepherders I've killed out on the border."

In February 1908, Miller killed Pat Garrett, the legendary lawman who had killed the famous outlaw Billy the Kid over twenty-five years before. The controversy over the killing—Garrett and Billy the Kid had been friends, and Garrett shot him without warning in a darkened room—made Garrett lose the next election, and he took up ranching. For the next twenty years Garrett ranched, served as a captain of Texas Rangers, again as a New Mexico sheriff, and as a collector of customs appointed by President Theodore Roosevelt. For five years he raised race horses in Uvalde, Texas, where John Garner, a young friend of his, would later become vice president of the United States.

By 1906 Garrett had a little ranch in the Organ Mountains east of Las Cruces, New Mexico. The land was coveted by W. W. Cox, a neighboring rancher, who could not get Garrett to sell. Somebody hired Miller to kill Garrett so Cox could get the land. Miller's price for this killing was $1,500.

Garrett was shot in the back of the head on February 29, 1908. He had been traveling toward Las Cruces in a buggy, accompanied by Carl Adamson. Wayne Brazil joined them on the way on horseback. Five miles from Las Cruces, the buggy stopped, and while Garrett was urinating someone shot him in the back of the head. He fell to the ground, dead, and he was shot again in the stomach. Brazil and Adamson went on to Las Cruces, where Brazil turned himself in to the sheriff, saying he had shot Garrett in self-defense. Adamson backed up his story.

Captain Fred Fornoff of the Territorial Mounted Police investigated the murder scene after the sheriff picked up the body. He found where a horse and rider had waited nearby for some time, leaving two spent .44 Winchester cartridges in the sand.

At a farce of a trial in which the jury heard only Brazil's story of shooting in self-defense—Garrett's heavy driving glove was still on his right (gun) hand and his fly was open—the jury acquitted Brazil. Captain Fornoff was never produced as a witness.

With the proof that the horse that waited beside the trail had been borrowed by Jim Miller and that the bullet that entered the back of Garrett's head came from his rifle, it is not surprising that most historians agree that Miller killed Garrett.

Miller spent the rest of 1908 back in Fort Worth gambling. Late that year he heard that his old friend Mannie Clements had been killed. He swore he would avenge the killing, but he had already been hired for another job, this time in Oklahoma. The fee was the highest he had ever been offered—$2,000.

Ada, Oklahoma, the scene of Miller's last killing and his own death, had a little over 3,000 people and thirty-six murders in 1908. Gunfighters from two powerful factions had been feuding for years. Angus Bobbitt led one faction; Joe Allen and Jesse West led the other. Finally, Bobbitt forced Allen and West out. They moved their cattle herds to Hemphill County, Texas, and brooded like wounded rattlesnakes. The killing of Pat Garrett hastened their decision on how to strike back.

In late February 1909, a frock-coated man was seen riding near Bobbitt's home a few miles from Ada. In late afternoon on February 27, Bobbitt was driving home with a wagonload of meal cake for his cattle. A neighbor, Bob Ferguson, followed in his own wagon. Just before sundown, they met a lone rider who talked a few minutes with Bobbitt and then rode on, passing out of view as he crossed over a hill behind them.

Just after sundown, about a mile from Bobbitt's ranch, a double-barreled shotgun sounded twice. Bobbitt, struck twice, toppled from his wagon, dead. Ferguson recognized the man they had met earlier on the trail as he galloped away.

The sheriff followed the killer's tracks to the farm of young John Williamson. The shoes worn by the mare Williamson had rented had been removed but were found under the kitchen floor. Williamson withstood a lot of pressure before he identified the rider who had rented his horse as his uncle from Fort Worth, Jim Miller. More investigation revealed that Berry Burrell, an old friend of Allen and West, was intermediary between them and Miller and had spotted Bobbitt for the killer. Miller was arrested on March 30 near Fort Worth. Burrell had already been arrested in Fort Worth. Afraid that Allen and West would fight extradition, the county attorney sent them this telegram at Canadian, Texas: "You and Joe come to Ada at once. Need $10,000, Miller."

The ruse worked, and Allen and West were arrested in Oklahoma City, just after stepping off the train to be greeted by their lawyer. The preliminary hearing was held on March 19. Some of Ada's citizens didn't wait for the trial.

At two o'clock in the morning of April 19, a group of vigilantes cut off Ada's electric current. In the darkness they overpowered the jailers and removed Miller, Allen, West, and Burrell. They took them to a livery stable and hanged all four. They saved Jim Miller for last. He refused to confess, merely saying, "Just let the record show that I've killed fifty-one men."

Miller was as unconcerned about his own death as he had been earlier about each of his many victims. The vigilantes stood him on a box, adjusted the noose around his neck, and told him to step forward to the edge of the box. Miller slipped a diamond ring from his hand, directing that it be given to his wife. He made other dispositions of his property.

"I'd like to have my coat," he said. "I don't want to die naked." He must have believed it would still make him invincible.

They refused, so he asked for his hat. They jammed his Stetson on his head.

Miller laughed. "Now I'm ready. I don't want this rope to knock my hat off. You sure you got it set right?"

The vigilantes looked on with amazement as they nodded their heads.

"I always knew I was born to hang," Miller continued. "They never was a bullet that could kill me."

He moved forward to the edge of the box. He looked down and laughed again.

"Let 'er rip," he shouted as he leaped forward.

Some people said Miller's conduct on the box showed his courage. Others said it showed his total depravity and inhumanity.

One of the vigilantes draped Miller's coat over his slumped shoulders as he hung there in the barn. "It won't do him no good, now," he said.

SOURCES

Outlaw Tales of Oregon
The DeAutremont Brothers

Outlaw Tales of New Mexico
Vincent Silva

Outlaw Tales of Oklahoma
The Two Faces of Ned Christie
Henry Starr
When George Birdwell Robbed the Wrong Bank

Outlaw Tales of Nevada
John Richard "Rattlesnake Dick" Darling
Ben Kuhl

Outlaw Tales of Washington
Lawrence Kelly
Johnny Schnarr
Jake Terry

Outlaw Tales of Colorado
Lou Blonger, Overlord of the Underworld

Outlaw Tales of South Dakota
Stella and Bennie Dickson
Helen Sieler

Outlaw Tales of Wyoming
John "Badeye" Santamarazzo
George A. Black
George Cooke

Outlaw Tales of Missouri
The Gangs of St. Louis
The Pendergasts
The Union Station Massacre

Outlaw Tales of Texas
John Wesley Hardin
Bill Longley
Jim Miller

Outlaw Tales of Idaho
Caleb Lyon
Henry MacDonald
Ferd Patterson

BIBLIOGRAPHY

The DeAutremont Brothers

Chipman, Art. *Tunnel 13.* Medford, Ore.: Pine Cone Publishers, 1977.

Cohen, Norm and Cohen, David. *Long Steel Rail.* Champagne: University of Illinois Press, 2000.

DeAutremont, Ray. "Ray DeAutremont's Confession." June 23, 1927.

Vincent Silva

Bryan, Howard. *Wildest of the Wild West: True Tales of a Frontier Town on the Santa Fe Trail.* Santa Fe: Clear Light Publishers, 1988.

De Baca, Carlos. C. *Vincent Silva: New Mexico's Vice King of the Nineties.* Las Vegas: Smith-Hursch, 1938.

L'Aloge, Bob. *The Code of the West.* Las Cruces: Yucca Tree Press, 1992.

McGrath, Tom. *Vincent Silva and His Forty Thieves.* Santa Fe: Fray Angélico Chávez History Library, 1960.

Simmons, Marc. *When Six-Guns Ruled.* Santa Fe: Ancient City Press, 1990.

Stanley, F. *Desperados of New Mexico.* Denver: World Press, 1953.

Therp, N. Howard. *Bandits of New Mexico.* Santa Fe: Fray Angélico Chávez History Library.

"The Worst Outlaw." *Santa Fe Reporter,* August 13, 1981.

The Two Faces of Ned Christie

Harmon, S. W. *Hell on the Border: He Hanged Eighty-Eight Men.* Muskogee, Okla.: Indian Heritage Association, 1971.

Shirley, Glenn. *Heck Thomas, Frontier Marshal.* Norman: University of Oklahoma Press, 1981.

Speer, Bonnie Stahlman. *The Killing of Ned Christie.* Norman, Okla.: Reliance Press, 1990.

Steele, Phillip. *The Last Cherokee Warriors.* Gretna, La.: Pelican Publishing Company, 1974.

Henry Starr

Harmon, S. W. *Hell on the Border: He Hanged Eighty-Eight Men*. Muskogee, Okla.: Indian Heritage Association, 1971.

Nix, Evett Dumas. *Oklahombres: Particularly the Wilder Ones.* Lincoln: University of Nebraska Press, 1993.

Shirley, Glenn. *Last of the Real Badmen: Henry Starr.* Lincoln: University of Nebraska Press, 1976.

When George Birdwell Robbed the Wrong Bank

Smith, Robert Barr. *Tough Towns: True Tales from the Gritty Streets of the Old West*. Guilford, Conn.: Globe Pequot Press, 2007.

John Richard "Rattlesnake Dick" Darling

Folder 0004, Box NSP 0001. Nevada State Archives.

Nevada State Journal, August 25, 1883.

Virginia City Evening Bulletin, September 14, 15, 1863.

Virginia City Territorial Enterprise, May 16, 26, 27, 30, July 1, 1866; November 15, 1872.

Ben Kuhl

Carson City News, December 14, 1918.

Elko Daily Free Press, December 6, 1916.

Elko Daily Independent, December 12, 13, 1916.

Nevada State Journal, May 9, 1945.

Nevada State Prison inmate case file 2018, Ben Kuhl; Nevada State Library and Archives.

Reno Evening Gazette, December 10, 1918.

Virginia City Chronicle, December 11, 1918.

Lawrence Kelly

Seattle Post-Intelligencer, May 15, 1909.

Clark, Cecil. *The Daily Colonist*. April 8, 1962.

Cummings, Jo Bailey, and Al Cummings. *San Juan: The Powder Keg Island.* Friday Harbor, Wash.: Beach Combers, 1987.

Davenport, Marge. *Afloat and Awash in the Old Northwest.* Tigard, Ore: Paddlewheel Press, 1988.

Dirks, Farmer. "Ship Owned by Pirate Kelly Discovered Here." *American Bulletin.* Anacortes, Wash.: September 2, 1955.

———. "Case of Missing Tools When Kelly Was Alive." *American Bulletin.* Anacortes, Wash.: September 9, 1955.

———. "Smuggler Kelly a Bad One, But Paid His Debts." *American Bulletin.* Anacortes, Wash.: September 12, 1955.

Jones, Roy Franklin. *Boundary Town: Early Days in a Northwest Boundary Town.* Vancouver: Fleet Printing Company, 1958.

McDonald, Lucille S. "Kelly, the King of the Smugglers, Guemes, Sinclair Islands were headquarters of notorious operator in years long past." *Seattle Times,* March 29, 1959.

———. *Making History: The People Who Shaped the San Juan Islands.* Friday Harbor, Wash.: Harbor Press, 1990.

———. "Old records tell how Puget Sound customs men went about tracking the smugglers." *Seattle Times,* July 27, 1952.

Richardson, David. *Pig War Islands.* Eastsound, Wash.: Orcas Publishing Company, 1971.

Short, E. T. "The End of Lawrence Kelly." *Tacoma Times.*

Telephone interview with Pat Nelson, great-granddaughter of Lawrence Kelly, August 18, 2000.

Johnny Schnarr

Mortenson, Lynn Ove. "Black nights and bootleg booze." *Peninsula Magazine.* Summer, 1993.

Newsome, Eric. *Pass the Bottle: Rum Tales of the West Coast.* Victoria, BC: Orca Book Publishing, 1995.

Parker, Marion and Robert Tyrell. *Rumrunner: The Life and Times of Johnny Schnarr.* Victoria, BC: Orca Book Publishing, 1988.

Jake Terry

Bellingham Bay Express, July 28-30, 1891.

Dugan, Mark. Tales *Never Told Around the Campfire.* Athens, Ohio: Swallow Press/Ohio University Press, 1992.

Dugan, Mark, and John Boeseneckker. *The Grey Fox: The True Story of Bill Miner—Last of the Old Time Bandits.* Norman, Okla.: University of Oklahoma Press, 1992.

Jones, Roy Franklin. *Boundary Town: Early Days in a Northwest Boundary Town.* Vancouver: Fleet Printing Company, 1958.

Seattle Post-Intelligencer, October 6, 1905; July 5, 1907–July 6, 1907.

Lou Blonger, Overlord of the Underworld

Parkhill, Forbes B. *The Wildest of the West.* Denver: Sage Books, 1957.

Stella and Bennie Dickson

Cecil, Charles F. *Remember the Time.* Brookings, S.Dak.: Charles Cecil Publishing, 2002.

Elkton Record, September 1, November 3, 1938.

Interview. Dr. Matthew Cecil, professor of journalism, South Dakota State University, Brookings, S.Dak.: April 2007.

Newton, Michael. *Encyclopedia of Robbers, Heists, and Capers.* New York: *Facts on File,* 2002.

Helen Sieler

Daily Argus-Leader, January 1, 2, 3, 4, 5, 1937; February 27, 28, 1937; May 20, 22, 27, 1937; July 28, 1938; January 13, 1939; September 6, 1946; March 20, 24, 27, 1954.

Caleb Lyon

Limbaugh, Ronald H. *Rocky Mountain Carpetbaggers.* Moscow, Idaho: University Press of Idaho, 1977.

McConnell, William. *Early History of Idaho.* Caldwell, Idaho: Caxton Printers, 1913.

McFadden, Thomas G. "We'll All Wear Diamonds," *Idaho Yesterdays,* Summer 1966, pp. 2–7.

Ferd Patterson

Davis, Hester. Personal recollection, dated "1866 or 1867," in files of Idaho Historical Society, "Crime and Criminal" folder.

Hart, Arthur. *Basin of Gold: Life in Boise Basin, 1862–1890.* Idaho City, Idaho: Idaho City Historical Foundation, 1986.

Idaho Statesman. "Early Idaho Feud Nearly Started Territorial Civil War," February 27, 1930.

Johnson, Clyde L. "Ferd Patterson," unpublished and undated report in files of Idaho Historical Society, "Crime and Criminal" folder.

Henry MacDonald

Adams, Mildretta. *Historic Silver City.* Nampa, Idaho: Schwartz Printing Co., 1969.

D'Easum, Dick. *Sawtooth Tales.* Caldwell, Idaho: Caxton Printers, 1977.

Hanley, Mike, with Ellis Lucia. *Owyhee Trails.* Caldwell, Idaho: Caxton Printers, 1975.

Welch, Julia Conway. *Gold Town to Ghost Town.* Moscow, Idaho: University of Idaho Press, 1982.

John "Badeye" Santamarazzo

Frye, Elnora L. *Atlas of Wyoming Outlaws at the Territorial Penitentiary.* Cheyenne, Wyo.: Wyoming Territorial Prison Corporation, 1990.

Newcastle (WY) *Democrat:* August 15, 1895; April 23, 1896.

Stevens, Serita D., and Anne Klarner. *Deadly Doses, a Writer's Guide to Poisons.* Cincinnati: Writer's Digest Books, 1990.

Weston County State Court. Case file A-121.

George A. Black

Albany County State Criminal Court. Case file #464.

Brown, Larry K. "Fingered by the Fire." *NOLA Quarterly;* October–December 1995, p. 29.

———. *You Are Respectfully Invited to Attend My Execution.* Glendo, Wyo.: High Plains Press, 1997.

Cheyenne (WY) *Daily Leader:* February 26–27, 1890.

Frye, Elnora L. *Atlas of Wyoming Outlaws at the Territorial Penitentiary.* Cheyenne, Wyo.: Wyoming Territorial Prison Corporation, 1990.

Wyoming Territorial Supreme Court. Docket 2–76.

George Cooke

Albany County Criminal Court. Case file #181.

Beery, Gladys B. "He Died Game." *Real West.* Yearbook, Fall 1984, p. 31.

Brown, Larry K. *You Are Respectfully Invited to Attend My Execution.* Glendo, Wyo.: High Plains Press, 1997.

Cheyenne (WY) *Daily Leader:* December 1, 1883; December 8–9, 1883; December 6, 1884; December 12–13, 1884.

Frye, Elnora L. *Atlas of Wyoming Outlaws at the Territorial Penitentiary.* Cheyenne: Wyoming Territorial Prison Corporation, 1990.

Laramie (WY) *Weekly Sentinel:* December 1, 1883.

The Gangs of St. Louis

Kefauver, Estes. *Crime in America.* Garden City, N.Y.: Doubleday and Co., Inc., 1951.

May, Allan. "The St. Louis Family," CrimeLibrary.com, www.crimelibrary.com/gangsters_outlaws/family_epics/louis/1.html (accessed February 5, 2008).

Mormino, Gary. *Immigrants on the Hill: Italians in St. Louis, 1882–1982.* Columbia: University of Missouri Press, 2002.

St. Louis Post-Dispatch, April 2, 3, 1923, and July 29 and 30, 1928.

Waugh, Daniel. *Egan's Rats: The Untold Story of the Gang That Ruled Prohibition-era St. Louis.* Nashville: Cumberland House, 2007.

The Pendergasts

Christensen, Lawrence, et al. *Dictionary of Missouri Biography.* Columbia: University of Missouri Press, 1999.

Dorsett, Lyle. *The Pendergast Machine.* Lincoln: University of Nebraska Press, 1968.

Larsen, Lawrence, and Nancy Hulston. *Pendergast!* Columbia: University of Missouri Press, 1997.

McLear, Patrick. "'Gentlemen, Reach for All': Toppling the Pendergast Machine, 1936–1940," *Missouri Historical Review* XCV, No. 1 (October 2000), pp. 46–67.

Reddig, William. *Tom's Town: Kansas City and the Pendergast Legend.* Columbia: University of Missouri Press, 1986.

The Union Station Massacre

Clayton, Merle. *Union Station Massacre: The Shootout That Started the FBI's War on Crime.* New York: The Bobbs-Merrill Company, 1975.

"Famous Case: Kansas City Massacre—Charles Arthur 'Pretty Boy' Floyd." Federal Bureau of Investigation database: www.fbi.gov/libref/historic/famcases/floyd/floyd.htm (accessed December 12, 2007).

Unger, Robert. The *Union Station Massacre: The Original Sin of J. Edgar Hoover's FBI.* Kansas City, Mo.: Andrews McMeel Publishing, 1997.

John Wesley Hardin

El Paso Times, April 17, April 24, 1895.

Hardin, John Wesley. *Life of John Wesley Hardin as Written by Himself.* Norman: University of Oklahoma Press, 1961.

Jennings, N. A. *A Texas Ranger.* New York: Charles Scribner's Sons, 1899.

John Wesley Hardin Collection, Southwestern Writers Collection, Texas State University, San Marcos, Box 174, Folders 1, 2, and 4.

Bill Longley

Bartholomew, Ed. *Wild Bill Longley: A Texas Hard Case.* Giddings, Tex.: privately published by Woodrow Wilson, 1953. Reprint, 1969.

Cunningham, Eugene. *Triggernometry: A Gallery of Gunfighters.* Caldwell, Idaho: The Caxton Printers, 1952.

Killen, Mrs. James C., ed. *History of Lee County, Texas.* Quanah, Tex.: Nortex Press, 1974.

State of Texas v. William P. Longley, Case No. 100, Criminal Minutes Book A, District Court for Lee County, Texas, 1877, 1878.

Jim Miller

Shirley, Glenn. *Shotgun for Hire.* Norman: University of Oklahoma Press, 1970.

Sonnichsen, C. L. *Ten Texas Feuds.* Albuquerque: University of New Mexico Press, 1957.

———. *Tularosa.* New York: The Devin-Adair Company, 1961.